Advance Prais
Tell It by Heart

"In *Tell It by Heart,* Erica Helm Meade brings together the timeless-ness of myth and the immediacy of personal story to create a richly compelling mosaic of healing and human possibility. Beautifully done."

— CHARLES M. JOHNSTON, M.D.
Author of *The Creative Imperative*

"This book restores story to its rightful place: the healing circle, the everyday and the ordinary life."

— DEENA METZGER
Author of *Writing for Your Life*

"Erica Helm Meade is a remarkable weaver of images. Each one of the stories in this book is like a shiny pearl offered to the heart."

— MALIDOMA SOMÉ
Author of *Ritual: Power, Healing, Community* and *Of Water and the Spirit*

"Erica Helm Meade's process of working with women is as fasci-nating as the stories told. Her twin passions for privacy and truth create an extraordinary field of intimacy for the reader. It's a coura-geous, delicate, delightful—and very moving—book."

— NOR HALL
Author of *The Moon and the Virgin*

"Clean, crisp, startling, intelligent and fun, these fictional case stud-ies show that life imitates art—and that art tells the deeper truths."

— JAMES HILLMAN
Author of *A Blue Fire* and *Revisioning Psychology*

"Meade's method of healing through storytelling is refreshing and inspiring. *Tell It by Heart* describes the magical reconciliation between story and hard reality that too often is overlooked. Meade's work sheds light on the powerful, revitalizing force of story as soulmaking."

— BRENDA PETERSON
Author of *Living by Water* and *Nature and Other Mothers*

"I am so moved by this use of *real woman* stories held in the context of the archetypal myths. Meade is writing precisely what we need now: telling soul stories in the immediacy of daily life. I felt hungry for more!"

— SHERRY RUTH ANDERSON, PH.D.
Author of *The Feminine Face of God*

"A remarkable book and an important one. Erica Helm Meade trusts story. With wisdom, caring, and great personal strength Erica holds up one well-chosen tale at a time and encourages individuals to look through into their own troubled interiors. Much more than a sum of its parts, the case studies and insights on using story-as-therapy meld into a beautiful reading experience. This is a hopeful collection of minor miracles which should be read by educators, healers, storytellers, and all who minister to other healing humans."

— MARGARET READ MACDONALD, PH.D.
Author of *The Storyteller's Sourcebook*

"Erica Helm Meade shows us how our life is filled with stories and mythic figures who provoke growth and reveal inner hidden truths. . . . an excellent resource guide to illustrate how storytelling can be used in personal, professional, and therapeutic contexts."

— ANGELES ARRIEN, PH.D.
Author of *The Four-Fold Way* and *Signs of Life*

Tell It by Heart

Women and the
Healing Power of Story

ERICA HELM MEADE

OPEN ✸ COURT
Chicago and La Salle, Illinois

Dreamcatcher

Open Court's Dreamcatcher series features personal stories
of discovery, healing, recovery, and inner development.

OPEN COURT and the above logo are registered in the U.S. Patent and
Trademark Office.

© 1995 by Open Court Publishing Company

First printing 1995
Second printing 1996

Printed and bound in the United States of America.

Library of Congress Cataloging-in-Publication Data

Meade, Erica Helm, 1954-
    Tell it by heart : women and the healing power of story / Erica
Helm Meade.
        p.   cm. — (Dreamcatcher)
    Includes index.
    ISBN 0-8126-9301-9 (cloth). — ISBN 0-8126-9302-7 (paper)
    1. Folklore—Therapeutic use.   2. Storytelling—Therapeutic use.
3. Women—Folklore.   I. Title.   II. Series.
RC489.F64M43 1995
616.89'165—dc20   95-32763
                                                              CIP

*To my husband and fellow teller,
Michael Meade, and to the mare of fate
who brings us together,
for though he goes his way and I go mine,
we tend to make camp
at the same watering holes.*

To be real is to be surrounded by mystery.

—James Joyce

There is . . . a kind of geometry underlying myth, a mathematics of wholeness as there is in music . . . The storyteller unfolds the story, and simultaneously, in those who partake of it, the story infolds . . . The tale reverberates between teller and hearer, and both are awakened to ponder its meaning, for themselves and for the community in which it has arisen and been handed down from generation to generation.

—Martha Heyneman,
The Breathing Cathedral

Contents

Acknowledgments

Due to the modern belief that progress and wonderment cannot co-exist, the art of storytelling nearly fell into dereliction. The word *myth* came to mean fallacy or *falsehood*, rather than *hidden truth*. Fortunately, myths and fairy tales now resume their rightful roles as works of art, subtle teachers, healers, and spiritual awakeners. Many individuals, and organizations have aided in their rescue. I wish to acknowledge: the brothers Grimm, Lady Charlotte Guest, Andrew Lang, Marie-Louise Sjoestedt, Heinrich Zimmer, Mircea Eliade, Edith Hamilton, Lady Isabella Augusta Gregory, William Butler Yeats, Carl Gustav Jung, Erich Neumann, Johann Jakob Bachofen, Marie-Louise von Franz, Joseph Campbell, James Hillman, Carl Kerenyi, Zitkala-Sa, Karen Blixen, Hilda Doolittle, Elsie Elles, Robert Graves, Idries Shah, Robert Bly, Verena Kast, Barbara Sproul, Christine Downing, Ann Baring, Jules Cashford, Gertrud Mueller Nelson, Thomas Kinsella, Octavio Paz, Diane Wolkstein, Elaine Wynne, Jackie Torrence, Gioia Timpanelli, Laura Simms, Catherine Wellner, Connie Martin, Samuel Jackson, Spencer Shaw, Morris Berman, Christina Feldman, Peter Blue Cloud, Michael Meade, Deena Metzger, Jerrome Rothenberg, Richard Erdoes, Ella Clark, Joanna Cole, Alfonso Ortiz, Merlin Stone, Russell Lockhart, Vi Hilbert, Floating Eagle Feather, Anne Cameron, Barry Lopez, Clarissa Pinkola Estes, Rudolfo Anaya, Nor Hall, Linda Leonard, Jean Shinoda Bolen, Alice Walker, Isabelle Allende, Polly Young-Eisendrath, Margaret Read MacDonald, Milbre Burch, Cathy Spagnoli, Billy Sego, Stephen Mitchell, Caitlin Matthews, Brenda Peterson, Merna Ann Hecht, Celia Coates, Lee Wallas, the National Association for the Preservation and Perpetuation of Storytelling, Seattle Storyteller's Guild, *Parabola, Common Boundary,* and *Storytelling* magazines. Space does not permit a more thorough list of those persons, known and unknown, whose contributions range from modest to grand, scholarly to elemental, poetic to scientific, in the restoration of storytelling in contemporary culture.

On a more intimate note, I wish to thank my husband, Michael Meade, for encouraging loyalty to the muse, and for long ago glimpsing the fiction writer in me, before I knew she was there. Without his dedication to our shared dreams this book would not have been written. Michael provided the saucy limerick for the final story. Many thanks to my beloved stepchildren, Oona, Aram, Bran, and Fionn, who through their great appetites for stories provided the best training possible, demanding at least one bedtime story per night all the way through grade school, listening always with appreciative ears. As adults, they provide soulful support, artistic spark, and keen criticism their writing parents thrive on.

Thanks to my parents whose faith in me has lifted me up after many a fall: my mother, Susan, and her passion for singing—her savory ballads feed my imagination still—my father, Franz Peter, a small-town dentist with a knack for engrossing patients in stories, distracting them from pain at key moments. Thanks to my grandmother, Florence, "The Mother of All Living" whose poetry and life adventures inspire all sixty-plus members of our extended family. Thanks to my aunt, Jef, for modeling a writer's daily discipline and for diligent proof-reading. Thanks to my sister, brother, aunts and uncles, and our dozens of cousins for vitality, love, and spirited talk.

Thanks to David H. Campbell and Stephen Silha, editors, soul-brothers, fellow writers, guardian angels of this project, who graciously critiqued draft after draft. Thanks to Gary Hillaire who first suggested this book, and to dear friends whose art, dreams, and thoughts nourished it: Rick Simonsen, Barbara Thomas, Susan Plum, Elaine Hanowell, Cathy Goetsch, Sobonfu Somé, Miguel Rodriguez, Diane Hillaire, Linda Medley, Karin Brusletten, Bill Freese, Charlie Murphy, and Merna Ann Hecht.

Writers and healers who read early drafts and whose comments helped shape the book include James Hillman, Tom Pace, Judith Gordon, Carol Caughey, Leela Miller, Janine Canan, Nor Hall, Sherry Ruth Anderson, Emily Fischer, Carol Jung, Susan Childers, Kate Grutz, Kathleen Jennings, David Hufford, Carl Robinson, Mary Ann Schwarz, Kathy Gildea, Mary Liz Callan, Jeanne Streick, Mary Ellen Walker, and Jody Alieson. Thanks to Tom Jay for his words about the muse as a "curious energy" which compels artists, to Peggy Pace for astrological information, and to Ned Leavitt for encouraging stories not essays.

I'm indebted to several mentors whose insights have shaped my perspective, thereby influencing this work: Louise Bode, James Hillman, Joseph Campbell, Louise Mahdi, Tom Bannen, Florence Crandall Helm, Bill Wahlberg, Robert Bly, Ruth Bly, Russell Lockhart, Terrill Gibson, Jack Kornfield, Gloria Aranoff, Linda Smith, Barbara Gibson, Edith Harrison, Judith Minty, Lillian Dodd, Maxine Thompson, Peggy LaCrone, and Verena Kast. Thanks to Megan Lawler-Yeager and Sheila Smith, administrators extraordinaire who've provided years of unwaning support for therapeutic storytelling in their agencies.

Many thanks to Freddie and Charlotte LaCrone for drawing out the youthful storyteller in me many years ago. Sincere appreciation to all the women I've worked with, whose life stories, like myths, have been my true teachers. Gratitude to the ancestors who loan us the stories. Thanks to editor Kerri Mommer at Open Court Publishing Company for sound judgment and persistent excellence.

Introduction

Stories . . . are like the small bag of magic food that is given and when taken by the heart is never used up.

—Gioia Timpanelli

Knowing and telling myths by heart was once a virtue which assured Irish bards a place in Heaven. Indigenous people around the globe still tell ancestral stories to evoke healing spirits and inspire change.

As a therapist working in many capacities in the human service field, I've found storytelling to be invaluable. Some years ago, I began teaching the use of healing stories to other therapists. Whether they were working with wounded kids, young adults, adults at midlife, women in menopause, chronically ill patients, or families facing death, they found stories to be enriching additions to their medicine bags.

Colleagues began requesting a book on healing stories. The idea intrigued me, and over the next few years, I wrote. What started out as a collection of essays has evolved into a collection of stories—cross-breeds between case studies and passion plays. The tales are not intended to confine myths to a single interpretation. They aim to give readers a taste of a mythic process in which new meanings hatch each time a story is told. The first tale, *Peas and Beans*, contains scenes from my childhood which reveal the origins of my passion for storytelling. It and the final tale, *By a Thread*, were inspired by three elder storytellers in my life, my grandmother and two of her close friends. The rest of the stories were inspired by therapeutic work with women of various ages and ethnic backgrounds, each of whom embraced a story as her guide through a process of meaningful change.

My favorite definition for myth was offered by author Gertrude Mueller Nelson's young daughter. As a candidate for kindergarten

1

she was asked to define mythology. She pondered for a moment, then explained that a myth is a story that's true on the *inside,* but not true on the *outside.* This definition is as useful today as those I've heard from mythologists and philosophers, so I go by it. Likewise, the tales in this book are true on the inside, but not true on the outside, so as to protect the privacy of real-life protagonists. I've worked to reveal essential *inside truths,* while inventing fictional circumstances and characters to carry them.

Storytelling is a natural outcome of speech, and to a certain extent, everyone is a storyteller, whether they know it or not. My mother and grandmother insist I was telling tales before I could walk. But I recall becoming a storyteller at age thirteen when I baby-sat daily for a neighbor's young son and daughter. Storybooks were their favorite pastimes, and each day they jumped into my lap with a stack for me to read. This soon bored me to tears, so I began allowing variations to unfold. I pretended to be reading, pausing while turning the pages, when in actuality I was drifting, grasping at tales which hung like moods in the air, or pictures on the wall. Sometimes the threads of a tale gathered in the children's faces. Other times they arose from an unseen source in my belly. We got used to having our fill of this type of soul food each day. Once when I reverted back to reading from the page, five-year-old Freddie covered my eyes and said, "Don't read by your eyes. Do it the other way. *Tell it by heart."*

Three years later, when he lay stricken with leukemia in a hospital bed, I visited him when visits were allowed. Once the nurse handed him the funnies and said, "Here, Erica can read you *Snoopy."*

Freddie barked, "Not comics! I want a *real* story!" After Freddie died, I returned to the hospital every Saturday morning at seven A.M., as a "candy-striper" volunteer in the kids' ward. I learned that neither hangovers nor adolescent heartbreaks interfered with my tongue's ability to yield up a tale for kids too sick to sit up and play Monopoly. In fact, my storytelling to sick kids was sometimes the only thing in the course of a week that made sense.

A shy person by nature, I couldn't have stuck with storytelling if it hadn't continually nourished me. At church camp I prided myself on a reputation for inventing great tales, even though I didn't really invent. I'd take a thematic suggestion from a cabin mate, such as two girls lost canoeing in the far reaches of the lake. All I had to do was close my eyes, picture the two in the canoe, smell the sultry water, and their adventure would begin to unfold. Scenes invented themselves in my mouth, and as long as my self-consciousness didn't get in the way, a story rolled out.

Our cabin throbbed with fresh hormones, and my imagination didn't have to stretch any farther than the boys' cabins to speak the stuff of young desire. These stories were a delicious late supper which lubed our dreams, heightened our fantasies, and made church camp a mysterious initiation into the eroto-sacral. Where else could twenty girls shower together knowing that through the trees twenty naked boys also showered? Morning prayer was an after-shower sacrament. If we girls knelt quickly, for a brief second while the boys in the pew before us remained seated, we inhaled sweet moisture from their freshly scrubbed necks. I'd pray with all my heart to the luscious, wet curls on the back of a certain neck, and that night's story would start brewing inside—not so much a product of invention, more a natural fermentation of surplus virginal longing.

There were times my mother thought perhaps she'd told too many fairy tales, nursed me on too much milk from the other world. Her concern peaked when I confided that when alone and troubled, I was sometimes visited by "the mare of fate," a velvety white mare with pink nostrils and steamy breath who appeared in my room, or in the woods near our home. Through nudging and licking this mare imparted tremendous comfort and peace. Mom feared the mare roamed far outside the bounds of "normal fantasy." But as the years went by, she saw it didn't interfere with church or school, so she stopped worrying.

Years later, as a mythology student in college, I came to understand the white mare as the Celtic ancestral Goddess, still very much alive in the earth and in my blood. In her earliest form, she was the mother goddess, Epona. The Celts sculpted her image on sacred stones throughout Europe. She appears again in the Welsh story of Rhiannon. Each day Rhiannon set out on the back of her mare, and traveled all day at a gentle pace. Many horsemen tried to join her, but none could ever catch up, no matter how hard they ran their horses. She and her mare continued at this leisurely pace, mystifying everyone as to how the best horsemen on the speediest mounts kept receding farther and farther behind her. When asked where she was bound, she replied, "I journey on my own errand." This has been for me, the single most nourishing myth to live by. It reminds me that as long as I stick to my own errand (my own purpose), a leisurely pace will do. This helps temper the urge to wear out mighty steeds rushing toward someone else's goals.

More Celtic nourishment came from my father's side of the family. I was allowed full access to the library he'd inherited from his father, even though the pages of his precious old books were moth-wing frail. Hand-bound leather volumes from Austen, Brontë, and Eliot, to Wordsworth and Yeats enticed me to drift through the ancestral haunts of English castles and Irish meads, sipping the exquisite drink of our mother tongue. My father's mind remains a library of anecdotes and fishing stories he dishes out generously to any ear that stays put long enough to hear.

His mother, my grandmother, is a ninety-four-year-old poet, still going strong. She serves soul food in the form of narrative verse, offering a buffet of adventures from her life as a vagabond teacher. Her tales span the century and stretch from Dublin to the Caribbean, to the Great Lakes, the Great Basin, and the Pacific. Like my parents and grandparents, I desire to pass on nutrients to future generations. The shorter tales in this book offer brief tastes of the mythic experience, while the longer tales require digestion and aim to gratify hearty appetites. I thank the ancestors who left the banquet table full for us, and invite others to partake in the feast.

— 1 —

Peas and Beans

The Seeds of Storytelling
in Childhood

It doesn't take much for the seeds of storytelling planted in childhood to resurface in my memory. An odor, a texture, an image, can conjure the voices of elder neighbors and loved ones whose healing tales blessed my youth. Today I planted a row of sweet peas. I poked finger holes into the moist earth, dropped one seed in each hole, and patted the dirt solidly over each. Bees droned in the apple blossoms over head. Memories swarmed like dreams. The soothing voices of those tellers washed over me, drawing me back to the source of this passion I bear for stories.

When I was five, a quiet white-haired lady named Cora lived at the end of our cul-de-sac. Cora was my grandmother's closest friend and she was always willing to make me a big plate of pasta in the middle of an interminable afternoon when no one else was around. Our cul-de-sac was surrounded by thick woods and ravines, so the backs of the houses were hemmed by the wild where we kids met raccoons, possums, centipedes, and tree frogs. The best entrance to the jungle was the hidden threshold behind Cora's house, where the brambles opened just enough for the passage of a coon, or a kid on all fours. I tailed my older brother and his friends up trees and into bogs. It was important to be fearlessly bold, but boldness had a price. The bogs sucked at our shoes. Tree branches tore at our shirts and raked our skin, which didn't go over well with our parents when we got home. Cora understood. She hosed us down, toweled us off, and dabbed our scrapes with salve so we looked halfway decent when we took our places at dinner that night.

Our cul-de-sac was the civilized world, and it bore what struck me as a very civilized name, *Pencraft Court.* It was nestled at the edge of a university town, proud of academic traditions. My grandmother explained that *Pencraft* means *writing.* Cora was writing a book, so it made perfect sense that she lived in the best house on Pencraft Court, the one at the very end that faced out from under a tangle of trees. All the other houses sat in a row like steps leading up to hers. A mulberry bush draped the arbor at her gate and inside, her house was full of nooks with old rugs and chairs where a person could sit quietly and make a book.

Cora wasn't making just any book. She was writing for Bobby who was sick next door. Bobby used to be a brat, taking everyone's toys and whining about it when we took them back. But now he'd stayed in bed so long, we could barely remember his pouty face. Cora said he'd stopped eating. Bobby was wasting away, and that's why his mom's eyes were always red from crying. The houses were close together on Pencraft Court and we heard most loud things, like Lonnie's dad yelling, so I found it perplexing that we didn't hear Bobby's mom cry. "She does it in a pillow," Jackie Smith explained. Jackie was a big girl with a blonde ponytail and a training bra. She read comics about ladies who cried a lot. She also played baseball with boys, so I believed she knew everything. I pictured Bobby's mom pressing her face into a pillow. The sound went hush, but big tears came out the sides gleaming brightly like in the comics. I felt sure Cora's book held the key. It would help Bobby eat and get well.

Cora let me help make the book. She put the pages together and let me staple it by banging hard on the black knob. She put the words down on the pages, and drew pictures above the words. She let me color something round on each page. First it was large, then as we turned the pages it got smaller and smaller. Then it gradually grew large again.

When we finished Cora told me the story. Naturally, it was about a boy who'd stopped eating. The longer he went without food, the tinier his stomach got. First it was the size of a softball, then it was the size of an orange, then it was the size of a lemon, then it was the size of a golf ball. The boy wrinkled his nose each time the mother in the picture brought him a big plate full of the kinds of food I would have eaten in an instant and asked for more. The problem was, the longer he didn't eat, the less he felt like eating, the more his stomach kept shrinking until it was the size of a dot: a small green pea that was hard to color it was so small. Finally he agreed to try one bite of cereal. That first spoonful of cream of wheat led to another, and soon his stomach grew back to the size of a golf ball. Then he ate soup, then noodles, and soon his stomach grew to the size of an orange, and so on. After a while he was well again. He got out of bed and went outside, smiling grandly in the sunshine. Cora's book was without doubt the most important book I could imagine. Reading it made me hungry. We went into the kitchen and Cora cooked up a big batch of vermicelli with butter.

None of us kids were allowed to see Bobby. I could only imagine Cora sitting at his bedside, showing him the pictures and reading the story. I hoped it would work, even though he was bratty. When your stomach is as small as a green pea, it's a terrible thing. You must eat and get better, whoever you are. I didn't think my stomach would ever be the size of a green pea. I bet when I was full it stretched to the size of a cantaloupe, or a squash. But *not* the size of a watermelon, like my mom's, before my sister was born.

I didn't see Cora for a while. We had Easter egg hunts, a Maypole, and ball games at the other end of Pencraft Court. Then one day when we were playing Indians with no shirts on, Bobby's mother called us over. She looked overjoyed like one of those queen-for-a-day ladies on TV with a new washer, only it was Bobby she was happy about. She wheeled him down the sidewalk in a fancy push-chair my brother and I wanted to play in right away, but we knew that wasn't nice. Bobby was all squinty and whiny, but he was outside and we knew that meant he was better.

"It worked," I told my brother later, "That book we made. Okay, *Cora* made it, really, but I helped." My brother said I was dumb and nobody got better from a book. But I knew he was just saying that. He'd made a book, too, one he kept under the mattress. He'd drawn pictures of volcanoes and airplanes in it. It was a book about expeditions. "What's expeditions?" I asked. "It's something boys do that girls can't," he said. That made me more determined than ever. Not only would I make books like Cora, I would for sure go on expeditions.

At the age of six, I came down with a fever that wouldn't let up. It was accompanied by listlessness and delirium, and was eventually diagnosed as histoplasmosis, an infection of the lung and respiratory system. For months I dwelt in a half-dream that was not altogether unpleasant.

Whenever I woke up, my sheets were damp from sweat. Mom knew I didn't like the feel of it. She changed the sheets each day. She'd roll me over to tug the bottom sheet, out from under one side, and then roll me back to the middle again. It was like floating on a raft, rocking in the wake of a passing boat. Her chocolatey arms moved competently over me, under me, and all around. The new sheet was always rough in a comforting way, just off the line, with pinch marks still on it where the clothespins had gripped. Her black hair fell forward and brushed across my arms and legs as she smoothed the bottom sheet. She smoothed the sheet with big sweeps—the way God made fields, I supposed. The bed jiggled as she made her way around it, bumping it with her knees like a dolphin nudging my raft. The top sheet would fly open like a startled angel, then billow wide, and settle silently like a cloud smelling of sunshine.

One afternoon I was more awake than usual. Mom let me sit in the living room while she had coffee with a strange lady. As soon as the lady was gone, we were going to have a story. I didn't mind waiting because some wrens were building a nest under the eaves. I watched them carry string and grass back and forth past the window.

The lady wore a pressed white blouse. She had thin lips and glasses hanging at her bust line on a gold chain. She leaned toward me with her saucer on her knee. She bugged her eyes and exaggerated her lip movements the way adults do when they're trying hard to impress a kid. She exclaimed loudly that I was a big girl and a very good girl. I was unimpressed, as she hadn't seen enough of me to judge my size or my character. She talked softly to Mom about me not being in school—about me *getting behind*—something worse than fevers, it seemed, by her inflection. Everything went black for a moment. I felt like throwing up.

The lady tried again to impress Mom with the extent of her concern. Getting behind leads to social and academic stigmas she explained, consternation digging creases at her brows. Mom nodded like she was beginning to see the light. I knew she wanted the lady to leave so we could have a story.

Everything went black again. I felt like I was falling into a dark pit—a well, or a volcano. All the kids my age were in school learning important things. I was far behind in the dark—the only kid who didn't know what those important things were. If I ever did go to school, stigmas would make me stand out like someone wearing their shoes on the wrong feet.

Thank goodness when I next opened my eyes Mom was closing the door and the lady was clomping down the steps saying goodbye. Mom and I snuggled on the couch. She propped the book on her tummy and read the names of all the fairy tales so I could pick one. I chose *Jack and the Beanstalk*, because a bean is a small magic thing, much like the pea in Cora's book. A bean can help you, just like a pea. Jack was a boy with numerous stigmas who was very far behind. Even his mother believed he was stupid. I wasn't *that* far behind, and it was comforting to know someone else's troubles exceeded my own.

Jack knew the beans were magic, so he traded his cow to get them. His mom called him "Dunderhead" and tossed the beans out the window. That was just the beginning. After that, a huge beanstalk grew from the spot where the beans had landed. At the very top was a castle, and who should live there but a wicked giant who happened to be causing trouble throughout the town. Unlikely as it may seem, Jack himself climbed the beanstalk again and again until he'd bested the giant. People realized then that Jack was quite clever in his own way. Of course, that was my favorite part, being that I was clever in my own way, too.

Dad took me to the hospital again. As usual, I had to stand up
and lie down with no shirt on in front of a big machine that took
pictures of my chest. The lady in the green coat told me, *hold still,*
Eureka, as if I were a vacuum cleaner. Then she rushed out of the
room like something bad was going to happen. I could see her behind a window, pushing the button that made the machine groan
so it could take a picture.

Later Dr. Gomez showed me the pictures he called X-rays. They
looked black until he clamped them to a blank screen and switched
it on. Then you could see my skeleton and lungs. Dr. Gomez always
put on his glasses and studied the pictures closely before talking to
me about what was wrong inside. I liked Dr. Gomez because he
let me stay with him the whole time he studied the bone pictures.
He asked me about my favorite animals and my favorite stories.
When I told him about Jack, he understood right away. He pointed
at the picture and said my spine was like a tall beanstalk. My lungs
were a big castle at the top, and the blotch on one lung was an evil
giant making me sick. He said I was like Jack. It was up to me, and
me alone, to best the giant. He believed I was winning slowly but
surely. He showed Dad the pictures from last year, so we could see
how the giant was getting smaller.

Dad was so happy to hear the news, we drove home the long
way, past the pony farm, and stopped for ice cream cones wrapped
in paper. He let me pick them myself right out of the freezer.
Drumsticks, he called them, just like my favorite piece of a fried
chicken.

Dr. Gomez was right. Some months later, the giant in the last
bone picture faded into a very small shadow, so I was able to start
school. Mom assured me the school was not a hospital, though it
looked like one. She took me into a room where there were lots of
kids standing up to paint pictures. All the kids had their own paints
on special painting stands called easels. Now I began to see the
important things I'd gotten behind on. I vowed to make every effort
to catch up, and get rid of all my stigmas as quickly as possible.

Mom said good-bye. We kids all had a snack, and I learned that
orange juice tastes sour if you drink it after eating graham crack-

ers. I asked a boy with freckles if they always had that snack. He
nodded. That was one lesson out of the way. Then we lay down on
rugs to take a nap. I asked a girl with pigtails why we napped on the
floor. The teacher said I talked out of turn and had to take a time-
out. Time-out, I learned, was a closet where you had to sit by yourself and think about what you'd done wrong. I sat there feeling bored,
and tried to think about my stigmas, but I still didn't really know
what they were. I wore a jumper my mother had sewed, while other
kids wore store-bought clothes. That could be a stigma. There was
a small window in time-out. It looked out on a honeysuckle bush
with shriveled blossoms. I wished I had a handful of magic beans.
I'd toss them into the grass and climb skyward on an instant
beanstalk.

Soon the teacher said I could come out. She handed out Dixie
cups and opened a big bag of dirt. She said we were going to plant
beans and watch them grow. What a stunning stroke of luck! She
said I could be first to fill my cup with dirt and pick out a red or
white bean to plant. When I went up front, she told everyone to be
nice to me because I was *new*. I was glad she didn't say *behind*. I
scooped some dirt and chose a red bean. I poked a hole in the dirt
and stuck the bean in it. Then I covered it up and poured some
water on. It wasn't a magic bean, just a regular one. I knew about
regular beans, because I'd helped in the garden at home. Some kids
didn't have gardens. I showed them how to do it. The teacher said,
"Very good, Erica, now sit down." I took my seat next to the girl
with pigtails.

At the end of the day we all lined up. I could see Mom just outside the door. The other kids bolted and ran. Mom and I stood there
'til they were gone and the teacher invited us back inside. My teacher
wore a store-bought dress, while Mom wore jeans, which she called
dungarees. I wondered if that was a stigma. It seemed like one. I
had a sinking feeling about it. But my teacher said I was doing fine,
and I'd already learned not to talk out of turn. She let me show
Mom the beans in Dixie cups on the window sill. Mine had an "E"
on it, which I'd made myself. Mom and the teacher were silent for a
moment. "I'm only a little bit behind," I told them. I already knew
how to plant beans.

When I was seven we moved to a rural spot on a northern
lake. My siblings and I made friends with dragonflies and
turtles and learned to handle a heavy old rowboat. But school
didn't go so well. Once again the new kid in class, I ran into
trouble on the bus.

Mom asked why I didn't want to ride the bus. I wanted to tell her, but I couldn't say the words. Every day big kids on the bus pulled up my smock and grabbed my crotch. But it was what they said that made me hate them. They laughed at my smock and said it was a maternity top. Mom had sewed it for me. I liked it because she'd put a giraffe on the front. But Tom Rader, a big kid with blackheads and greasy hair, said I was wearing it because I was going to have a baby. He pointed at Willie Tweedy and said Willie was the father. Willie Tweedy didn't say a thing. He just rocked back and forth like he always did with his head tilted to one side and drool hanging off his chin. When I got home I hid the smock under the stairs and hoped Mom wouldn't notice.

I was mad because the bus driver, Mr. Gibbs, didn't help. I told him Tom Rader was being mean. He said, "Don't be thin-skinned." When I got home I asked Mom, "What's thin-skinned?" She said, "Sensitive. *Over* sensitive." I was really mad then, and couldn't tell Mom because she and my brother already said that about me.

Anyway, I didn't care. I was happy because Gram's friend Vivian was coming from New York and she was a storyteller. Mom made a cot for me in my sister's room so Vivian could have my bed. I liked it when Gram's friends came to stay because they filled the house with talking and they sometimes left a nice smell in my bed.

Vivian came in a big black car. She hugged us the minute she stepped out. It was impressive the way she already knew our names. She wore heavy earrings that pulled on her big jiggly lobes. Her hair swooped up high in a firm bundle of loops and curls that didn't move a bit, even when the wind blew. Even when she bent over, it stayed in the shape of an Easter basket. I knew right away her powdery smell would linger in my room after she'd gone.

She was a professional storyteller. By the way the adults talked, we kids knew this meant something more special than Mom's,

Gram's, and even Cora's storytelling, but we didn't know what. Besides being a storyteller, Vivian was a *librarian*, which meant she had a zillion books. I bet she read every one. But when it came time for stories, Vivian told them by heart and never used a book. I was amazed to find out there were things about storytelling none of us knew yet. But with Vivian around, we would learn.

First off, there was an aura about the very word *New York*, which rubbed off on Vivian because she lived there. I wasn't altogether sure of specifics, but I knew it was a tremendous city where people did lots of fancy things we'd never seen at home. I pictured libraries as tall as the Empire State Building, and lots of librarians in mink stoles with firm hairstyles and seams up the backs of their stockings. With very tall high heels on, these librarians probably rode escalators, or maybe elevators, from one important place to the next. Their nails were always long and polished, which looked perfectly elegant when they handled books. I bet they had storytelling every day.

Gram was always lively, but more so with Vivian around. If Gram lived in New York, she'd polish her nails and probably smoke, too. New York brought out the worldliness in a person, and that's why Vivian told stories with an accent. I quickly figured out that an accent is the way people talk, like a New York person has a New York accent, and so on. Vivian told fairy tales from Europe, so she talked like a person from Ireland or France to fit the story. It made perfect sense. But the most amazing thing was when she told about the princess who slept on a pea. This famous story came from Hans Christian Andersen, who grew up poor, but later got to live in a castle in Denmark because of his excellent storytelling. Vivian's accent was wonderful. Instead of saying "the real princess" she trilled, "Zee **re-e-e-e-el Pre-e-e-een**-cess."

The prince wanted to marry a princess. She would have to be a real princess, but how could you tell? The queen had a clever test. Like Cora, she knew how helpful a pea could be. She placed a small green pea under the mattress. All kinds of girls who might look like princesses could sleep on it, and not notice a thing. But then, a girl like me who maybe didn't look so much like a princess, felt the pea though it hid under twelve mattresses and three featherbeds.

My sister asked, "What's so big about feeling a pea?" Vivian said
that one day the princess would be a queen and a queen has to
understand things, not just on the surface, but underneath, way
below the surface. "A queen has to be keenly sensitive," Vivian said.
There was that word *sensitive* again. But Vivian didn't mean *thin-
skinned*. She meant something good by it. I suddenly felt very strong.
"Peas are alive, Vivian," I said, "I bet that's why a real princess can
feel them." Mom nodded, Gram did too, and Vivian said, "Yes, peas
are alive."

Now I understood why grownups told stories about peas and
beans. Peas and beans are growing things. You can eat them to
help you grow, or you can plant them and watch *them* grow. But
they're also magic, and can help a person in surprising ways. Before Vivian even got to happily ever after, I pictured a book I would
make. It would have mattresses stacked like pancakes and a girl
like me, way up on top. She would be sensitive, but not thin-skinned.
I would draw little creases by her eyes to show that she could feel
that pea even though it was way below the surface.

I suddenly felt as if I understood something about the past and
the future, though I couldn't put words to it. Things which had been
murky now became crystal clear. Tom Rader was a big jerk, and I
would tell him so. If he touched me I'd scream so loud Mr. Gibbs
would have to stop the bus. It seemed like everything would turn
out fine, maybe better than fine, maybe excellent. After all, people
like Vivian came all the way from New York just to see us. And a
regular girl who feels *way below the surface*, might grow up to be a
queen, or something else important. A storyteller, maybe.

2

The Giant's Secret and the Sword of Truth

The fairy story communicates to the child an intuitive understanding of his own nature and of what his future may hold if he develops his positive potentials.

—Bruno Bettelheim

Loose Stuffing

Geena was seven when her mother Nel first brought her to the counseling center. Nel dragged Geena by the hand to the waiting area where other anxious moms tried to manage their kids. It was Halloween. A small boy dressed as Dracula chewed plastic fangs and stared at Geena and Nel. His mother jerked on his cape to snap him out of it, but he stayed mesmerized. At his age I'd have stared too.

It was hard to tell if Geena and Nel were costumed or not. They both bulged out of ill-fitting rumpled neon sweat suits: buttons, zippers, and shoes all spilling open. Fuzzed bunches of red hair sprang out in places on their heads, betraying botched home perms. Other spots lay flattened as if slept on. Geena's eyes bugged out and rolled in different directions like a lizard watching flies.

I was a green intern at the time, my head full of theories about childhood trauma. I was to interview Geena and Nel to help determine whether the girls' group for young survivors of domestic abuse was right for Geena. The plan was for me to co-lead the group with my supervisor, Dee, who'd picked me from the available interns because of my storytelling. Dee wanted a fairy tale to follow snack time each week, and asked for tales on the theme of recovery from family trauma. She had no idea how easy that was. Out of the fifty or so fairy tales I knew, I couldn't think of one that *wasn't* about healing from family trauma.

Scanning Nel's and Geena's hefty files stood my hair on end. Scrawled case notes from numerous social service agencies revealed trauma beyond belief. I attempted to collect myself by checking and double-checking supplies, making sure I had the right paperwork, plenty of pencils, and the key to the consultation room. I told them it was time for our meeting. Nel stood up and nodded apologetically, as if she understood my dismay, and felt truly sorry that their mere presence caused wear and tear on others.

Before we got down the hall, Geena started shrieking at the top of her lungs, "Momma, I gotta get Bunny! Bunny's in the car, Momma! They'll kill 'em, Momma!" She clutched her mother's hand and yanked violently without letting up. It was hard to watch and even harder hearing her earsplitting wails. I wished I could empathize from a pleasantly detached bubble—one that Geena's terror couldn't pierce. But her shrieks went through me like wind through the trees. Dracula boy felt it too, and hid behind the couch.

"See what I gotta put up with, Doctor, see? They wanna take my Geena away cause they think I can't handle her like I'm crazy or I made her this way, only *she* makes *me* crazy! Now wouldn't that make you crazy too, Doctor, if your girl was this way day in and day out? Wouldn't it?" I felt sick for Geena and sorry for Nel. I'd have to choose a calmer moment to say I wasn't a doctor.

Being an intern with no seniority, I got the consultation room in the mobile unit across the parking lot. Staff called it "the bunker." The three of us walked to the car to get Bunny on our way there. Nel's rusted blue station wagon looked like it had come from a desert war zone where sand and wind had eaten the paint job. Bunny was fine, aside from frayed fur around the ears and a hole in the toe where his stuffing fluffed out. Geena's fuzzy hair trailed like loose stuffing. Her translucent skin and pudgy face couldn't conceal the slightest nuance of emotion—flushing pink, then waning pale—scrunched with grief, then suddenly sublime. Now, with Bunny in her arms, she cooed over him, exalting him with kisses.

My anxiety soared at the thought of seventy-five minutes alone with Geena and Nel. Walking across the parking lot I tried to visualize calming images. I aimed for a mare grazing. When that didn't come I tried for an old growth cedar, but the picture that stuck in my mind's eye was the Wanted poster from Geena's file: the scraggly hair and crazed eyes of the suspect, her father, wanted for the cult murders of two young women. Social workers believed Geena witnessed the murders, but kicking the leg of her chair, she swore she "never saw nothing."

Supposedly, the father had twice phoned Nel and threatened to kill her and take Geena. Nel was constantly on the move, changing jobs, addresses, and phone numbers. "If we stay put he'll find us," she said. But her social worker suspected Nel had other reasons to flee. What those might be, no one knew for sure. She was hard to pin down. Her terror was genuine and for all we knew she may have been doing a brilliant job of living incognito on the run and keeping them safe. Both mother and daughter seemed loony. But if their story was true, they'd have to be insane *not* to be made crazy by it. That was the sort of logic they lived with, and we who wished to help them were stuck with it, too.

I twice asked Geena who was going to "kill Bunny." The first time she said nothing, but broke the red crayon she was peeling. The second time she rhythmically pounded her head against Nel's shoulder and chanted, "No-bo-dy, no-bo-dy, no-bo-dy."

"It's Bad, Doctor, Bad"

How Dee and our director decided Geena was right for group was beyond me. Too optimistic maybe, or the need to fill a quota. The agency seemed to run on subtle principles I didn't yet grasp. Geena looked shell-shocked when Nel dragged her to group two weeks later. They both looked frazzled with their red hair sticking out here and lying flat there, as if they'd been in K-Mart, trying on sweater after synthetic sweater, until their hair was loaded with static. I hated the way their mere presence made me queasy.

"It's been bad, Doctor, bad. Geena hasn't slept through the night all week. Has to sleep with me of course and I know I can tell you—and you won't tell the social worker—that my boyfriend don't like that! He's never gonna marry me if she keeps carrying on this way."

I glared. "Nel, that's something to talk to your counselor about, that's what she's there for." (What did I know? I didn't know if she should talk to her counselor about it, or the social worker, or the state-appointed psychiatrist. I just knew it wasn't right to blurt it out in front of Geena.)

"Well yes, Doctor, I know. But I knew you'd understand, you knowing Geena and all. And besides, you're the one here tonight. Can't just call my counselor every minute, now, can I?" From her side it made perfect sense. But it made me crazy she was still calling me "Doctor" after I thought we'd straightened that out. "Doctor" implied more authority than I wanted in the situation, but Nel was too burnt out to bother with details. She was a decent woman, coping as best she could. I felt a strange gratitude to be stuck with my problems and not hers.

The other girls, all trauma survivors between seven and eleven, sat on the floor in a circle. Knees, elbows, and Nikes sprouted everywhere. "Momma, stay with me, Momma!" Geena begged, her eyes as big as Orphan Annie's.

"I'll be right outside, Dear, in the waiting room," Nel said, trying to pry loose Geena's grip on her purse and wrist.

"Momma, give me the car keys so I know you won't go."

I worried how Nel would handle that one. Was she going to be the parent and hold onto her keys, or give in because it was easier? She looked at me like I might have some magic to ease parting.

"Geena," I said kneeling so my face was level with hers, "Dee and I will be here with you the whole time. Your mom will wait outside. We're going to have cookies as soon as you sit down with the other girls." She released her mother and took my hand. I led her toward Dee, who patted the carpet beside her. The door should have closed behind Nel by now, but it didn't. The girls were all watching, wondering why the one mom was still at the door. I turned back to see Nel paralyzed in the doorway. Now it was she who couldn't let go.

"It's okay," I said. She nodded and turned, letting the door swing closed as she walked back down the hall toward the waiting room.

The Giant's Secret

A few weeks later, group had jelled into a compatible unit. The girls looked forward to snacks and stories and sitting cross-legged on the floor, knee-to-knee with their pals. Some tender friendships had formed. Dee said it was time for a story on secrets, because so many of the girls were stuck with ugly or dangerous ones. I chose *The Giant's Secret,* a tale I'd learned while living with a group of artists in Islas Canarias off the coast of Morocco. My friend, Sandra Ruiz, an artist from Colombia, got it from her grandmother, who got it from a Spanish sailor. Sandra used to tell it to her daughter at bedtime, and now it would get inside the ears of several girls who might also pass it on. Like kisses, flu bugs, and recipes, this is how stories get around.

We opened group by chatting about the difference between fun secrets such as planning a birthday surprise, and painful secrets like being coached not to tell you've been beaten or raped. The girls had plenty to say about being taught to hide bruises, and being bribed not to tell on parents and siblings who hurt them in secret. There was great relief for them in sitting together with other girls whose homes were torn by rage and twisted love.

After snack time the girls urged me to get on with the story. Waiting for listeners to prod is an old storyteller's trick. You avoid saying, "Hush up and listen." Instead you wait for them to say, "Hurry up and tell it!" That way they're committed. They draw it out of you as if drinking from a straw.

There was once a father with three lovely daughters. They lived in a big house high on a hilltop, overlooking the city, the harbor, and the sea. The father was a rich merchant who made his wealth by buying and selling beautiful things from distant lands. He owned his own

**fleet of ships and sold goods in many ports along distant
shores.**

**One day when he was preparing to set sail, he asked
his eldest daughter, "What gift would you like me to bring
you when I return?" She thought for a moment and then
replied, "Please Father, bring me . . ."**

I paused and looked at the girls. By now they were accustomed
to storytelling pauses. It meant they'd be asked to improvise. They
usually improvised with natural ease, for a word such as "gift" conjured quick pictures in their minds. They knew the pause meant I'd
choose one of them to name the daughter's wish. Emily looked like
she had it pictured and waiting on the tip of her tongue, so I pointed
to her and she took it from there. "Please Father, bring me a . . . bring
me a expensive, really excellent ring with a matching bracelet and a
necklace too, with diamonds and gems and stuff that sparkle real
bright." I nodded and picked it up again, weaving her words into
the story.

**She said, "Please Father, bring me a really expensive,
excellent ring with matching bracelet and necklace with
sparkling gems and diamonds."**

Emily nodded her approval, and the story rolled onward.

**Then the father asked his second daughter what she
would like. She thought for a moment and then replied,
"Please Father . . ."**

I looked around. Melody whispered, "I know, I know, I know." I
pointed to her and she said, "Please Father, please Father, please
bring me one of those jump-up-and-down things like they have at
the girl's and boy's club."
The other five girls chimed, *"Trampoline!"*

**The middle daughter said, "Please Father, would you
bring me a *trampoline* to jump up and down on?" Then
the merchant went to his youngest daughter and asked,**

"What gift would you like on my return?" The youngest daughter replied . . .

Geena cocked her head to one side with exaggerated longing, giving me a "don't I ever get a turn?" look. I pointed to her and she said, "Please Father, please bring me a bunny. No a *kitten!* A *real live* kitten. A *little, teeny, fuzzy, cuddly* one."

It was my job to blend Geena's kitten into the story alongside the other two gifts, and to remember them, for they'd be important to the story's unfolding. But more than that, they were expressions of longing from three girls starved for father-love.

The youngest daughter said, "Father, please bring me a kitten, a little, teeny, cuddly, fuzzy, real live kitten."

Geena beamed at her kitten's prominence in the story. The pleasure was mutual. The girls made old stories new for me. Keeping tales fresh with pathos and surprise, they kept me on my toes, and made me grateful to be a teller.

The three sisters wished their father well. He kissed them each good-bye. They watched his ship sail away from the harbor, until it was just a dot on the horizon.

The merchant stayed gone for many months. He filled his ship with beautiful goods from around the world, including fine jewelry for the oldest and a trampoline for the middle daughter, but he hadn't found a kitten for his youngest.

One day the daughters gazed out the window at lunch and spotted their father's ship returning to the harbor. They jumped for joy. They knew a driver would be waiting on shore to bring their father home. When his baggage was loaded on the coach, he and the driver set out riding through the streets of the city, toward the big house on the hill. The whole time the merchant stared out the window wondering what to do about his youngest daughter's gift. As the coach slowed down at a crossroads, the merchant grinned with delight at what he

saw. There on a stone wall beside the road, sat a fuzzy little kitten.

He told the driver to stop. "Hello, little kitten," he said. "Do you have brothers and sisters? Where's your master? You look so forlorn all alone. Perhaps I can take you home to my daughter. He scratched the kitten's ears. The kitten seemed glad to see him. The poor thing looked abandoned sitting there all alone on the cold stone wall. The wall surrounded a very large mansion, with acres of green grass and well-kept gardens. The merchant saw no sign of a caretaker or anyone else. "You must be lost, little kitty," he said. "You look like you haven't been fed in days. The best thing for me to do is to take you home to my daughter where you'll be properly fed and cared for."

He picked the kitty up and put it inside his coat. But just as he turned to go, a shadow fell over him. He thought it was a big bird or a storm cloud overhead.

But on the ground in front of him stood the biggest pair of boots he'd ever seen—as big as fruit crates! And those boots were filled by a huge pair of feet. It took socks the size of sweaters to cover them. Those feet were attached to bulging legs that towered like pillars. Before the merchant could tip his head back to look up at the face, the words, "How dare you take my kitten!" boomed down on him like a thunderclap. It took every ounce of courage the merchant had, to look up at the mean face, for he knew he was standing in the shadow of a . . .

"Giant!" chimed the girls.

Yes, the merchant knew he was standing in the shadow of a giant. He felt so frightened his legs turned to jelly. "Excuse me, Mr. Giant, Sir, I was only trying to help. I thought the kitty was abandoned. I only wanted to buy it from you. I'll give you a good price, you see, I *promised* my youngest daughter a kitten."

"Daughter! Did you say daughter?" bellowed the giant. "There's nothing I value more than daughters, besides kitties, that is. Don't think you can steal my kitty and get away with it! A thief caught red-handed doesn't just pay and go free.

"You can take the kitty home to your youngest, but in exchange, you must send one of your other daughters to me! A kitten for a daughter: It's only fair."

"It's hardly fair, Mr. Giant, Sir! A rich man like you must own many cats, and those cats will have many kittens, but a daughter is a rare treasure who cannot be replaced!"

"You're a crooked thief!" bellowed the giant. "You would have stolen my kitten if I hadn't caught you! You're in *no* position to bargain! Only I can say what that kitty is worth to me and I say it will cost you a daughter! If you don't send your daughter to me by this time tomorrow, I'll . . . I'll . . ."

Cheryl cleared her throat and furrowed her brows. Mustering the giant's intimidating tone she said, "If you don't have your daughter here by tomorrow, I'll curse you with a really bad stomach ache!"

I copied Cheryl's intimidating tone and amplified its threat.

The giant said, "If you don't have your daughter here by this time tomorrow, I'll curse you with a double-over-and-die stomach ache!"

Cheryl hugged her knees and grinned, approving the intensified version.

And then the giant stormed away, leaving the merchant dumbfounded. When he got home his daughters ran out to greet him. The eldest was very happy with the gleaming jewelry, the middle daughter delighted in her trampoline, and the youngest loved the kitty. But the merchant didn't smile, his eyes didn't sparkle, and he walked as if a terrible weight burdened his shoulders. The daughters asked, "Father, what's wrong?" He tried to keep his worry from them, but they kept asking and the more they asked, the harder it was to hide. At last he told them the whole story of the kitty, the giant, and the dreaded curse.

The eldest daughter said, "Father, we couldn't get along without you. What would we do if you died tomorrow? It would be the end of us. I will go to him. I'm the oldest and most fit to get along on my own." She packed a few things and no matter how much the merchant protested, her mind was made up. The next day they said a tearful good-bye and the eldest daughter went to the giant.

When she arrived, he showed her around the place. Outdoors she could do whatever she liked: stroll in the magnificent gardens, ride horses, swim in the pond, or fish in the stream. Indoors she was offered nothing but comfort, beauty, and splendor. She had the full run of the house, the library filled with marvelous books and statues, sitting rooms with velvet couches and crystal lamps, game rooms, tea rooms and a sunroom full of exotic flowers.

There was just one room off limits. The giant said, "You must never open the door at the end of the hall. I keep the key hidden in my room. If you should tamper with the key, I'll know, because my magic apple will fall off the shelf." It seemed fair enough to the girl. She'd never seen such a grand place. It was fit for a queen. In the days to come, she enjoyed having the place to herself to do as she pleased. The giant was usually gone all day, giving her plenty of time to amuse herself.

One day however, she grew bored. She'd had enough of swimming and horses, fishing, reading, pastries and tea. She missed her family. She sat doing nothing and as she sat she couldn't stop thinking about the room at the end of the hall. The more she tried to put it out of her

mind, the more she wondered, until there was no stopping her feet from marching to the giant's room to find the key.

As usual, the girls stayed riveted to the story. It melded fantastic images with life dilemmas that were all too familiar. None of their fathers took an active parenting role. One was in jail, one was on the run, one was addicted to drugs, while others were building new families with new wives. Luckily none of our girls blamed themselves for paternal absences. The kindly merchant resonated with their view of a father. A father was someone who meant well, but was simply overpowered by "giants" such as alcohol, drugs, desperation, temptation, and bad luck.

And what of the absent mother, the merchant's unmentioned wife? This theme too, rang true. All of the girls had moms, but what sort of mothering did they get? Distracted mothering at best. Where were these mothers when their daughters were molested, and why had they failed to protect? Two of the moms were mentally ill, in and out of institutions. Others tried to make up for lost youth by living like party-girls. One had a history of beating her kids. Most were ambivalent about mothering. Being single moms meant too much responsibility, too many bills, and diminished desirability in the eyes of potential lovers and potential employers. They loved their kids, but felt deprived of love themselves. In a climate of deprivation, there's little to pass on.

The girls often adapted to their mothers' lives as best they could, sometimes taking the role of mothering Mother, snuggling and hearing her confidences when she was lonely, and backing off when her boyfriend returned. They were like the merchant's eldest daughter, eagerly adjusting or sacrificing to save the parent.

When the merchant's oldest daughter gave herself to the giant, she won instant privilege and lived like a queen. This too, was familiar to our girls. One had told about being allowed to stay up late and eat chocolate each time she gave herself sexually to Mom's boyfriend. There wasn't much in the tale our girls couldn't identify with. They quivered with anticipation each time the story mirrored their own hopes and fears.

The key was right beside the magic apple on the giant's shelf. The eldest sister didn't stop to think. Curiosity had the better of her. She reached up and grabbed the key. The moment she did, the apple fell from its place, hit the floor, and rolled across the rug. She rushed down the hall to the forbidden door. She placed the key in the lock and twisted 'til the door opened. Looking inside she went suddenly cold. What she saw frightened her so, she could barely stand up. The room was full of girls like herself, like her sisters, but they didn't move or speak. They looked like . . .

Geena's arm shot up. She waved her hand annoyingly in front of my face. I looked around to see if anyone else had any offers. A couple of others looked like they were trying to think up a picture, but Geena *saw* something already. I pointed to her.

"The girls did not move or speak," she said, her eyes rolling like they had when we'd first met on Halloween, the day the murderous "they" were "gonna kill Bunny." I prayed she could keep it together to give something to the story, and not blow it apart by evoking bedlam. It was obvious Dee was thinking the same. Only then did it dawn on me—of course Geena *saw* something—she'd witnessed cult violence, maybe murder. There was no turning back now. For better or worse, Geena had the floor.

"They were like frozen meat, all stiff and blue with their eyes wide open. But not dead. Just under a evil spell, okay? Like sleep. Not dead," she shook her head emphatically.

What a relief. Geena kept it together and gave us a great image. Dee remarked later that the "not dead" fantasy was her psyche's way of fending off the brutal finality of the murders she'd witnessed. We wondered what kept Geena from falling into a million pieces.

To see a room full of girls, blue and stiff as frozen meat, with their eyes wide open, was more than the girl could bear. She thought they must be under an evil spell, a deep sleep, and the same would happen to her

when the giant checked the magic apple. She closed and locked the door. She put the key back on the shelf and picked up the magic apple. It was bruised on the side where it had fallen. She turned the bruise to the wall and prayed the giant wouldn't notice.

Her heart pounded when he returned. He went to the shelf and checked the key. It was in its place. Then he checked the apple, and found it bruised. He didn't say a word to the girl. He just grabbed her by the hair, dragged her down the hall, and threw her into the forbidden room. He slammed the door without looking back. He didn't think twice about the merchant's eldest daughter. Instead he started thinking of what he wanted next. Do you think he was satisfied with just one of the merchant's daughters?

Together all the girls yelled, "No-o-o!"

What do you suppose he demanded?

Four or five hands went up, "The second daughter!" the girls cried, without waiting to be called on.

Yes, the greedy giant wrote to the merchant demanding the second daughter. What do you think he threatened to do if the merchant refused?

I pointed to Cheryl and she shouted, "Double-over-dead stomach ache!"

Yes. The giant wrote threatening the double-over-dead stomach curse if he didn't send the second daughter. What do you think she said when she saw the letter?

Desi lifted her hand, her face beamed. "She did like the big sister." she lisped through missing teeth, "I mean, she said, 'I'll go, Father.'"

Yes, the second daughter said, "I'll go, Father, just like my big sister." She packed her bags and went to the giant.

When she got there, the giant showed her around. He let her have the run of the whole place, all except for . . .

"The forbidden room!" the girls yelled in unison.

He told her about the key and the magic apple, and warned her he would know if she so much as touched the key. It seemed fair enough to her, but as the days went by, she grew bored. She began to wonder about her sister and thought she might learn something if she looked in the forbidden room. Her curiosity got the better of her. She went to the giant's shelf and grabbed the key. No sooner had she done so than the magic apple . . .

I looked around the group and pointed to Carrie. "Crashed, bonk! Smashed on the carpet!"

Her vigor spread like a virus to Geena who screamed, "Smash-o-rama! She's in big trouble now! Oh my god! Oh my god!" Geena cackled hysterically flailing her arms and head wildly, hitting Carrie to her left and Cheryl to her right. Her laugh was unnervingly loud and grotesque. It frightened the other girls. They gave Dee and me a "do something" look. Dee moved in beside her. Cheryl was all too happy to give up that spot. Dee slipped behind Geena, and without a word, lifted her onto her lap and wrapped her arms around her. Dee was trained in such moves. I knew it was called a restraint, though the way she did it, it always looked like a big hug. Geena quieted right down, to the palpable relief of the group. I forgot where we were in the story. We walked a fine line on the verge of bedlam. I'd probably encouraged too many whole group responses. But it was a tough call. If the girls didn't participate fully, they got bored and distracted. Lively participation kept them involved, but it also riled them to the edge. "Where are we?" I asked Dee, who was more at ease with bedlam.

"Smash-o-rama," Geena whispered. Her emotions ran wild, but her memory was sharp.

The magic apple fell to the floor for the second time. The merchant's middle daughter clutched the key and ran to the forbidden door. She jiggled the key in the lock 'til the door swung open. She was horrified to see her own sister as blue and cold as frozen meat. She shook her and cried, "Sister, why don't you move? Why don't you look at me? What sort of spell is this? I'm afraid he'll do the same to me!" She ran out of the room and used all her self-control to close the door and lock it as she'd found it. Then she went back to the shelf and replaced the key. She put the magic apple back and hoped the giant wouldn't notice the bruise.

When he came home the first thing he did was check the apple. The second thing he did was . . .

Emily waved her hand, "He grabs her by the hair and sticks her in the room and locks her up in there with the other ones!"

He grabbed her by the hair and stuck her in with the others. He didn't give her another thought. All he could think of was . . .

"Another daughter!"

He wrote to the merchant demanding the youngest daughter. The merchant wept, saying, "No, you cannot go. I shall be left all alone in my old age."

But the youngest daughter said, "Father, you won't have an old age if I don't go. Besides, I wish to learn what's become of my sisters."

The next day she went to the giant. He showed her around the place and made her welcome everywhere except the one forbidden room. He warned her about . . .

"The magic apple!"

And how he would know if she so much as touched the key. She was a curious girl, and wasn't much inter-

ested in the comforts and amusements of the mansion. She wondered about her sisters. She went to the shelf and looked at the magic apple. Then an idea came to her. She knew the apple couldn't fall if it was already on the floor. She set it on the floor and nestled it between two pillows, where it couldn't get bruised. Then she seized the key and headed for the forbidden door. She turned the key in the lock and the door swung open. She was flabbergasted at what she saw. Her own two sisters staring off into space, as motionless and lifeless as frozen meat. She tried to wake them from the spell, but it was no use. She knew she'd have to keep calm and use her cunning. She left them there for the time being and locked the door as she'd found it.

Cunning

Several girls nodded vigorously at the words, "Keep calm and use her cunning." As young survivors with limited muscle, they knew that direct confrontation of an offender was out of the question. They knew powerful wrongdoers must be fought strategically. They leaned forward, eager to hear how the cunning third sister would contend with the giant.

The merchant's youngest daughter reached up and replaced the key and the apple on the shelf where she'd found them. When the giant came home he was pleased to find the key in place and the apple unbruised. He told the girl she might be just the kind he was looking for. She pretended to be happy. She offered to join him upstairs after his bath, to sing to him, and comb his wet hair. While the giant bathed, she took a large sword from his room and hid it behind the couch. After his bath she said, "Come sit on the couch and let me comb your hair." She sang sweetly to him and gently combed his hair until he closed his eyes and fell asleep. Then she lifted the sword in two hands, and with one sweeping blow, she lopped off his head.

This part of the story had worried me. I'd run it past Dee the week before to see if it was too violent. She surprised me by saying it was the perfect analogy for the moment of truth the girls faced with their offenders. She said it tells the story of stopping family violence from the abused child's point of view. From where they stood, stopping abuse seemed to require the most violent gesture of all, telling. She said telling meant raising the sword of truth against the giant.

The girls taught me that telling was hard no matter how you cut it. They all had various authorities trying to protect them, but even when authorities had their hearts in the right place, telling posed a nightmare for the girls. With child abuse, there's seldom hard evidence, so intervention depends solely on the child's story, often on the witness stand. In that position the girls felt the weight of an unbearable responsibility. They weighed the sword of truth in their hands, knowing that raising it could mean sending the breadwinner to jail, splitting up the family, humiliating Mother, and costing siblings what little security they had. And yet, when young victims opted for silence, they knew full well they'd endure years more abuse. Neither option offered true solace. Usually the deciding factor was what they thought was best for their loved ones.

Most of us like to think the truth is easily told, and justice is easily won. It's sometimes hard to see why survivors opt for silence. But, in the years to come, as I continued to work with such families, I never met a survivor who wasn't terrified by the potential to alter the family's fate in one violent blow, that of speaking the truth.

The giant's head rolled to the floor. But do you think that was the end of him? Do you think it's *that easy* to kill a giant?

"*No!*" clamored the girls, knowing habitual cruelty dies hard.

From the middle of the rug the head shouted, "How dare you try to harm me! First you'll repair the harm you've done, and then you'll pay. Go into the cabinet where I keep my potions. Bring the *Heal-All* at once!'

She went to the cabinet and searched until she found the Heal-All. Beside it was another bottle she thought might be useful in reviving her sisters. It was called . . .

Wake-Up Medicine

Several hands went up. Dee pointed to Desi. "It was called *Wake-Up-Girls* medicine stuff!"

She put the bottle marked *Wake-Up Girls* medicine stuff into her pocket for later. Then she went back to the giant's shouting head.

"Put my head back on my shoulders and apply the Heal-All ointment!" he ordered.

She did as she was told. She put the head on the shoulders and slathered on lots of Heal-All. You might be getting worried that things were going too well for the giant just then. Don't worry. The merchant's youngest daughter glued his head on *backwards*. He jumped to his feet and tried to lunge at her, but when he tried to go forward he went back. He was so confused he knocked over furniture and slammed into walls. He fell right through the window and met his death on the ground below.

The youngest sister made haste to the giant's shelf. She knocked that old apple out of the way, grasped the key, and rushed to the secret room. Once inside, she went to her eldest sister first. She put two dabs of Wake-Up medicine on her palms and rubbed vigorously over her sister's face and hands. Soon the warmth came back to her fingers. The color returned to her cheeks. She started to breathe. Her eyes regained their shine. Soon she smiled and began chattering joyfully. The two went to their middle sister and revived her in the same way. Then they went from girl to girl all around the room until all had the roses back in their cheeks, the motion back in their limbs, and the ring of their voices filled the room.

The three sisters set out for home, and as for the other girls . . .

Melody raised her hand, "They were invited to go up to the merchant's house and live there together, all of them."

Emily whispered, "They can't all live there. What about their parents?"

"I mean they all went there for a big party. Then they went home," Melody amended.

They all went to the merchant's place for a big party. They laughed and cried and made fun of the giant, until they were pooped. Then they went home.

And that's the story of how the merchant's daughters got free of the giant and started a new life.

The girls clapped and cheered. Their enthusiasm bounced off the walls. They asked for a party. They asked to act out the story, and before Dee and I could think about it, they argued who would play whom. Dee looked at me. I gave her a "why not?" shrug, and without further discussion, she became the director, and I the narrator. We gave the girls free rein on their dialogue, and over a period of three weeks, allowed everyone to try out each and every role. It seemed the girls would never tire of what became their group psychodrama. Neither Dee nor I could recall crying and laughing both at the same time as much as we did during those weeks. Dee said we could stick with the one story because secrets and abuse of power were their core issues. I was eager to use the other tales up my sleeve, but Dee said we were going for depth, not breadth.

The girls gave passionate expression to their deepest hopes and fears by enacting and reenacting *The Giant's Secret* with a surprise twist every time. Some of the girls loved being the heroine but hated being the giant. Others loved standing on chairs, stomping, waving fists and bellowing as only a giant can. One improvised a whole new scene where the youngest daughter says, "Daddy, when you come home this time, I want you to bring me a mommy." An argument erupted around the questions, "Do we have a mommy?"

and if so, "Where is she?" Some wanted an ideal mom who'd taken sick and died tragically, while another said, "Mom ran off with a fast crowd, and never called us or nothin'—not even on Christmas." We enacted both, and out of that came a third scene where Mom tries to come back. Naturally, that split too. One girl insisted Mom mends her ways and returns, restoring family harmony. Another said Mom only comes back for Dad's money, and the girls shun her.

We had one week left. Dee said she wanted the moms to come to the last group. The girls asked if we could have a little party and one suggested we "do a play" for the mothers, enacting *The Giant's Secret*. That lit up the entire group. Dee agreed, and we planned some special touches including simple costumes and props. Geena begged to play the youngest daughter. Dee asked me if I thought Geena was up to it and I said yes. She had a knack for drama, and we wanted her to carry good memories of group with her wherever she and Nel traveled next.

Geena and Nel showed up along with all the others. Emily showed the moms where to sit, and we began. Dee gave a brief introduction telling the mothers that the story was analogous to the girls' struggles with painful secrets. She said group had helped them break the spell of silence and vent their feelings about abuse. A few of the mothers looked satisfied with that, but some looked skeptical, and one rolled her eyes as if we didn't know the half of it.

As narrator, I described the house on the hill, the harbor and ships, and the father's departure. The daughters gave sappy goodbyes and waved him off. From there we shifted to his return months later. Desi mimed the horse-drawn coach, and Carrie played a wonderfully boisterous giant with a lisp. We got the merchant back home where he reluctantly told his daughters he'd be killed unless he sent one of them to the giant. Cheryl as eldest daughter had barely spoken the words, "Father, I'll go," when Geena lunged on her screaming, "No Momma, no! I won't let her go!"

I tried to smooth the way forward saying loudly, "The youngest daughter adored her older sister and didn't want her to go." I tried to take Geena's hand, and pull her off poor flattened Cheryl, but Geena gripped with all her strength. She kept screaming so loudly I thought the receptionist down the hall would call 911.

Aghast, the mothers looked at each other. Geena shrieked more and more desperately, "Momma! I won't let 'em get her, Momma!" Her panic was real. Nel looked as confused and distressed as the others. Dee moved in behind Geena and deftly gave her the big hug. Geena went limp, curled into Dee, and sobbed.

I didn't need Dee to tell me what had happened. Geena was protecting Nel. She couldn't bear subjecting her mother to the scene where the giant claims a daughter. That struck too close to home, resembling her father's threat to take her from Nel. I hurt for the whole uneasy lot of us, felt ashamed for contributing to this disaster, and furious at Dee for not somehow preventing it; after all, she had been leading groups for years.

Dee lifted Geena and plunked into a chair, still holding her, but now rocking her like a baby. Geena's thumb went into her mouth. Nel looked slightly relieved. Dee rocked Geena and turned to address all of us, "Each time we acted out the story, we learned something new. We've learned about loneliness, fear, and anger. Tonight I've learned how powerfully protective Geena can be. She doesn't want to ever see another kid hurt, even in a play."

Dee's explanation calmed the mothers somewhat. The girls wanted to get on with the play. Their hearts were set on it, but Geena stayed put. It was clear Dee was leaving the narration up to me. "I'll do Geena's role as the younger sister," I said finally. Geena didn't protest and the rest looked relieved.

Our drama had never been so pat as it was that night. After Geena's outburst, the girls seemed to want to prove how normal they could be. They played their parts like bored grade-schoolers who'd obediently learned lines by rote. Afterwards, Geena climbed out of Dee's lap and said to me, "You kept saying, 'frozen girls,' but it's supposed to be: girls as stiff and cold as frozen meat, remember?"

We all ate cookies and drank punch. The mothers made polite conversation, careful not to set Geena off.

We said sad, restrained good-byes. Dee and I would miss the girls—even Geena—and they would miss us. Some of the girls exchanged addresses. Geena said loudly, "I can't give out my address," though no one asked her for it.

Redefining Success

A week later, Dee and I reviewed the group with our consultant. I still felt ashamed. The consultant asked why. "Don't you think we did a disservice to Geena and Nel?" I asked. "I mean, we put them in an embarrassing situation. I don't think Geena was ready for this group!"

We spent an hour going over it with a fine tooth comb, and I faced three disappointing facts. Firstly, more intensive care would have better served Geena, but with limited funds, none was available. Secondly, I learned we can't shield people from themselves. Geena embarrassed Nel in the grocery store. So it was a bit presumptuous to think we could somehow prevent embarrassment in group. Thirdly, with Nel and Geena moving again so soon, there'd be no real way to tell whether group had helped or hurt them.

Dee and the consultant seemed unruffled when I said that our final group had been a fiasco. They shared an attitude I'd earlier perceived as simple optimism, but now it seemed clear their years in the field had lowered their expectations. They honed in on subtle successes I never would have noticed. They said the girls learned something important from Geena: that they could keep their bearings, despite someone freaking out in their midst. Dee said, "Geena helped them practice holding tight to their selfhood, despite craziness around them. That's something they can't do when things blow up at home." I didn't say so out loud, but I knew what Dee was talking about. I'd practiced this too, by visualizing cedar trees and grazing mares during Geena's eruptions.

"Still feel ashamed?" the consultant asked.

"A little," I said. "I hadn't realized how much I'd wanted the mothers to enjoy the play. I thought if they saw their daughters in that playful, creative mode, exuding confidence, they'd feel encouraged themselves. Instead I think they went away scratching their heads, wondering if we'd done their daughters any good at all."

"You're absolutely right," Dee said. "And you've hit on the one thing which bothered me. Inviting the moms in at the end kept them too distant. What we need is a moms' support group that meets the same night as the girls' group. If the mothers don't get support, how can we expect them to protect their kids? Next time, we'll do a moms' group . . . You come up with a story, and I'll start writing the grant."

I came to understand what every grad student hears, but still has to learn the hard way: that in the end, success is measured by what you've learned from your failings. Success hides between the lines. It's the Wake-Up medicine that restores our humanity from whatever kept us numb. The girls woke me from my naive hope to simply train abused kids to keep safe. They helped me see the enormous task that lay ahead: that of nurturing the seeds of empowerment and protection in wounded parents and kids at risk.

With Light Streaming in: An End to Terror

Years went by. The mothers' groups challenged and frustrated us even more than the girls' groups, but we knew it was the right thing. At first, despite our efforts to be empathic, we kept finding ourselves lecturing them on how to be good moms. They yawned a lot and found all kinds of excuses not to come. When we finally learned to connect with the wounded daughter within each mother, their life stories began flooding forth, and group became their lifeline.

We never heard from Nel and Geena, and I often wondered what had become of them. It was easy to picture them on the run, cheap hotels and odd jobs, in and out of community mental health programs. They had taught us a great deal. Occasionally I thought to include them in my prayers, but that didn't seem enough.

Then one day, I walked into the teen residence where I led weekly story groups for older girls, and there was Geena. She didn't recognize me at first, but I'd never forget that translucent face. She stood taller and bigger of course, but she was unmistakably Geena.

I walked up to her, "Hi, Geena, I'm Erica, the storyteller here. We knew each other from a different story group when you were just seven. Do you remember?"

Her eyes lit up. "Yes, I remember you. You were my storyteller." She looked around and announced loudly to whomever might be listening, "Erica used to be my storyteller!" New to the treatment center, Geena was overjoyed to claim something familiar from her fragmented past. "That Giant story was my favorite!" she gushed. "I told it to myself every night. It made me feel safe when I was scared. Do you remember the kitten? I used to pretend I had that kitten. Really I had a stuffed rabbit, but I pretended it was a kitten and I was the heroine of the story. I remember the whole thing by heart. Maybe they'll let me tell it here."

Over the course of Geena's stay, the gaps in her life story filled. I learned she had indeed witnessed her father load the stiff, naked corpses of two young women into the trunk of his car. "Dad drove around like that, 'til the car stank," she said, "Then he buried 'em in the desert." She was able to describe the grave site well enough that local officials found the remains, though the identity of the victims was yet unknown. Geena didn't talk about any of this until authorities provided proof that her father himself was dead and the cult disbanded. Now as a teenager, Geena wasn't crazy by any standards. She was a nerd and a scapegoat in the eyes of her peers, and an irritant in the eyes of her teachers, but not crazy.

Nel was contentedly remarried. But the mother-daughter unit was still charged with anxiety. They pushed each other's buttons and perpetually got stuck in the "agitation" cycle. Neither knew how to live peacefully, but split apart they could learn from others. They visited on weekends, and everyone agreed: Short visits were best. In her years at the teen residence, Geena refused to remain a scapegoat. She confronted her peers again and again, in house meetings and in story group. Eventually she carved out an acceptable niche for herself and made friends.

One day during a free period at the center, it struck me that Geena would be okay. She sat in a bay window with light streaming in. Another girl sat behind her, smoothing her tangles and braiding her hair. Geena looked out the window. Her eyes didn't roll separate ways like they used to. "I think I'll be a vet," she said, "take care of animals. Or maybe a counselor for kids in a place like this." No longer under a reign of terror, Geena now saw herself as a likely healer for the vulnerable creatures of this world.

3

Rage
and Mercy

Story is and always has been a telling of good over evil. Not in a
didactic or religious way—it's just the human condition. We want
goodness over evil, light over dark, strength over weakness.

—Merna Ann Hecht

Alola was thirty-four years old, and trying to be a good mother to
her four kids. She wasn't keen on the idea of therapy, and she let me
know right off the bat that she'd only phoned because the state required it. "If I want to keep my kids, I have to prove I can protect
them. Otherwise they'll be sent to a foster home."

Alola's protective skills were in question because she'd failed to
prevent her husband, Oscar, from molesting her eldest daughter,
Hana. Hana had confided to her school counselor that Oscar had
raped her countless times over a period of four years. Oscar confessed, and eventually pled guilty to the crime. He was now on probation, in therapy, and living outside the home until authorities
deemed it safe for him to return. Alola wanted my stamp of approval to reunite her family. She said she and the caseworker had
gotten off on the wrong foot. She didn't like being judged, and she
hated being lectured about how to be a good mother.

This kind of case gets heat from all sides. A woman in Alola's position feels pressed to jump through hoops and conceal problems in order to get the state off her back. The violated daughter is usually sunk in a morass of self-defeating patterns ranging from substance abuse to self-mutilation. She's typically pressured by siblings to "get a grip and behave herself," so Dad can come home. The community at large scorns the family's resolve to get Dad back under their roof. Dad is pinched between shame, new strains on his wallet, and the tight rein of probation. Therapists feel pressured by the state to act as "tough guys" policing moral decency, while the families expect therapists to expedite reunification. Everybody wants big changes fast, while the actual healing may creep along at a snail's pace, costing more heartache, time, and money than any of us care to budget.

I interviewed Alola alone to get family history. They were a native Hawaiian family with ancestral threads leading back to Taiwan and the Philippines. Oscar was father to Alola's two youngest, and stepfather to Sam and Hana, Alola's children from her first marriage. The family had moved to the mainland six years earlier, because Oscar got a job offer he couldn't refuse. Alola had never worked outside the home in Hawaii, but after they moved, she trained to be a hotel desk clerk. She had a knack with both staff and the public, and was offered a management position. She didn't accept, however, because it would have meant leaving the children on their own too much. Suspecting she might be exaggerating her maternal devotion, I checked into her story, and found it to be true.

I interviewed Alola with the four children to observe the dynamics. There was no question in my mind that she was a caring mother who wanted what she felt was best for her children. Her good parenting was evident in the basic well-being of her three younger kids. She got along well with all but the violated daughter, Hana, who fumed in my office, whether alone or in the presence of her mother.

Hana felt her mother down-played her pain and all too readily dismissed the incest. She was furious with Alola for not siding with her against Oscar. The other children obviously loved their sister, but they wished she would ease up on Mom, and let bygones be bygones. There was clear consensus that Hana was the disruptive factor—the one who caused the upset—first by reporting the incest, and then by remaining staunchly unforgiving. They felt Oscar had been wrong, but they felt Hana brought problems on herself by binge eating and purging. The family was more appalled by her bulimia than by the incest, and they saw her anger as the biggest problem of all.

All the kids had been interviewed by a child protection caseworker who concluded that Hana, alone, had been molested. Hana was sent to individual psychotherapy for the incest and the eating disorder. In accord with standard procedures, all four kids received self-protection training. But even so, the caseworker believed that if Oscar came home the incest would recommence—if not with Hana, then with one of the others. The caseworker said Alola's lack of indignation indicated poor mothering, and suggested Hana would receive more sympathy in a foster home. At this, the entire family clamored together in opposition. Even Oscar, who'd heard it through the grapevine, said he'd rather live elsewhere until the children reached adulthood, than force his stepdaughter into exile with strangers. Hana herself was dead set against it. She hated her parents, but she didn't want to lose them.

I had to assess where the wounds lay, and which would be most accessible to healing. Old wounds lay hidden inside Hana, Alola, and Oscar, but the most urgent wound—in the one that continued bleeding daily—was the injury to the mother-daughter bond. This wound called for immediate care, and I told the family as much at our fourth meeting. The three younger children seemed relieved. Sam, the twelve-year-old, asked, "Do we have to come? Can't Mom and Hana work it out? We have other stuff to do." They had homework, scouts, and band to think about. Their instinct to duck out of therapy was a healthy one. Alola sighed and patted Hana's shoulder, "Let's see if you and I can get something out of this, Sweetie, what do you say?"

Feigning reluctance, Hana shrugged and mumbled, "Okay, if we have to." But her posture gave her away. She leaned into her mother's caress like a calf who wants out of the wind.

The tenderness of that moment was short-lived. In the weeks to come, mother and daughter dug battle trenches to defend opposing camps. Hana lashed out, attacking her mother with scathing accusations. Alola turned away, fighting the flames with icy detachment. It was painful to endure. I wanted Alola to accept her daughter's rage. I believed a reservoir of sadness lay beneath it, and that once released, her tears would wash and cleanse. But Alola couldn't honor her daughter's fury. I suspected that doing so would expose her own unseen frailty—something she couldn't face—and so we were stuck. The colder the mother, the more scalding the daughter.

With a bit of time and effort, each clearly articulated what she wanted from the other. Hana said, "Everyone who really cares about me hates Oscar for what he did. They don't harp on me about forgiveness! My therapist just wants to make sure I don't turn my anger against myself. But Mom doesn't care. She didn't even believe me at first. If she was a real mother she'd kick him out for good!" After much venting along these lines, Hana identified her chief desire. She wanted Mom to rage on her behalf. She wanted the flames of Alola's wrath aimed at Oscar with an intensity that would make him shrivel.

Alola too, groped her heart for her chief desire. "It's difficult for an oldest daughter, I know. I was the oldest. A lot was expected of me, but I knew the family came first, and I did what I had to do. I wish Hana would see what's best for the family, and give us a little mercy. It's tough on all of us when she's so hot-headed."

Alola's words rattled my memory, calling to mind two goddesses: Kuan Yin, the Chinese goddess of mercy, and Pele, the hot-headed Hawaiian volcano goddess. What a stroke of luck! We now had a goddess for each camp. Hana's heart cried out for Pele's fiery, vengeance, while Alola longed for the blessed mercy of Kuan Yin. The goddesses could lighten the weight of expectation from the overburdened mother-daughter bond.

It was my job to gently ease the goddesses into the dialogue. "You both voice very significant human needs: the need for eruptive anger, and the need for mercy. There are stories about these needs. In the fiery rage department, the Hawaiian goddess, Pele, comes to mind," I said, looking at Hana. "And in the mercy department, well, Alola, you may already know of Kuan Yin, the Chinese goddess of mercy."

"Actually," Alola said, "we know them both. When Hana was little, I read her lots of Hawaiian legends. Do you remember that, Hana? Pele, the volcano goddess?"

"Yeah," Hana nodded, "and I remember that picture you brought from Taiwan—of that lady with swirly scarves and chubby angels all around her."

"Yes," Alola said proudly, "That was Kuan Yin. My grandparents had that hanging above the family altar in Taiwan."

I asked Hana what she recalled about Pele.

"She was really beautiful," Hana began. "Whenever hunters saw her in the woods, they went after her and tried to catch her, but when they crossed the line, she showed her angry side. She turned into a wild boar, or a river of hot lava. Then they were sorry." Hana grinned at her mother as if the story added incontestable clout to her side of the argument.

"And you'd like your mother to turn on Oscar like a river of lava, to make him sorry he crossed the line."

"Exactly," Hana said, crossing her arms over her chest.

"That makes sense to me," I said.

"It's obvious . . . to everyone except Mom," Hana glared. We both looked at her mother.

"I understand better than you think!" Alola defended, becoming tearful for the first time. "I've been hurt, too! And so has Oscar! If you must know, my uncle raped me, and Oscar's grandfather raped him!" Alola hunched over and buried her face in a pillow. Hana's face froze in disbelief. I'd suspected as much, but each time I'd asked, Alola had assured me there had been no prior incest in the family.

"When I was a girl, Uncle Harvey took care of the whole family. It was tough back then. My father was disabled with no pension. Harvey was a big generous man, who expected special favors. I was his favorite niece. My parents sent me to clean his house and take care of things. He made me have sex with him right up until I married your dad. I didn't like it any more than you, but I had to do it for the family. Why do you think I married your dad? Not for love, you can bet on that! Marrying him was my only way out."

Alola's ripe confession educed mercy in her daughter's heart. Hana reached over to touch her shoulder and said, "Mom, why didn't you tell me?"

"I never said a word to anyone. Not my mother, not your father, not even Oscar, until this came out. My parents wanted more for me, but they had no alternative." Alola now raised her head and looked into Hana's eyes. "Hana, it wasn't that bad. I got over it. I would never insult my family by making a public stink about it. I still can't believe you did that to me."

Hana looked devastated, as if the earth had just dropped away from beneath her feet, and she were falling into a bottomless pit. For months she'd felt justified, even righteous in her rage toward her mother. Now she saw her mother as a victim like herself who'd suffered in silence her entire life. She looked as if she wanted to take back every harsh word, every hateful thought, and shower her mother in sweet mercy. They hugged and bawled, saturating each other in love and sorrow.

In the months to come, Alola made efforts to respect her daughter's position, but also expected Hana to respect her mother's. Often it seemed we were nearing détente, only to have the gulf between them suddenly widen. Alola would raise the banner of merciful Kuan Yin, while Hana swore allegiance to fiery Pele. Hana insisted that incest was the ultimate injury, shattering her self-image, her sense of safety, trust, and family, as well as her standing among her peers. Alola vacillated between accepting Hana's word, and arguing that the real problem came with "broadcasting it," subjecting the family to public scorn, and criminalizing a basically decent parent who was himself a victim.

As Alola bared her soul about her own incest, she reached strong conclusions. She said blowing the whistle on her uncle would have thrown her family into economic chaos, and she bore no shame at having endured incest for the cause of family stability. She felt no rage toward her parents, only pity. For Hana, who looked to American values and norms, Alola's view was deplorable.

Finding it impossible to maintain neutrality, I consulted an Asian counselor who told me not to judge Alola, for in parts of Taiwan and the Philippines incest is accepted under certain terms. I complained that Hana was expected to protect her parents, not the other way around. My Eastern colleague said that while Western textbooks might call this dysfunctional, mutual dependence between parent and child contributes to the strength of Asian society. He advised that it would be ineffective and counter-therapeutic for me to show cultural bias or disrespect.

With all this in mind, I later asked Alola to consider that she and Hana had each tried to cope with incest in ways that seemed culturally correct. Each had behaved in accord with the prevailing ethics of the time and place. Both had wanted to walk the moral road. For Alola, that meant silent resignation, while for Hana it meant outrage and punishment. As Alola studied this new angle, a subtle shift occurred in her way of thinking. She began to realize there was more to Hana's mode than simple disrespect. It was her attempt to uphold American values. Alola even admitted that in the long run, this made sense, seeing as how the family was here to stay. She said she was sorry Hana had endured such moral confusion, and she hoped Hana's future children would never have to suffer it. This wasn't the full apology I'd hoped for, but it was a step in the right direction.

Luckily, Oscar was in therapy, too, working on painful boyhood memories of being raped and humiliated by his grandfather. His personal discoveries further tipped the family attitudinal scales. During their Friday night dates, Alola and Oscar discussed their own childhood incest and its impact on their lives. The more feelings Oscar uncovered in therapy, the more he realized his molestation had injured him deeply. It had made him hate himself. It had caused him to feel small and powerless. But worst of all, it had cultivated in him the compulsion to gain sexual control over someone small and dependent. The more he reclaimed his childhood pain, the greater his remorse for violating Hana.

After several months, he realized that Alola hadn't helped him by letting him off the hook. He couldn't break the chain of wrongdoings if his wife kept sweeping them under the rug. He'd done irreparable damage to Hana, and couldn't make peace with himself, or restore his role as husband and father, if Alola kept minimizing the crime. His contrition wouldn't mean much unless Alola would take a stand as the outraged mother.

Alola was baffled. Both Hana and Oscar sang the same tune. Victim and perpetrator were united in a campaign to make a tempest in a teapot, when all she wanted was to get her family back together and get on with life. Oscar lumped Alola together with his own mother who had failed him by looking the other way. He said that whether Alola knew it or not, her mother had failed her, too. The way Oscar saw it, family sores would continue to fester unless a fierce mother figure could spit fire to cauterize the wound.

Oscar wrote to the younger kids saying he, and he alone, was responsible for the mess the family was in. He told them in no uncertain terms that he had wrongfully violated Hana, and that she had done the right thing by telling. He said he couldn't come home until he'd paid for his wrongs, and until he felt certain that it would never happen again. The other kids started expressing solidarity with Hana. Even the youngest understood, and asked, "Mom, why didn't you make him stop?" Sam said, "This wouldn't have happened, Mom, if you stayed home with us kids, instead of working." For the first time, Alola was furious at everyone but Hana. Being lectured was the one thing that made her dander fly.

Alola called me to schedule an emergency appointment. She came in fuming. "How dare Oscar prompt my children to lecture me! Did I molest them? He destroyed this family, not me! I was an incest victim, too, but did I turn around and do it to my children? Absolutely not!

"It wasn't as if he was deprived either! I never denied him—not even when I was dog tired from work!" Oscar's insolence had lit a fire. Finally, Alola's indignation flared. I must say, I was grateful.

"He has the nerve to lecture me after what he did to my daughter! He's the bad parent! He's the one who should be lectured!" Oscar had crossed Alola's line. Lecturing her was like stripping away her adulthood status. It brought up painful memories of all the years she'd endured parental lectures in silence. It was like cornering Pele, and it 'roused the same response. She who'd been docile and sweet, suddenly spit fire.

I pointed out that she'd joined forces with Pele. "I have to be very firm with my kids, and also on the job, but I've always been soft with Oscar. That's got to change. From now on, when it comes to Oscar, I'm Pele!" she fumed. "We left our home and family to be with him! It hasn't been easy for my kids in the schools here, either. It's pretty racist, you know. But if there's one thing I've learned in the past few months, it's that we're survivors. We could get along without Oscar, if we had to, and if he makes one wrong move with any of the kids, I'll divorce him. I mean that."

She sighed and said, "I should have seen the signs, I know. First no appetite, then gorging like a vulture. Crying for no reason . . . Begging me to take her with me everywhere." Tears spilled down Alola's face as she spoke. "You must think I'm a terrible mother, but I didn't want to know. I didn't want anything to spoil our happiness. For the first time, we had real security and a decent home. Oscar was good to us. It was such a happy change from Hana's father who beat us. I just didn't want to know," Alola sobbed. Her whole body heaved and jolted with sorrow.

In the weeks to come, Alola scheduled several extra sessions. She came alone, carrying with her a small prayer card picturing Kuan Yin. The radiant saint floated on a cloud, her face glowing serenely, surrounded by a swirl of colorful shawls. The image comforted Alola, and Kuan Yin's sad story helped her access her own long-denied grief. Kuan Yin was a pure-hearted girl whose greedy father tried arranging a wrongful marriage so he could gain the dowry. When Kuan Yin refused, he turned upon her with murderous cruelty. Sometimes Alola wept for Kuan Yin, sometimes for Hana. At other times she seemed to weep the unshed tears of previous generations. A few times, she even admitted to weeping for herself: "I refuse to say anything disrespectful about my parents," she said. "They did their best to be honorable people. It was fate which treated me cruelly."

As Alola grieved, she found within herself the mercy she had longed for, and was able to channel some toward her daughter. Hana softened like brittle grass after a rain, and their affection resumed. Under these conditions, Hana found it easier to eat in accord with physical hunger, rather than bingeing to stave off emotional drought.

When Alola's grieving began to subside, she said she had but one regret, "If someone in my family had had the *Pele-fire* to stand up for me, maybe the incest would have ended right there. It can only happen if you let it happen." But instead of dwelling on past regrets, she looked to the future. In taking the Pele stance now, she felt she was guarding the safety of future generations. Eventually, the child protective agency gave permission for Oscar to have supervised visits with the kids. Like Pele, Alola guarded against Oscar crossing the lines. Over the months to come, as the family gradually satisfied the requirements for reunification, she remained especially sensitive about how changes effected Hana. Alola slowed things down when she noticed Hana starving or bingeing. Oscar remained sincere in his desire to heal, and was grateful to have Alola take charge.

When Oscar finally moved home, he continued individual and group therapy for sex offenders. Hana stayed in individual therapy and started group therapy for incest survivors. Alola stayed with a mother's support group she'd joined some months earlier. It seemed every night someone was in therapy. Oscar worked extra hours to pay for it all, and they often joked with me about being professional clients. But it kept them from being isolated with their problems, and helped them stay on track. After a while, the mother-daughter bond held firm, and they stopped seeing me. They sent me Christmas cards each year, and occasionally came in for a session or two at the suggestion of Hana's therapist when they hit a rough spot.

One spring I got a note from Alola saying Hana would complete high school and go on to college that year. She said each spring her support group put on a picnic for their daughters. Several of them would be graduating, so the mothers wanted to plan an extra special picnic. They decided to invite a storyteller, and she'd suggested me. She told me to expect a call from the group facilitator.

A few days later the facilitator called and I said yes.

The picnic was on a Saturday. It was held on park-like grounds behind the church where the support group usually met. The setting was quite impressive, with picnic tables nestled beneath huge laurel, alder, and madrona trees in full bloom. The trees looked like giant bridal bouquets being tossed by the wind. The moms had carefully tacked down their tablecloths and weighted their paper plates. I grew concerned that a few environmental factors might get in the way of storytelling. Most tellers prefer indoor, acoustically favorable settings because gusty winds disrupt the carriage of the voice, sunglasses cut off eye contact, and, worst of all in my case, pollens irritate my nose and throat. I had no choice now but to make the best of it.

It was a pleasure to see Alola and Hana. They'd obviously weathered the storm of incest and had settled on kinder shores. Hana had become a radiant, young woman who'd make any mother proud. With the clouds behind her, and the wind lifting her hair, she resembled Kuan Yin, and it was hard to remember what she'd looked like when anger had consumed her. Alola exuded the kind of competence one would expect of a seasoned mother and hotel desk manager. She presided over the charcoal grill with the ease of a gracious host.

What happened next could have been a storyteller's nightmare. Between the pollen and the smoke, my eyes began to water. I looked up through tears at the bright sky where pollen dust filled the air like fog. Soon my throat and nose were inflamed. I looked around at the others. Some sniffled and looked mildly annoyed, but no one else seemed to be having an all-out allergy attack. My sinuses throbbed. No way was I going to tell stories. I pulled Alola and the facilitator aside. It didn't take us long to agree that Alola would do the storytelling. She said she'd tell the stories of Kuan Yin and Pele.

The facilitator had one of those brass meditation bells which sound so elegant indoors. But outside, competing with the wind and the cross-table chatter, she had to whack it four or five times to get everyone's attention.

Alola stood at the head of the table with Hana on her right. She folded her hands over her belt buckle and composed herself. She began speaking as if leading a hotel staff meeting. Luckily, she loosened up gradually, as she became intrigued with her own story. She was surprisingly candid about her past failure to protect Hana, and asked her for permission to tell about it. "Go ahead, Mom, I trust you," Hana said.

The others listened respectfully while Alola's personal story led seamlessly into the myth of Kuan Yin.

> **Kuan Yin's father didn't care what was best for his daughter. All he wanted was to marry her off to a rich man so he could collect the big dowry for himself. Kuan Yin did not want the marriage. She begged her father to let her go to the Temple of the White Bird, where she could lead a simple life as a novice nun.**

Alola's voice shook with emotion, as if telling the story to a group caused her to recognize how closely her story paralleled Kuan Yin's.

> **The father was the sort of man who raged when his will was crossed. He vowed to punish his daughter. He intimidated the nuns until they agreed to force Kuan Yin to do all the hardest tasks. She slaved night and day. But at night, while the nuns slept, the animals came to help her. The serpent cooked and the tiger hauled wood. Even the peacock took mercy on Kuan Yin and swept the temple floors with his splendid tail. When her father learned his plan to punish her had failed, he grew en-raged and set the temple on fire.**

Alola's face tightened and quivered. Tears pooled up in the corners of her eyes and rolled down her face. She'd always maintained that her parents had not been cruel when they'd forced her into sexual servitude with her uncle. She couldn't permit herself to be angry with them, but the story's cruelty was so blatant, it gave her permission for anger and tears.

Others looked at me, wondering if I could take over and relieve her, but Hana, touched her hand and said, "That's beautiful Mom, keep going." Alola's words erupted from a deep place in her belly.

> **The fire spared Kuan Yin, so the cruel father hired a swordsman to kill her. The swordsman caught her and raised the sword to strike off her head, but before the**

**sword hit her neck, it broke in two. When the swords-
man reported this to the father, he went completely mad
with rage. He chased after Kuan Yin himself. When he
caught her, he choked her to death with his bare hands.
Naturally, her soul drifted off to the land of the dead.
There she found that all the souls were still suffering
because they'd received no love and understanding . . .**

Alola grasped Hana's hand and held on for dear life.

**Kuan Yin prayed for the suffering souls. She sang
sweetly to them and released their spirits from agony.
The Lord of Death did not like what was going on.
Kuan Yin received too much gratitude and love from the
dead. He wanted to get her out of there. So, he sent her
back to the land of the living.**

Another surge of emotion came over Alola. Her face glistened
with the fluids of sorrow and rage. They flowed generously from
her eyes and nose. By now the listeners took the tears as an integral
part of her storytelling. She wiped her face with a napkin and went
on, determined to tell it all in full.

**To this day, Kuan Yin lives on a distant island in the
sea. Her goodness could never be rubbed out. Not by
cruelty—not even by death. Kuan Yin still prays and
sings to us, She is our immortal mother of mercy who
lightens our worries and releases our despair.**

Alola paused. The others started to clap, but she made clear she
had more to say. She said her job as a mother was to learn "when to
be Kuan-Yin-soft, and when to be Pele-fierce." She entered into the
myth of Pele, almost incanting the words as Hawaiian kahunas do.

**Pele is the fiery mother of the sacred earth. She is the
forest and the volcano. She is beauty, and all that we
love, but she will not be crossed. A hunter who invades**

her boundaries will pay. Pele demands respect for the earth and for *women!*

Suddenly the wind gusted, blowing the charcoal aflame. Like a true storyteller, Alola seized the moment for a powerful end. Spreading her arms she cried,

Pele's fire crackles! She's here to ignite our hearts. Our daughters will never be harmed again.

She clapped her hands over her heart, and sat down quickly, leaving us all a little breathless.

We looked at each other. A common response seemed to be surging up from our feet. We jumped up to clap and cheer. At first we sounded like football fans, but soon rounded a bend into owl hoots, gypsy ululations, wolf howls, and bird calls. We whooped like the night animals who helped Kuan Yin. We whistled like birds in Pele's forest.

Hana and Alola hugged. They held hands and sat down. The rest of us sat down too, invigorated, in need of breath. I felt Pele's coals glowing in my belly, and forgot all about the allergy which had incapacitated me half an hour before. I wept, too, and so did others, but these were tears of celebration for resilient women, past, present, and future: our grandmothers and mothers, Alola and Hana, and all our daughters, and granddaughters. The wind let up, allowing a moment of stillness. Everyone grasped hands in silent prayer. I felt the mercy of Kuan Yin wrap around us like a great silk shawl.

That day I went home feeling I'd seen something vital yet unnameable. The feeling stayed with me like a subtle perfume—the complex essences of mercy and rage. I remembered how silk, the most delicate of fibers, yields cloth of iron strength. I thought of the volcanic soil of fertile Hawaiian farmland, and recalled its origin in Pele's raging heart. That day it was as if I'd seen the commonest of miracles, the secret of women making strong cloth from fragile threads—the secret of seeds that sprout in the ashes of old rage.

4

Creation Songs

Before our world became reified and compartmentalized, the doctor, artist . . . and storyteller were united in one role, that of shaman or healer.

—Celia Coates

No Muse Blues

One morning I got a long phone message from Ginny. She described herself as a seasoned journalist taking time off to write poetry. She'd moved to a northern island to live in the woods and find her muse. There she'd met several local women artists who gathered weekly to discuss everything from politics, to mothering, to marketing their work. They'd welcomed Ginny with open arms, and she was touched by their fast friendships. She wanted to show the group her gratitude by treating them to something unique. That's where she hoped I'd come into the picture. She'd attended my workshop, "Creativity and Creation Myth," the previous year, and she wanted me to lead a similar weekend retreat for the group at her island lodge.

Any other time I would have said yes in a heartbeat, but that winter I was up to my ears in child abuse cases, and kept finding myself on the witness stand advocating for kids. Storytelling sat on the back burner while my tongue finessed a new language: *legalese,* a pedantic oratory, once a kissing cousin of Gaelic poetry. Believing justice and inspiration spring from the same source, ancestral poets memorized laws as well as stories, but in my heart the two clashed. I found expert testimony was best received when laden with pseudo-scientific jargon, a form of speech that by its very nature, seeks to deny the mythic imagination. I had the sinking fear that if I opened my mouth to tell a creation myth, my tongue would betray me by spinning diagnoses instead.

Ginny called again with enticing details. The arts group included a potter, a musician, a writer, a sculptor, and a retired dancer recovering from cancer. The lodge sat high above the ocean amid two hundred wooded acres. Such an excursion might win back my muse. Another call firmed up the plan. It seemed half my brain had to be put on ice while the other thawed out. I felt like a cheating wife: all week wedded to *fact,* but running off with *metaphor* on the weekend. If there was a meaningful challenge in being torn asunder, I was too tired to see it.

My husband understood this schism. As he helped me pack the car early Friday morning, he said I'd find the muse on the road north. A sculptor once told me the difference between an artist and a technician is the "curious energy" which compels the artist. At the time it had struck me as a fine definition for the muse: a compelling, curious energy. According to Webster's, the verb *to muse* means to ponder. In earlier times it meant to gaze, or to be amazed. But who or what amazes us and catches our gaze? To muse on something also meant to catch the scent of it, to whiff a trace of it in the air. As I set out for Ginny's, I neither gazed at nor whiffed this curious energy.

The winding roads and the wait for the ferryboat resembled a tour across lonely parts of Ireland to the Aran Isles. Heavy mist drizzled upon boggy pastures dotted with bedraggled cows and sheep. I put Van Morrison on the stereo, hoping to raise my spirits, but the sweet lightness of the tune, "You Make Me Feel So Free," skipped over me like a love letter for someone else. *I yearn for my mistress calling me, that's the muse, that's the muse. But we only burn up with that passion when there's nothing left to lose.* I cranked up the volume and sang along but my voice wavered with a frailty I didn't want to hear. I'd been strong in the courtroom all week, so where was my strength now when it came to creativity? If Van had written "The No Muse Blues" it would have suited me better.

Ginny expected knowledgeable guidance in the realms of creativity. I wasn't inspired, but at least I could remember my plan. Greek myth says *memory* is the mother of the muse. Maybe courting the mother would win back the daughter. Hopefully, it would make me more receptive to the curious energy I was looking for.

Mapping Creation

I'd begin the evening by telling the myth of the Pelasgian creator, *Eurynome* (you-RIN-o-me). Ginny recalled the myth from the workshop, and felt it would deepen the group's understanding of the creative process and enrich their weekly talks. Hopefully, they too, would identify with Eurynome's creation cycle: her grasping for form in Chaos, experimenting with raw materials, birthing creation, suffering betrayal, followed by her re-imagining creation, reworking it, offering it as a gift, and at last, taking time to rest.

After telling the myth of Eurynome's creation, I'd sketch a "map" showing nine major "regions" of her creation:

(1) Rest
(2) Chaos, Disorder, and Confusion
(3) Improvisation; Experimentation, and Play
(4) Ecstasy, Birth, and Grandeur
(5) Betrayal, Exile, and Failure
(6) Contemplation and Reflection
(7) Revising and Reworking
(8) Presentation: Contributing to Culture
(9) Commitment (the ingredient required to brave the others)

I'd explain that these are the same areas visited by artists engaged in the creative process. This had become evident through years of working with creative people, interviewing artists, and reading artists' biographies while at the same time studying creation myths and tracking my own struggles. The creation cycle requires us to enter these regions. Each one evokes a different atmosphere, a different psychic geography. This is why artists so often use landscape metaphors to describe the creative process. We speak of entering the forest, the abyss, the depths. We seek solid ground, mine the mother lode, cross thin ice, navigate rough waters, descend into darkness, get lost, go into exile, seek open vistas, rise to a zenith, or return home. *Eurynome* means wide-wandering, and creativity requires us to cover a lot of ground. Other artists have told me that when entering these textured landscapes, and performing the tasks required there, they're sometimes seized and guided by forces greater than their own individual egos. Some artists are cautious about words like *muse* which imply a transpersonal presence, and yet when asked, they still describe an unseen force which arrives unexpectedly and supplies momentum toward unintended destinations.

Once the group understood the nine regions, I'd roughly divide the cycle into two hemispheres: one where spontaneous, unplanned acts tend to occur, and one where intentional acts tend to form around a basic plan. Creativity requires action in each. An artist can function with a foot in each hemisphere simultaneously, like a jazz musician whose every move combines impeccable technique with free-flowing impulse. An artist can also divide time between the two, following a free-flowing impulse one day, conforming to an outline the next. There's no 'correct' route for navigating the two hemispheres. The point is to work toward one's own greatest fluency.

A heavy rain began to pour. I gripped the steering wheel while rounding sharp curves on the swamped two-lane road, which was getting more like a river by the minute. A string of logging trucks barreled past, inundating my small car. I couldn't see where their lane ended and mine began. The sky darkened. I broke out in a cold sweat. The rain turned to hail, pelting the car with stones as hard as golf balls. I searched desperately for a bit of shoulder to pull off the road, but there was nothing to the right but the ditch and the abrupt edge of the forest.

I fumbled for a different tape, hoping another song from "Van the man" would get me through. The tune, "Haunts of Ancient

Peace," swelled gently like steam rising off a meadow—a weird contrast to the storm. *Beside the garden wall/We walk in haunts of ancient peace* . . . A truck careened toward me, blaring its horn like it owned the road. Van sang on, *Here in this wondrous way we keep, These haunts of ancient peace.* This song used to inspire me. Now it sounded like new age fluff. How could Van keep singing of ancient peace while ancient forests are slashed to extinction? How could he keep recording placid tunes when so many kids are at risk?

The next song seemed equally out of touch. *Holy Magnet* . . . *I was attracted to you* . . . *Take a walk with me down by Avalon, Oh my common one with the coat so old, And the light in her head* . . . *I will show you, It ain't why, It just is.*

A logging truck suddenly, lurched around a blind curve and lobbed toward me, hogging both lanes. I had only a few seconds to save myself from sudden extinction. Time stretched elastically, filled with near-death lucidity. I pumped the brakes as steadily and de-liberately as if making love. I slowed way down, and just before the truck hit me head on, I swerved right to plant my Honda's nose into the ditch. I precalculated the damages—at best, whiplash, a tow truck bill, and serious front end repairs—at worst, head injuries, unconsciousness, and a totaled car. Instead, I came to a swift, safe stop, as if Van's "Holy Magnet" saved me by placing a roadside pull-off in that exact spot. I burst into tears, relief sweeping through my bloodstream like an elixir. Giddy and grateful, I bellowed along with Van those words my sobs would allow, *Oh my storytime one, Take a walk with me* . . . *It ain't why* . . . *It just is* . . . *Oh my high in the art of sufferin' one* . . . *It ain't why* . . . *It just is.*

The phrase "high in the art of suffering one" softened some-thing in my belly—releasing a tightness that had been there for months. All year I'd been absorbing the pain of hurt kids. The need to look for reasons suddenly vanished. Now I recognized that in the timid, hopeful eyes of those children, and in my own fears and frustrations, there flowed a warm, curious energy. I began to see clearly as if a fog was lifting. It dawned on me that I hadn't been exiled from the muse, I'd just failed to recognize her in the court-room. I'd wrongly presumed that when I couldn't smell the bouquet of inspiration, she was gone when in actuality she'd been there at

every turn. Memories flooded over me of times on the stand
when the right words had come at the right moment. How could I
have failed to get a whiff of the muse in those moments?

My heart brimmed with gratitude. I wanted to hug my children
and sing their praises, squeeze my husband 'til he hollered, and
send valentines to everyone else. I wanted to renew my commitment to the muse wherever her curious energy might lead. In an
instant all regrets about the courtroom vanished, and life revealed
itself as a garden bursting with possibility. I recalled the good things
which had come to me as a result of my commitment to tend the
garden, and realized what Goethe meant in saying that when one
commits oneself, providence moves too, and help arrives from inexplicable sources. Van sang on and on for what felt like twelve
minutes. Gradually the chorus wound down. Van whispered, *Listen
to the silence. Can you feel the silence?* The storm had cleared. Yellow light streamed through the haze. I opened the car door to get
some air. It was so quiet outside I could hear the mushy hailstones
seeping into the earth as they melted. I stretched and felt every joint
in my body move fluidly for what felt like the first time. Starting the
engine again, I realized all the riches in my life—the love and creativity—had blossomed from commitment—from my ability to
hang in and persist, even when I couldn't remember why. The vow
to the muse was like marriage: When the passion wanes, commitment sustains us until the juice comes flooding back. I'd tell Ginny's
group that commitment is the *global currency* which funds our
journeys into all the regions of Eurynome's cycle—most importantly,
those forays into painfully conflictual arenas like courtrooms, where
travel extracts an emotional price.

In the end, I hoped to get the group making something—a ritual,
a poem, a doll, a mask, or a play—something to honor the one *with
the light in her head.* I'd often told students that the creation goddess and the muse are *archetypal, metaphorical, symbolic;* but such
words have a subtle way of dishonoring things sacred, as if to say
they exist only as a trick of the mind. From that moment forth I'd
never forget the urgency to live one step closer to these powerful
forces acknowledging them as the living essence of the world. I
hoped to get Ginny's group outdoors to hand-gather the sorts of

earthy materials which house the muse-spirit—lichens, fungi, feathers, bark, sticks, vines, leaves, seed pods—the textured, scented stuff of her body. I could hear the rustle of swift hands shaping dolls and masks. I felt like a fasting monk headed for a feast.

It had been dark for an hour by the time I finally arrived at Ginny's. The lodge was made of heavy old logs supported by huge unhewn fir beams. A crackling fire lit the stone hearth and warmed the interior with a tawny glow. The first floor was one big open room with a lodge-style kitchen against one wall, separated from the dining and main lounging areas by a long lunch counter. At the other end of the room, another lounge area stretched across the worn wood floor. Big, frayed overstuffed chairs and a sofa faced large windows. By day they probably looked out across the water, but at night, backed by the wet darkness outside, they acted as huge mirrors to the glow within.

Ginny greeted me with a hug. Her blue eyes sparkled behind wire-rimmed glasses and her short red hair curled softly around her rosy face. She introduced me to Ann and Marcia, who tended a huge steamy soup pot on the stove. Ann, a willowy, dark woman in Punjab pants extended a long arm and elegant hand—nothing like the hand I expected of a sculptor. Marcia's silver braids hung draped over her generous bust and terminated at her waistline in silver clips. She stepped forward to welcome me with a potter's firm embrace, as if my coming this far made us instant kin. Her bracelets clanked across my back.

Ginny showed me to my room upstairs with its queen-sized bed neatly covered by a thick down comforter. I could see air mattresses arranged on the floor in a room down the hall. Obviously not all the digs were as plush as what she'd given me. Jovial voices bantered in that room, giving off the chummy feel of a girls' slumber party. After showing me the bathroom, Ginny called to the jovial voices, and they invited us in. Louise, the writer, was a strikingly tall grey-haired woman with dark eyes and a wide, friendly face. Julie, the musician/composer, probably in her early thirties, bounded athletically across the room to give me a generous handshake. Adelle smiled and greeted me from her seat on the edge of a narrow bed. A delicate, elderly woman with white hair swept into a French twist, she was, no doubt, the retired dancer.

After filling our bellies with rich mussel stew and sourdough rolls, we gathered at the hearthside. Louise served us tea in one-of-a-kind mugs, made by Marcia. I picked up my tambourine and shattered the pleasant silence with cutting slaps and jangling rings. Eurynome's creation begins in Chaos, the dark unknown place where all things begin. This myth has never shown me a way to ease in gently, but only to blast and shatter the daily sense of order with the vertigo of Chaos. The lodge's open rooms and bare wood walls produced just enough echo to invoke a mythic voice. Larger and more forboding than my personal voice, it moved through the air gathering momentum as it rolled like a huge cold wave destined to leave its mark on the shore. The crackling fire threw undulating shadows on the walls, coaxing images out of the knots in the wood. I danced rhythmically while incanting the beginning of the myth. Each time I crossed before the fire my shadow loomed from floor to ceiling. There are times and places which welcome the mythic voice. This was one of them. I felt I was serving the muse, and she in turn was fueling me.

In the beginning there was only Chaos . . . coiled serpents in cold darkness. In the beginning there was only cold and tangled Chaos in the dark. The only sound was Eurynome's breath skirling through the twisted nothing where it all began. The only heat was the breath steaming in her breast. The only notion was the no-notion of her dream. She reached out and seized hold of two tails of Chaos, one in each hand. She stretched and awoke from her dream. The first tail of Chaos was fluid and light. She released it above and called it Sky. Sky spread across the Great Above covering all. "It is good!" cried Eurynome, Sky Maker. She held the second tail of Chaos in her other hand. She released it below and called it Sea. Sea tumbled downward. Fluid and heavy, falling across the Great Below, covering all. "It is smooth, and it is good!" sang Eurynome, Sea Maker.

Then Eurynome began to dance. She danced along the Sea, whirling and kicking, casting water beads against Sky. She reeled harder and faster, plowing deep furrows where water meets air. "It is good!" sang Eurynome, First Dancer. The faster she danced, the higher the wake rose up behind her. When she danced swiftly, the air followed, caressing her skin, tickling her. When she leapt swiftly to the North, she produced the North Wind. The swifter she turned, the harder the wind whipped and furled her hair. She seized hold of the wind, fought it, twisted it, kneaded it, braided it. Out of wind she made bone and flesh: the great serpent of the North Wind, Ophion.

Louise beamed a broad smile, letting me know she liked Eurynome's bold strokes. Ann looked a bit startled to see the soft-spoken guest she'd just met at dinner disappear into this loud, imposing myth. Adelle looked more elderly and frail than before. She scowled at Ginny as if to say, "What are you subjecting us to!?"

If there's a boundary between storytelling and ritual mythtelling the firelight had pulled me across it, for I'd entered a region where the teller steps aside and ancient voices come through. They'd taken over the room, and everyone could feel it. Julie and Louise looked ecstatic, Ann looked confused, Adelle looked terrified, Ginny looked caught in between, and Marcia looked around wondering what to think. Perhaps it had been unfair to yank them suddenly into the boggy chaos of precreation. Most tellers avoid primordial myths, as audiences prefer "listener-friendly" folktales. In tribal settings, most origin myths are reserved for seasoned elders. But Ginny's group members were seasoned elders, or at least seasoned artists. The myth was unsettling, because it echoed an ancestral truth all artists know in their blood, "Once you make a commitment to creativity, you're working for powerful muses, older and larger than yourself." As mythteller, it was my job to remind them so, by letting the old voice resound. As listeners, it was their job to remember.

Eurynome and Ophion danced together on the Sea. She changed herself into a dove and flew high above to

swoop down to him. He surged from under the waves to rise up to her. He entered and entwined her. She enfolded him with her wings and engulfed him with her dark folds. Swooping and surging. Entering, entwining, enfolding, engulfing. Eurynome, First Dancer, played and coupled with Ophion, until exhausted, she floated on the Sea and fell asleep. Eurynome swelled large and ripe with the fruits of their bond. She awoke alone, spread her dove wings and cried. Spasms churned through her, opening her flesh, thrusting the egg of the universe from her womb. It floated on the waves of the Sea. Eurynome, First Mother, sang, "Open, sweet egg, open." She ached to see what would hatch. She nudged the egg, pushed it, tapped it, kicked it. But the egg held firm.

Eurynome called at the top of her voice, summoning the serpent of the North Wind. Ophion came to her from across the Sea. "Ophion," she sang. "Coil 'round the egg. Rend it in two!" The great serpent coiled 'round: one, two, three. He squeezed tightly, but the egg held firm. "Ophion, coil 'round again." The serpent wound again: four, five, six, squeezed tightly, but the egg held firm. "Ophion, you have one length left. Coil 'round again and squeeze!" The great serpent coiled 'round. The seventh time he wrapped around, the world egg cracked in two. The seventh time the serpent wound, the world egg fell in two.

The two halves of the world egg floated like pearly bowls on the Sea. Eurynome watched to see what emerged. The stars flew out and scattered like seeds across the Sky. The Moon drifted up to center Sky shedding infinite, ghostly petals on the Sea. Then the bold Sun shot out, blinding the Sky. The planets drifted up and found their places. Earth spilled forth with its mountains, valleys, plains, and rivers. Eurynome stepped upon the Earth. "It is firm, and it is good!" sang the Mother of All Things.

Eurynome and Ophion climbed to the highest peak in the center of creation, Mt. Olympus. They basked under Sky's new brilliance. They savored the fragrance of Earth, adored the sweetness of honey, and the songs of mating birds and rushing brooks.

But Ophion grew bored with beauty and pleasure— bored with the drone of bee to poppy, hummingbird to lupine, stag to hind, blossom to fruit, fruit to seed, seed to Earth, sprout to tree and 'round. He wanted more than to be part of creation. He wished to claim authorship. He began whispering to birds, "Creation is mine." Soon he hollered from hilltops, "I am Ophion, Maker of All Things! I rose up from Chaos. I made Sky and Sea. I produced the egg of the universe! I am Ophion, creator of Heaven and Earth. All things come from me!"

Eurynome—she who separated the limbs of Chaos, produced the wind, created the serpent, laid the egg of the universe, and gestated all things—had no patience for the braggart or his false claims. Right then and there, she kicked him in the teeth and banished him to a pit at the edge of the world. He may be there still.

Eurynome looked out from Mt. Olympus, and gazed upon creation. For the first time she noticed something was missing. Earth's creatures lived with mates and families. The mare had the stallion, the goose had the gander, and the lion had her pride, but the great eternal planets stood alone. They kept to their solitary, sterile courses in the Sky. Eurynome, too, stood alone. Ophion was not with her, he was of her. Her true companion was longing, and out of longing, she completed creation.

She made a queen and a king to rule each planet, crafting pairs to meld poles: She and He, north and south, attracting, gravitating, whirling, uniting. Male enveloping female, female penetrating male—one gestating the other's seed—ruling together in harmonic dissonance, tender disagreement, fiery union.

Eurynome stood back to look at the planets. "It is good!" said the Mother of All Things. "They dance and turn—they quarrel and make up. It is good." Then

Eurynome was satisfied. She gazed out from Mt. Olympus and she rested.

The group clapped and cheered, expressing their participation in the myth's exuberance. Louise spoke first, bubbling over with questions about where the story came from, how I'd found it, and learned it. I said the *bones* of the story came from Robert Graves's *The Greek Myths*, volume 1. The myth belonged to an old tribe that had once farmed the region now called Greece. The sensual details, the story's flesh and blood, had taken shape over the years. "Each time the story gets told it reveals itself in a new way," I explained.

As a writer, Louise was tickled at the thought of digging up and reviving an old myth, but Adelle looked skeptical. She wanted to know where I'd gone to school and obtained training for this unorthodox art. Ginny had forewarned me Adelle might seem snobbish at first. But a bit of skepticism was to be expected. After all, why should any of them trust me on Ginny's word alone? Adelle's skepticism was fair enough, but I tossed her a response with my own special twist. "First off, Adelle, I try to follow Mark Twain's advice not to let schooling interfere with my education."

Marcia and Ginny chuckled, encouraging me to take the ball and run, so I kept going: "But I had training nonetheless, and it started early. As a girl I had the good fortune to have elder tellers in my life. My mother taught me Celtic ballads, and I spent afternoons lazing through my grandfather's books. My grandmother told poems as we picked berries and beechnuts. She's ninety-one and going strong, so it must not be hazardous to the health." They all chuckled at that, so I kept on. "As a teenager I took care of an imaginative little boy. Illness kept him confined, and storytelling was his greatest joy. Later on, in *chaos* . . . I mean in *college*, I wound up with two majors: a serpent in each hand, you might say."

Julie, Ann, and Louise burst out laughing. Adelle laughed too, more out of want for inclusion than enjoyment of the joke. She seemed won over for the most part, but I couldn't stop there. The chaos/college slip of the tongue was a sure sign of the muse. I had to see where she would lead.

"So, Adelle, to answer your question, I found myself in college choosing a major. In one hand I grasped myth and poetry, the ancient arts of soulmaking through listening and telling. In the other hand I grasped psychology, the contemporary art of soulmaking through listening and telling. For better or for worse I chose both writhing serpents, and they've become the sometimes turbulent, sometimes peaceful landscapes of my life. Throughout grad school and to this day, I remain a student of both. I like to think the muse comes through both channels if they open to her. In my life, the therapist sometimes quarrels with the mythteller, but like Eurynome's king and queen, they sometimes make up and harmonize."

This impromptu vita satisfied me. A gift from the muse, it won the group's acceptance, and also healed the schism I'd been suffering all winter. Adelle looked around, sizing up the pleasure in her friends' faces. Smiling, she turned to me and said, "Well, at least you don't get bored, do you? I know what it's like to be torn. For years I was torn between modern dance and ballet, and I've certainly known what it's like to be torn between two men!" The group cracked up laughing and Adelle flashed me a wink fit for an old pal. She seemed too smart to ruin her weekend by deciding not to like me.

Suddenly everybody wanted to talk about the business of living with a serpent in each hand—the business of polarities, harmonies, and dissonances—those between men and women, those between art and other aspects of life, including everything from family and social responsibility, to politics, finances, and falling in love. This was indeed the lively, intelligent group Ginny had promised. Around midnight, as our talk wound down, I told them the basic plan for the weekend, and asked them to remember their dreams in the morning. Finally, our exuberance gave way and exhaustion led us to our pillows for the night.

Swimming with Dolphins

I woke up early remembering this dream: *I was scheduled to testify in court, but when I arrived, it was not a court at all, but an aquarium where I'd once told sea creature tales. A group of expectant listeners waited for me to speak. Suddenly dolphins swam through our midst, and it was difficult to tell if they were swimming in air, or if we all sat submerged under water. The dolphins circled me invitingly. I had a feeling I should trust them and follow their lead. I soon found myself swimming with them, grasping their dorsals and catching swift rides, delighting in the sensation of breathing underwater.*

The dream seemed to be reminding me I'd been invited to Ginny's, not subpoenaed. It urged me into Eurynome's playful waters, and encouraged me to respond spontaneously to the surprises of the moment. It suggested I'd survive just fine, swimming in unknown waters, and should trust the spirit of the moment as my guide. I showered and put on an arty blouse, the kind I'd never wear in the courtroom.

We ate breakfast muffins and sipped coffee in front of the large windows. Sun poured through wet cedars magically lighting silver spider webs under the eaves. Ravens flapped and swooped outside the glass, reminding me of the dolphins in the dream.

Marcia began telling her dream. There was something wonderfully surreal in the animation of her lips and tongue, stained purple with blackberry jam. She now wore one silver braid down the middle of her back. Her strong potter's hands danced as she talked and the heavy bracelets on her wrists clanked back and forth with each gesture. "I was walking along the path to my studio so I could fire up the kiln to fill my Nordstrom's order. Halfway up the trail I saw our white mother cat run under the studio porch, where she'd left her kittens. A big fat raccoon was running away from the scene with something bloody in it's mouth. I could see a white tail dangling and I knew it was one of the kittens. Momma cat hissed and chased after him. I bent down to see if the other kittens were okay. Then I woke up."

"That's depressing!" said Adelle. "All I can recall is a silly recurring dream about finding my toe shoes all mildewed and falling apart. It used to upset me to the point of waking me up. It's funny, but I don't seem to mind any more. I just went right on dreaming, though I can't say what."

"I didn't have much of a dream either," Ann said. "All I remember is that Dean kept asking, 'Do you want to get married or not?' And even though we've been married for sixteen years, I kept deliberating, 'should I or shouldn't I?' You know that awful feeling, what's it called?"

"Ambivalence?" I asked.

"Yes. Ambivalence. You can't decide, because you want to make a commitment, but if you do, you may be giving up a golden opportunity that's just around the corner." Ann ran her long fingers through her thick black hair and sighed, "But everyone's getting sick of hearing me say that. Dean says I'm too old to keep my options open." Making a noisy fuss outside, two ravens nearly hit the window. They fought over a tasty scrap which fell to the ground and was quickly snatched up by a third. Everyone laughed as if this scene were the fateful moral of Ann's dream.

Julie gave it voice. She flapped like a raven and squawked, "Too bad, Ann. There goes your golden opportunity!"

Ann burst out laughing and held a napkin to her face to avoid spitting coffee. This further amped the group laughter to include spasmodic flails and pants-pissing moans. Ann seized upon the first lull to dab the corners of her mouth, and pretend to compose herself with exaggerated "high tea" decorum. She looked like Scheherazade doing a Miss Piggy imitation. The group broke up uncontrollably. The joke was obviously built on a history of generous self-mockery and friendly jibes. Their humor was like balsamic vinegar, tangy and rich, but stinging nonetheless when it hit a nerve. Clearly it wasn't the first time they'd all joked about Ann's ambivalence, but she was in the mood for it—a good sport which permitted us to laugh, no holds barred.

When the air cleared enough for her to get a word in, Ginny turned to me and said, "So you see Erica, we're sort of a stodgy, intellectual bunch."

"Maybe Erica can help us loosen up," said Louise, removing her glasses, wiping away laugh-tears. "But, back to this dream thing. You think Marcia's dream is depressing—I dreamt there was an ants' nest in my computer. There were teeming hordes of them pouring out of the slot where the disc goes in. There was nothing on the screen but asterisks and dashes. It was a nightmare! My entire novel was reduced to stars and dashes, and more stars and more dashes."

"I know the meaning of this dream!" Marcia quipped. "It's about your new Gertrude Stein haircut. I can hear your next reading," she puffed up pretentiously to do a Stein imitation. "'A dash, is a dash, is a dash.'"

"That's not funny, Marcia," Louise defended, "unless you want to play Alice B. Toklas and take dictation. Then I wouldn't need a computer."

Ginny piped up, "Girls, girls don't squabble. At least you had dreams to argue about! I don't seem to dream at all . . . or if I do, I don't remember. I must have a dream block to match my writer's block. Julie, what about you? Did you dream?"

Julie nodded hesitantly. She tossed back her leonine hair to reveal veins pulsing in her slim, muscular neck. "Yeah. Yeah, I dreamt I was playing at an improv club in an all girls' band. I had a crush on the leader, a blonde singer/songwriter. But she kept ignoring me. After the gig, I asked her if she wanted to play with me at a jazz club in Vancouver. She said she liked jamming with me, but couldn't see me as a musical partner for the long haul." The mood perched suddenly on a sharp edge. Clearly, the dream touched a nerve for Julie, and the group knew it. Nobody had looked surprised when she mentioned having a crush on a female band leader, so her being a lesbian was not news. I leaned toward her slightly, noting the obvious, "The dream hit a nerve?" Noting the obvious is an old therapist's trick. It's a code meaning, you don't have to change the subject. We can talk about it.

Julie nodded. Her eyes reddened and tears welled. She stiffened and pulled herself taller, giving off a double message: Her eyes said *help, I'm in pain,* while her voice tone and posture said, *I can take care of myself.* "They all know what the dream's about," she said gesturing toward her friends. "It's not a symbolic dream. It's biographical. My girlfriend and I were a duo 'til last month. We went to L.A. to make a CD with a producer who flipped over her voice. He promised to launch her career, which is exactly what we'd hoped for. But after four days in the studio, he kicked me out. He said he wants Maggy to record with known songwriters, doing top-forty type stuff. He said my sound is too esoteric. He didn't come right out an say it, but he refused to promote an openly lesbian duo. To make a long story short, I got dissed, and her CD comes out in six weeks. We're talking about a major brush off, musically and personally."

Louise jumped in, "Just to give you some background, Erica, I rented my cabin to Julie and Maggy last summer, so I heard them rehearse night and day. Their music is quite dynamic, because Julie's a fabulous composer and Maggy's got a fabulous voice. But since Maggy hooked up with this producer, well, I have to say it, her new sound may hit the pop charts, but it's really quite mediocre." The rest of the group agreed, and Julie obviously appreciated their support, but it was a small consolation for the loss of her collaborator, her lover, and their dream of shared success.

"Last night while you guys were sleeping," Julie went on, "I tossed and turned and basically felt like shit! I couldn't sleep, so I just lay there in my sleeping bag. One part of the myth kept coming back to me, the part where Ophion betrays Eurynome. That hits really close to home. It's so ironic. Ophion's got everything, right? *Paradise.* Who could ask for more? He's part of a really harmonious thing, but that's not enough for him. He's got to have fame, and that ruins everything. It's the fame thing that came between Maggy and me. It's totally ruined what we had.

"Anyway, I finally got up about two o'clock and came down here. The clouds parted and moonlight poured in. I watched the moon sparkling on the water, like in the myth, and it sort of energized me, so I picked up the recorder and started to play. I hope I didn't disturb you guys, but a tune just came to me and I felt like I had to play. It's the first piece I've written since Maggy ditched me. It's important 'cause I've felt artistically dead since then, and it was like finally coming back to life." She blushed and gave her hair a prideful toss as if to shake off the emotion flooding through her. "Anyway, I hope I didn't wake anyone." She guardedly glanced around, as the group assured her they'd slept like logs.

Love Apples on My Tree

Everyone sat still except for Ann, who reached behind the couch for the recorder and handed it to Julie. She looked tentatively around the group. Everyone urged her to play. She turned deeply interior, like a high diver preparing to plunge. Rocking slightly to find her rhythm, she lifted the recorder to her lips. First she played a pleasing tune that evoked for me the image of swallows dipping and swooping between green hills. Then it slowed and her face strained. Again, she looked deeply interior. A few discordant notes fell like blots of acid rain, and then a huge torrent of shrill, penetrating notes attacked the air and whirled like a blustery storm, causing the group to tense and pull back. Finally, the piece ended with a sorrowful strain akin to the lonely woods outside.

Julie lowered the recorder to her lap, sighing deeply, obviously in intense pain. The group squirmed and looked unsure how to react. Marcia almost reached out, and then refrained. I wasn't sure if we were doing group therapy, or art, or both. The dolphins of the moment seemed to suggest swimming with the flow of Julie's emotions. I asked her if she wished to follow the feelings. She sniffed hard and nodded. A sense of confusion kept coming up for her around the sudden loss of Maggy. It left her feeling disoriented, and out of the disorientation flooded childhood memories of waking up one morning in a foster home, without understanding why. Over the next three years she lived in four different homes.

In order to survive the chaos of her childhood, Julie became a resilient, self-sufficient kid. She said she'd been a loner up until she'd teamed up with Maggy. Maggy had taught her how to collaborate and connect, how to reach out and rely on someone. Now that Maggy was gone, Julie's greatest fear was that she'd revert back to being as she was in the dream: a clever solo artist, fun to jam with on occasion, but no one's partner for the long haul.

She also feared the group would feel cheated because she'd strayed from the topic, *creativity*. Louise reminded her that betrayal was part of Eurynome's creation cycle. Marcia said the betrayal turned out to be valuable because it was the thing which got Eurynome to review things. Ann said she didn't feel cheated at all; on the contrary, she identified with Julie's pain, and respected her for facing it. It took a few minutes to get all that across to Julie, but she finally understood that we liked making time for her, even when she was in pain. This was something she'd never experienced as a child, and it took a few more minutes, and lots more tears before it sank in.

She seemed in a different place than when she'd begun, so I asked if she still felt caught in the "betrayal" part of the myth.

"I think I'm more drawn to the next part, where Eurynome wants to improve creation. I'd like to keep working on the piece, but I don't know what direction to take it. I'm dying to hear what others think, but . . . I'm terrified . . . about getting feedback, because I feel so fragile right now. I'm afraid I won't be able to take it in. I feel shaky, you know . . . like a newborn fawn on wobbly legs." The image of a newborn fawn was perfectly apt for the tentative feel in the air. I urged Julie to stay with it to see what might come forth. What came was the image of a mother doe, licking and steadying the fawn. Julie spent some time with this image. Her face became serene as she described the earthy tones of their coats, the doe's way of sniffing the air, and pricking up her ears to listen. The presence of the deer was now palpable in the room. We'd all grown alert, silent, and respectful as if we'd encountered them in their forest home. Chills ran through me. A particular atmosphere had coalesced, one that might be referred to as "ritual space." I knew that responding to it was imperative.

I read the situation something like this: Julie had unwittingly invoked a nature spirit. It was no surprise, really. Living in the woods, and being in emotional crisis, can make a person susceptible to the spirit realm our Irish ancestors referred to as "the other world." At times like this, I like to harken back to the teachings of my friend, Malidoma Somé, a ritual specialist, who warns not to invoke nature spirits unless you have a clear purpose in doing so. But one of the awkward things about working with women today is that they stumble upon nature spirits in dreams, through art, and in emotional turmoil. According to Malidoma, we would need to do the following: acknowledge the invocation and honor the nature spirit, enter into a meaningful dialogue with it, and intensify the experience with a soulful action or prayer. I held these steps in my mind, and over the next hour, tried to do them justice.

First, I said a few words to emphasize the presence of the deer, and to honor them as a muses and teachers. With a bit of encouragement, Julie opened a dialogue. The doe seemed to be telling her to renew and strengthen her commitment to music. Julie understood the value of this message, but her concentration began to wane, and the images dimmed. She wanted to take the doe's message to heart, but feared she lacked the ability to follow through.

We needed a swift recharge before it all fell flat. I let my storyteller's memory trace the mythic themes of Julie's story. I said that our ancestors revered the deer as the totem of the moon goddess, queen of the hunt. Last night, betrayal had stalked Julie. She in turn had hunted the moon, and snared a song—a song which called the totem beast to her. "If that's not *follow through*, what is?" I asked emphatically. That was enough to draw Julie out of inertia.

On the coffee table sat a large vase in which Ginny had arranged spring blossoms: plum, camellia, and quince. I knew quince boughs had once been used in processions honoring the moon goddess, and they also happen to be a favored delicacy of deer. I plucked a sprig of quince from the vase, and called it "deer browse," and "the moon goddess's love apple." I asked the others to silently send respect to the doe and fawn. They did this, with palpable emotion. Tears streamed down Julie's face. I felt a warmth spread across my back and shoulders as if a warm-blooded animal were breathing gently on my neck. In a voice akin to the mythtelling voice I said that one meaning for the word *ritual* is obligation or commitment, and asked Julie what obligation called to her now.

"The obligation to keep working, to be strong, and make good music," she said.

This readily translated into a prayer the group could sing, "May you keep working, may you be strong, and make good music. May you keep working, may you be strong, and make good music."

After several repetitions, Marcia broke loose into a throaty blues strain. The others were thrown off at first, but there was real soul in it, which caught the rest of us the second or third time through. We swayed and harmonized gospel style. Soon the prayer expanded, "May you keep working, may you be strong, may you live long, and make good music." We sang on, letting variations emerge until we lost time and lost ourselves in the song. Julie wept profusely. At a certain point, we all whiffed a change in the air and the song seemed to end itself. We sat silently, looking at each other, unsure what to do with the fullness we felt.

I asked Julie if she had a sense of how to close. She wanted to place the quince bough at the edge of the woods, in a gesture of offering and thanks. We all went to the foyer and quietly put on our shoes to go outside. Ginny opened the heavy door which looked out onto the back lawn. We looked through the dusty screen door, and to our amazement, saw a doe and two fawns nibbling quince buds from the bush beside the shed. We stood breathless. Julie stared like a stunned animal. The doe stretched her graceful neck, lifting her head. Her tail flicked straight up as she glanced our way. The fawns hadn't noticed us, but they noticed the doe's tail, and watched her for guidance. She made herself tall like a kangaroo. Her ears scanned this way and that. She seemed to conclude we were harmless, and went back to browsing. When she'd had her fill of quince buds, she led her two fawns to the forest edge, and sprang over the tall ferns in an effortless bound. The fawns followed soon after.

With quince blossoms in one hand and her recorder in the other Julie led us out the door. She walked to the spot where they'd entered the forest, and lay the blossoms across their path. She said she wanted to call the new song, "Love Apples on My Tree," and dedicate it to the doe and her fawns. As a final gesture of thanks, she played sweet strains on her recorder. Returning to the lodge, the rest of us could no longer contain our amazement at the way the ritual and the actual had overlapped. Words like "incredible," "unbelievable," "extraordinary," and "synchronistic," couldn't pass often enough through our lips. We ran out of words to describe what we felt, and we shook our heads, grateful that we'd all been there and seen it together.

Back at the lodge, Julie said, "I still need to hear feedback on the new piece." Now everyone had something to say.

Ginny went first. "I was moved by the way you went into yourself when you played. You disappeared into the music, and something larger came through. I found that larger thing both chillingly sad and hauntingly beautiful. I hope it's not trampling the fawn to say that I'm envious of your passion as an artist, because as a journalist, I've been trained to be a passionless observer."

Ann said, "At first I worried I'd put you on the spot by handing you the recorder. But the music exuded such intensity, it was like a trapped spirit meant to come out. Then I got completely caught in the terrible beauty of it. It had the same primal quality of the myth last night, and it brought up a lot of memories that I might mention later."

Adelle cleared her throat and said, "Your music always amazes me, Dear. The whole time you played I felt every nuance. It spoke to me of the very stage I'm in now, the autumn of life. I don't know if I'm reading into it, but I heard the theme of life and death. If I were younger, I could have danced to it. And if I may say so, being jilted is a kind of death, but you will get over it. You have so much life ahead of you."

Marcia said, "It reminded me of Eurynome kicking Ophion in the teeth. I got the sense of a huge, violent, destructive fury—quite vengeful, but also quite cathartic."

Louise said, "It was indeed cathartic. It was operatic, and seemed like a grand finale of sorts. It made me wonder if you're washing your hands of Maggy for good. It brought up the question, 'What if Maggy comes crawling back, begging for forgiveness?' but now's not the time to get into that."

Everyone had given feedback but me. I said, "Lucky for the muse, you're listening to her call rather than pumping out top forty tunes to please a producer!"

Julie laughed and looked around. "Everything you've all said encourages me to keep working, which is exactly what I need. I'm really touched by what you said, Adelle. It helps to put things into perspective to think of your long career, and how many betrayals you've gotten over. It makes me realize someday I'll be an elder composer, you know, with a whole history behind me, and this will all be just one episode of the story.

"Also, Adelle, I was flattered when you said you 'felt every nuance' of my music and could have danced it. I know you've danced to some excellent music in your day, so that's a real compliment. And . . ." Julie slowly tilted her head, grinning slightly, glancing around the group, "I saw you dance with Fred Heaney at the Salmonfest. You could still polka faster and lighter than anyone there, so, when you say you *could have* danced to my music, I have to say I think you *could* dance to it: *present tense*. But we'll get to that later.

"Lastly, I want to say that when Ophion betrayed Eurynome, it made her think twice, but she didn't get hung up on it. She had other things to think about, and it made her realize there needed to be more lovers in the world. Maggy ditching me makes me realize a few things, mostly how much I need love in my life. Hopefully, that's where I'm headed." Her voice broke, and tears flowed again. "I guess once the hard tears flow," she said, "the joyous ones flow more easily."

Hugs, affectionate chatter, jokes, and afterthoughts bubbled about. It was late morning already. We took a fifteen minute break. I wondered where we'd be headed next. If we'd stuck with my original plan, we wouldn't have explored betrayal until that evening, but following the dolphin-flow of Julie's emotion had taken us there and beyond during breakfast. A sequential expedition into the nine regions was now the furthest thing from my mind. The muse was leading us with her emissaries, the dolphin, the ravens, and the deer. I was grateful to follow and to accept whatever unfolded.

Dancin' Fool

When we resumed, Ginny brought up her problem with spontaneity: "You're all so spontaneous! I'm awed by the way Julie transformed her insomnia into a creative breakthrough. It's obviously a tremendous gift to spontaneously use the stuff of life to keep your work vital, but I don't seem to have a spontaneous bone in my body. Everything I do is from a recipe, an outline, or a formula. I can relate to every part of the myth, except Eurynome's dancing on the sea. Dance intimidates me, especially spontaneous free-form dance. I get caught up wondering if I'm doing it right. Then I become utterly stiff, and ridiculous. This happens whether I'm trying to dance, or write poetry, or anything free-form, for that matter."

As a diplomat's daughter, Ginny had grown up in foreign cities. She'd won top honors at elite schools. Her father had taken great pride in her precocious grasp of world affairs, and had made a point to include her in adult discussions. This made her feel loved and appreciated, but on occasions when she tried to dance or sing, he scoffed and said she should stick to books. She couldn't recall ever being encouraged to follow a creative impulse, but had plenty of humiliating memories of times she'd tried. Classmates mocked her efforts to dance, draw, and sing. As an adult, awkward self-consciousness still sapped the life out of each creative urge. She confessed that discussing it made her feel distant from the rest of us, who seemed at home with spontaneity.

For Ginny, spontaneity was a *dragon zone:* a remote corner of the creation map that appeared to be full of monsters and black holes. She needed to be welcomed into this region, but after feeling like an outsider for so long, it would be no easy feat for her to accept the welcome. Entering a dragon zone after long exile can be excruciating. I scanned my mind for a way to welcome her. It occurred to me that she was not a total stranger to spontaneity. She often visited this realm in conversation. "Ginny, let me guess . . . You're Irish, right?" She nodded. "I thought so. Part of you is so innately spontaneous, you take it for granted." She gave me a confused look, but at least I'd intrigued her. "Your spontaneous expression comes out in the Irish art of conversation. In conversation you're quite playful and not the least bit stiff."

She got the point, but dismissed it as flattery. Luckily, the others saw the truth of it. They recalled rich, spontaneous comments she'd made just that day. At last she conceded that she was easygoing—even artful—in conversation, but utterly stiff when she tried to write poetry or dance. The fear of being foolish held sway as her greatest barrier. I liked Ginny very much and wanted to banish the barrier by insisting she see it differently. I offered assurances that foolishness is valuable, even sacred. "Native American creators, such as Coyote and Raven stumble upon creativity through the very act of being foolish," I tried to make her understand this paradox, but it didn't carry much weight alongside fifty-two years of humiliation. As she talked further I had to accept the heaviness of her block, and acknowledge the pain of a child who never got to play, never got to be foolish or show off. Finally I asked her to close her eyes and focus inside. A memory emerged.

"I'm alone in a classroom sitting at a desk. Outside the window the other kids run around playing and yelling." Her humiliation deepened. She said she always found excuses to stay indoors at recess because outdoors her clumsiness glared. "You see, that's what's hard about this group. Everyone else is focused on their professional work, where their strength lies, while I'm trying to learn something new. It's like the old klutz-in-the-playground situation all over again. I really hope this weekend will help me get past that."

Ginny had only one memory of playing outdoors without embarrassment. It was at a summer camp where she volunteered to work with disabled youth. "Everyone else was in wheelchairs. I was the most able of the lot," she said. "It was heavenly." I asked if she could imagine a way to translate that idea to the group, to imagine conditions under which she wouldn't feel her clumsiness glared. After a minute or so, she said, "If others would try things they *weren't* good at, then I wouldn't feel the lone fool."

"Do you have a picture of how that would work?"

"Well, yes, sort of. If everyone would try something they can't do. I know Louise can't carry a tune, for example, so if she'd agree to sing . . . and Julie says she can't draw, so if she'd draw . . ."

Everyone got a big kick out of Ginny's idea. We broke for lunch, and while eating lox on sourdough, we planned how to spend the early afternoon playing at things we did poorly.

It turned out to be a strange sojourn into the experimental playroom, like a free-for-all at disabled day camp, yielding unexpected results. Adelle and Louise played with Marcia's finger-paints, and sang while doing so. It was bizarre to hear Louise, the erudite author, sing absurd ditties out of tune while she painted. She got stuck on her favorite childhood song, "It's a Long Way to Tiperary," and would have driven us crazy if it hadn't been so ironic. She and Adelle shamelessly ruined huge swaths of butcher-paper with hideous colors and hung them proudly above the door.

Reviewing our handicaps, Ann, Marcia, and I discovered that along with Ginny, we all shared dreaded memories of playground humiliation. We'd endured years of being last picked for team sports in grade school. It brought up a gnawing wish to be invisible. But

for Ginny's sake, we chose the most humiliating sport of all—baseball, a sport where flub-ups are hard to hide.

Ann happened to have her son's Nerf baseball gear out in the
car. She brought it in and we began. Marcia did an incredible imitation of Mae West kicking off the season by prying the crushed
nerfball out from between her breasts, and dedicating our game to
the "big boys on the bench," asking, "Is that a bat in your pocket, or
are you just glad to see me?"

It was surprisingly easy to hit and catch the big soft ball when it
came my way. I hit with a vengeance, imagining planting big spongy
blows to the egos of the naturally athletic classmates who'd lorded
their superiority over me all those years. It was like banishing the
Ophions of the world. Ann and Marcia felt it too, and there was
something joyous in the shared release of hostility. We laughed as
much as we played, forming a cathartic sisterhood of defiant klutzes.
Our unity undid old hexes. Our exuberance took on a life of its
own. Our bufoonery lifted us to artful heights previously explored
by a few lone geniuses the likes of Buster Keaton and Lucille Ball.

The mound became a vortex where the sacred and profane came
together: benedictions, genuflections, and signs of the cross com-
bined with chewing, spitting, crotch scratching, obscene tics, and
foul calls. Julie, who "couldn't draw," took markers to butcher
paper and immortalized our game with rough stick figures holding
balls and bats.

Ginny played my "Best of Van Morrison" tape and danced over
and over again to "Brown-eyed Girl," a favorite song from her
college years. For the first three rounds she walked rigidly like a
faulty mechanical toy about to fall over and break. Then she stayed
in one spot with her eyes bugged out as she bobbed up and down
like an alarmed prairie dog. But after the fourth or fifth time, the
free animal broke loose. She found a big swaying rhythm and
waltzed around like a dancing bear. She sang the "sha-la-la" chorus
in a strange, slightly warped tempo that seemed otherworldly. To
our astonishment she closed her eyes, and moved about without
hitting the furniture. Louise stopped painting. She stopped singing
"Long Way to Tiperary," and just watched.

At first the exercise had seemed like an insult to the muse, to all that was graceful and skilled. But what we discovered was the genius within the fool—the impulsive, unfamiliar muse who got freed when we set aside our skills, and dove headlong into areas of inferiority. At last Ginny turned off the music and sat down. "I can't say when I've felt better," she sighed with cheeks aflame and sweat dripping off her nose.

We gravitated toward the kitchen and made afternoon tea, chatting, laughing, miming each other, rehashing the choicest moments. We remarked how gratifying it had been. "Better than sex," said Adelle. "I feel like a new woman," Ginny said. "We must do it again soon." Julie said, "Look at us! We're happy as pigs in shit!" We realized how boring, how flat it can be to limit ourselves to established skills. We applauded Ginny for plunging headlong into her dragon zone and imploring us to do the same.

Personal Cartography

Hot tea and conversation stirred intellectual coals, and the next thing I knew, they were asking me to talk about dragon zones. I said the term *dragon zones* refers to the regions we avoid while *home turf* refers to the regions where we spend most of our time. I grabbed the markers and butcher paper and began mapping. I explained that Julie was very much at home in the region of *improvisation* and *play,* thereby making Ginny's dragon zone her home turf. Ginny on the other hand, could call regions such as *revising* and *presenting* her home turf. The group members perused the nine areas and began to identify those which felt like home turf and those which felt like dragon zones. They talked of how their work got stale when they stayed too long on home turf. They listened carefully to each other to glean pointers as to how to enter avoided dragon zones.

I told them that many of the "tragic artists" we love and admire simply got stuck in one place, and that any of the regions can become dangerous unless tempered and enriched by the others. Louise got excited about applying this concept to famous writers who'd died young. She said suicidal writers such as Virginia

Woolf and Sylvia Plath are often tormented by too much *reflection.* She thought of Jack Kerouac's alcoholism as an example of deadly engulfment in *chaos.*

Marcia said in her younger years she spent too much time *reworking* her pottery, destroying the life of the piece. Julie could see how getting stuck in the *betrayal/failure* area could leave a person paranoid and alone. She confessed that after Maggy left, she'd come close to resigning herself to bitter solitude. Adelle spoke of ballet prima donnas, and the danger of dancers getting stuck in the *grandeur/ idealization* area: "It's deadly when dancers get fixated on the *ideal.* They get addicted to feeling weightless, and literally kill themselves with starvation diets and amphetamines." Ann mused that Picasso's genius in the area of *experimentation and play* eventually did him in: "He'd flit from woman to woman until he had no one. He actually wound up dying alone—estranged from everyone—even his children."

We talked of the blessings of each region. *Chaos,* though difficult and confusing, is the fertile origin of creativity. *Experimentation and play* keep our work fresh and joyous, and renew us through cathartic release. *Grandeur and idealization* generate a sense of divinity and a higher purpose that inspire, motivate, and help us store up energy for the inevitable periods of depletion.

Exile, betrayal, and failure, though extremely painful, force us to confront inner conflicts, face losses and limits, and shed false elements which undermine integrity. *Contemplation and reflection* help us to envision a bigger picture, enabling us to catch glimpses of such things as the long-term impact of our work, and our own artistic destinies. *Reworking* is the essential act of improving, modifying, or transforming a piece, to bring it to completion.

Presenting allows us to offer our creations as gifts to culture. In the hands of the public, work takes on a life of its own, carrying meaning for the community. *Rest* enables our bodies and minds to relax, forget, and empty out, so we can begin again. *Commitment* to the entire process insures that we persist and endure these difficult themes so that the muses might continue to express themselves through our work.

That evening we chatted. Some of us ruminated further on our relationships with the various themes. Some rested. Some wrote in their journals new ideas evoked during the day. We talked of our dreams as indicators of our location on the creation map. I told them my dream called my attention to *spontaneity*, and what a refreshing call that was, in contrast to the staid courtroom demeanor I'd rehearsed all winter.

Marcia felt her dream of the coon preying on the kitten had to do with the way her line of production pottery ate up all her creative energy.

Pondering her dream of ants aswarm in the computer, Louise felt it reflected directly on the *chaotic* state of her current novel. After lengthy discussion, she decided to postpone a scheduled research trip, feeling it would only "add to the confusion" at this point.

Ann felt stuck in *contemplation and reflection*. She'd been "too long deliberating" whether to spend the year sculpting new works at her island studio, or to accept a position as set designer for a major theater on the mainland. She said her wedding proposal dream was the story of her life: "always feeling frozen when what's called for is decisive commitment."

Julie said she'd covered enough ground that morning, and didn't want to think. She played the recorder softly as others talked.

Adelle didn't make a connection between her dream and the creation map. She'd fallen asleep in the easy chair and we didn't have the heart to wake her until the last of us went off to bed. I assumed her dream of the dance shoes disintegrating had to do with her retirement and the "autumn of her life," as she'd called it earlier. Her dream seemed to come from the foggy place at the boundary between *chaos* and *rest*.

All the Rest

In the morning when we reconvened, a soft sadness hung over us. It was our last day, and the end of our expedition. Adelle was the only one who hadn't led us across her creation map. Everyone seemed to be wondering if she'd initiate something this morning. She seemed pregnant with her own thoughts. We kept glancing her way to see what might hatch. Julie poured her a second cup of coffee and said, "Adelle, I said I'd get back to the topic of your dance, and now seems like the time. Yesterday you said you could have danced to my music in your younger days, but it's obvious you could still do it, if you were willing, because, everyone saw you shake a leg with Fred at the Salmonfest, and you were dynamite."

"Well Dear, ballroom dance is something quite different from ballet. When I was a tiny girl my father stood me on his feet and whirled me around the room, until ballroom dancing became second nature. It's still effortless, and probably will be until the day I die. But the world of professional dance is quite another thing. You either live it one hundred per cent, or you retire. And after my surgery, I could see the dance world had indeed survived quite well without me."

"But I heard you were asked to consult for your old dance company and you turned them down."

"That's right. What's the matter? Can't an old lady with one breast take a breather? What's wrong with that?" Adelle's face reddened.

"Well, you're still so vital, and talented. It just seems a waste not to put it to use."

"I'm still on the board of the dance academy, and I sit on the damned arts council!" Adelle cried, slamming her mug down splashing coffee in all directions. "All my life, dance came first. It ruined two marriages. Finally, at fifty, I met Jacob, the one man worth my giving up dance. But by then I was so stuck on career I didn't know how to quit! Jacob and I had ten wonderful years before he died, and the only thing I regret in this life of mine is that I didn't retire sooner so we could have spent every last minute together.

"I know you young gals value worldly success—I certainly was obsessed with it in my day—but good Lord, after losing Jacob, and surviving cancer... Other things become more important, that's all. I know you mean well, and I don't mean to snap at you, Julie. It's just that I get frustrated when people pass judgment without seeing the whole picture."

Once again Adelle took a stand as our elder, showing us the territory would look different as we got older. It was time to highlight her advanced status. "Adelle," I said, "you're ahead of the rest of us, as a woman and as an artist. We're still trying to make our careers work, while you're wrapping yours up, and discovering the importance of other things. We very much need to hear your views on the whole picture."

She looked pleased to have formally been given the floor. "I love these girls, and at my advanced age, this group has become one of the important things. I see myself in all of you. Being here is like a mirror on the past. Sometimes I sit and listen and hear you say things I've said over the years. It's important for me to be here to support you all, and it's important to know my perspective is sometimes useful."

Others began to tell stories of how she'd supported them over the years. Marcia said, "Adelle, I saw your true colors that time several of my pieces got wrecked in the gallery fire. I was broke and the gallery hemmed and hawed about reimbursing me. I was in tears and you came over. Without saying a word, you picked up the phone, called the gallery and said, 'This is Miss Stanford calling for Ms. Gonzales. If her check for $4,000 has not arrived by Monday, you'll be hearing from our attorney, Ms. Crocket.' I never heard a peep from the gallery, but the next day I received a certified money order, express mailed. If I have half as much class at your age, I'll be happy."

More episodes unfolded, ending with Ann's which I'll never forget: "When you came home from the hospital, Adelle, everyone was getting used to the word 'mastectomy.' It was very difficult for me, because when I was a child in India, we were never allowed to discuss such things. As you know, after my grandfather died, my grandmother refused all treatment whatsoever for her breast cancer. No one in the family would say it, but, we all felt it was her way of committing suttee, traditional widow's suicide. This was an old family tradition which terrified my sisters and me, but we weren't allowed to question it. Mother said it was disrespectful of the dead. Anyway, childhood fears got stirred up for me when you got breast cancer. I was terribly uneasy and you knew it. You took it upon yourself to help me, remember?"

Adelle nodded and Ann went on, looking at me now, because I was the only one who hadn't heard the story. "My youngest son is very forthcoming and curious. He's fond of Adelle and he loves her pet birds. He went with me one day when she was recovering from radiation. He was very sweet and wanted to carry the basket in which I'd packed some nice teas and Adelle's favorite curry. When we got there, she was lounging under a blanket and he wanted to know why she was sick. Before I could hush him up, I could see Adelle was going to be very frank." Ann's eyes filled with tears. "She said her breast had been very sick, so sick, they had to cut it off to save the rest of her. I was almost nauseous, but my son took it very matter-of-factly. He said he understood because he helped his father cut a sick branch off our apple tree. He took it in stride, and asked if he could see it. Adelle looked at me. She looked a tiny bit unsure for half a second, then she said, 'Of course you can.' The next thing I knew her shirt was rolled up and my five-year-old was having a look. It wasn't horrible at all—just flat white skin and a big pink scar. He said, 'Like a boy on one side,' and Adelle said, 'That's right, like a boy on one side. It's not so bad, is it?' Jeffrey just shook his head, and asked if he could feed the finches, and that was that."

Ann turned to Adelle. "I don't know if you know it, Adelle, but that was a huge healing for me. I don't know what I'd expected a mastectomy to look like . . . something unspeakable. The imagination of it was far more dreadful than the actual sight. In that little encounter you and Jeffrey healed forty-three years of silent terror. I was grateful you could do that for my son, and you showed me how I could do him far more good by simply explaining things than by hiding them."

"Oh, Ann," Adelle said clapping her hands to her bosom, "It does me a world of good to hear you say that. It's taken me a whole lifetime to learn about being honest. We ballerinas learn so much about posing to conceal flaws, it takes a long time to learn that an honest look at things is the greatest gift of all. Jacob taught me that lesson by the way he saw through my poses and still loved me, flaws and all. I could just *be* with him for hours and days on end. That was more rewarding than all the rest, that and raising my two children, of course. A dance career is wonderful, there's no denying it, and I'd do it all again, given the choice, but love and family come first, hands down.

"And as for why I'm not going back to work, well, it's time I shed some light on the *resting* phase of Eurynome's creation. No one has said a word about it, and these days it's my home turf."

I said, "Please, Adelle, we're all ears." Her floodgate had opened and there was no stopping her stream of consciousness now.

"Well," she said leaning forward like a teacher about to divulge precious secrets, "Eurynome does her best with creation, but even after repairing it, she has to leave it rough—imperfect. It will just have to do, as is. That's the way of life. For years I wanted the dance company to be flawless, but now I see it never will be. I didn't understand that as a young woman, but I understand it now.

"I used to think sleep and *rest* meant nothingness, oblivion. I could never rest on tour. I wanted to be where the action was. Goodness, I wanted to *be* the action. But lately the other meaning of the word *rest* has taken on new significance. *Rest* means to relax and restore oneself, but it also means "the rest"—all that remains—the totality. I've discovered that when you really, truly rest and let go of things, everything of importance comes back to you. You have it all. Some people call that senility, living in the past, but I tell you, it's a wonderful way to spend your days with the blessings of past, present, and future aswirl in your head.

"So if I can get up and polka with Fred next year, fine, but if I have to sit it out, well, damn it, that's fine too. It will simply have to do. I don't know if I'm making myself clear, but you girls will someday discover the luxury of living like this. Some days, all I feel like doing is drinking tea and watching the birds, and that's exactly what I do. I make sure it's a damned good cup of tea, too, because it could be my last.

"You know I'm not a religious person, but that doesn't mean I'm not spiritual. After my father died, I always felt I'd see him again, and that's still what I feel. I believe I'll dance with him again—and hold Jacob again, when the time comes. I'm lonely sometimes, but not totally lonely, because I have you, and I have them waiting for me. This is the peace which elluded me when my heart and soul were all tied up in dance."

Julie reached out and snatched Adelle's hand, "Oh, Adelle, that makes so much sense. And here I was worried that you'd get bored. I can be such an idiot, sometimes."

"You're certainly not an idiot, Dear." Adelle said, "At your age I would have been bored watching birds."

Ann said, "Adelle, I feel so grateful to have you in my life. You said you see a mirror of the past when you're with us, and I hope I'm seeing a mirror of the future when I look at you. This is the kind of conversation I was never able to have with my mother and grandmother, and it means a great deal to me." The others said "Amen" to that.

"Well then," Adelle said, "since you appreciate my frankness, maybe now's the time to tell you about my living will. I can't speak for Ann's grandmother, but for myself, I've come to believe that death is kinder than prolonged misery. And who knows, your grandmother was a Hindu, and they know all sorts of secrets about death and the afterlife, now, don't they? Anyway, what I'm trying to say is . . . If the cancer starts up again, I won't take a thing but morphine next time. I've had enough surgery and sickening treatment. My son can't yet accept it, but my daughter is beginning to come around. I hope you girls will support me if it comes to that. You'll have to, because I've made up my mind."

Louise reached over and hugged her tightly, "You're the choreographer. We'll follow your lead," she said. Adelle pulled Ann and Julie closer and the three larger women drenched their tiny elder in tears. Everyone moved in close. For the next five minutes no words were spoken. The language of touch sufficed.

Looking Ahead: Where to Go from Here

We had three hours to go. I asked for their ideas about how the weekend might end. They agreed they now had a strong sense of where they stood on the map of creation and an inkling about where they needed to go next. Before going home, they wanted to focus on the new direction. With that in mind, I suggested we let the muse guide us in the making of a shrine for the new direction. We would get our hands on natural materials and let them speak to us as we worked. Little explanation was needed, as the group was quite at home with the intuitive approach. We put on boots and hats and a foraging mission unfolded naturally. With Ginny reminding us not to disrupt the forest, we entered the woods, fanning out silently, without a plan, probably the way our earliest ancestors had set out to gather roots and herbs.

I marveled at sumptuous lichens and brilliant mosses opulently bursting forth from rotted stumps. The forest was indeed a vegetative celebration of new life feeding on deadwood. It was otherworldly. The cells of my body hummed with the spirits pulsing in the earth and trees. And I wondered how the human race has become so out of touch with the divinity of nature. Living in the forest as she did, it was no wonder Adelle had grown wise and full of faith.

What kept grabbing me was the pale moon-glow of hanging mosses and lichens. Sea-green moss swayed in wisps like trolls' beards and nymphs' hair. I found a recently fallen limb and plucked those mosses already torn by the fall. Soon I had a huge woolly armload.

After an hour or so, we began drifting back to the lodge with our goods. Ginny had come back early with bird wings she'd found. Satisfied they were enough, she'd arranged a large table before the window as the altar for our shrine.

During the next hour, stubborn artistic heads butted a few times as ideas collided about how to construct the shrine. But all in all, things fell into place. The shrine was as beautiful as those I'd seen in the remote villages of other continents. For a moment we just stood back to admire it. Then I asked them to create a closing for our weekend by speaking to the new directions which called to them now.

Julie wanted to start. She explained how, poking around Ginny's shed, she'd discovered a heap of quince clippings from when the bushes had been pruned last year. Julie had gathered the dry ones and had broken them into hundreds of foot-long rufous twigs. She'd arranged them on the floor to define a stunning entry to the shrine. "These are love apple twigs," she said. "They were cut off and left for dead . . . betrayed, so to speak . . . But now they've been salvaged, and given new purpose. They call me to leave betrayal behind, and renew my commitment to music. That's my new direction: commitment."

Ann went next. She stepped forward and ran her slim fingers over the rust-colored cedar boughs she'd deftly twined to form a six-foot-high archway over the top of the shrine. "As you know, I'm stuck contemplating my options ad infinitum, and I haven't been able to settle on what shape my creative commitment will take. As I walked through the woods, these cedar boughs caught my attention. They'd fallen from a huge old tree which has probably been standing for hundreds of years. I could see charcoal in a cleft in the trunk, showing that it's survived at least one fire, and of course, countless storms. As I was dragging the boughs in, I kept thinking one thing. Both my options are excellent, so what am I afraid of? I could flip a coin, and be happy either way, and yet I feel frozen when it comes to free choice. Why?

"I had some strange sensations, dragging the boughs. It was like dragging branches for a fire, and I had a fleeting sense of what it must have been like to set up a suttee ritual. It really gave me the willies! I thought of my grandmother and all the other women who had no options at all, and probably nothing to live for. I realized that for their sake, as well as my own, I must choose, and get moving. I have a lot to live for. So, Julie, I'm right there with you. Maybe we can help each other with commitment, because that's my new direction too."

I was stunned by the way past and present came together in the making and telling of the shrine. Working with natural materials drew meaning out of scents, textures, and muscular exertion; evoking deep memories, and emotional release.

Ginny stepped forward. "I too, started something and pray I can keep going with it. Until yesterday, I'd never danced. It's embarrassing to say it, but I felt beautiful and spontaneous, as free as a bird. There were moments when I felt like I was Eurynome, herself. Today when I walked outside, I wanted something to symbolize that spontaneity. Right off the bat, I saw a dead bird," she held up two blue-grey wings for us to see. She turned them, gently exposing their white undersides and then set them back on the shrine, nested upon the sage-colored moss I'd gathered. "At first I found the dead bird disgusting—mutilated by a feral cat, no doubt. Most of the head and body were torn away, and just the wings remained, one broken, and one perfectly intact. I moved it off the trail with a stick and kept walking, searching for shrine materials, but nothing captured my eye. Later it began to dawn on me the wings were quite fitting. Eurynome became a bird when she danced, remember? Anyway, by the time I realized the wings were the perfect thing to honor spontaneity, I'd wandered quite a distance. I turned around and rushed back, thinking I'd never find them, but there they were, right beside the trail in the same spot. It also seems fitting that one wing is broken," she said with trembling lips. "One wing is the wounded side, and the other soars freely, as I did yesterday. Anyhow, I hope this means spontaneity is my new direction."

Marcia signaled her turn. "I want to go next, to talk about protecting spontaneity, because I'm realizing how fragile it can be. I found a marvelous place to dig clay, and brought in a couple boxes full. At first I had nothing in mind, other than to make something decorative for each side of the altar. I began shaping these large feline figures. As I worked, I thought about the mother cat in my dream and the raccoon devouring her kittens. I realized something fragile in my life is at risk: namely, my spontaneity. Every moment gets gobbled up by production work. I need to set up some free time in the studio, and then guard it like a mother cat. Hopefully my new direction will be spontaneity."

Louise got up to go next. She'd collected dozens of alder catkins and heaped them onto a tray she'd fashioned out of a large piece of dead bark. She'd placed it on the center of the table, where it looked like an offering. "I went into the alder grove south of the lodge," she began. "I kept getting hit in the head by these catkins dropping off the branches. It made me notice how tremendously prolific alder trees are. They seed prolifically. They sprout and grow like weeds. It made me think of my first two novels and how quickly they sprang to life.

"I picked up this hunk of bark, and began to fill it with alder catkins. You can see they're half disintegrated by now. That brought my present novel to mind. It keeps disintegrating. It's got complicated subplots played out over generations, which seem to crumble before they jell. Like these alder catkins, the new novel is excessive, overripe—and let's face it—a mess. That's what the dream of the ants was about . . . a chaotic force beyond my ken and certainly beyond my control. So, I guess I'm paying my dues to chaos. I still don't know if this novel's going to make it. But when I try to force structure upon it, it just makes things worse. So, if the novel is meant to be, it'll emerge in its own time, like Eurynome rising from chaos. I don't like that one bit, but I don't seem to have any say in the matter at this point. For me, new direction means patience with the chaos. I'll think of Eurynome, and instead of resisting chaos, I'll try to surrender."

"I'll go next," Adelle said. "Surrender is a key word for me. You all know that I'm refining the art of resting. I'm content to be like Eurynome, satisfied with my work and happy to put my feet up and listen to the birds, including these cacklers," she gestured toward the group and smiled fondly. "I found this walking stick." She stood up to demonstrate how nice it was to lean on. "It's starting to rot. You could say it's surrendering to slow decay, like me. It looks useless at first, but if you look closely, you see it's got beautiful green moss growing on it, and little colonies of mold, and these clusters of fungi standing out here." She turned the stick to make sure we all saw. "So many lives prospering from the old stick. Well, I thought to myself, a retired dancer is like an old stick. Students, children, grandchildren, and friends stay in touch because she still has something to offer. Are you with me, so far?" Everyone nodded.

"Okay, because there's more. The stick doesn't whine and say, 'Gee, I want to get back on the tree and be a supple young branch like I used to be!' It's got the good sense to enjoy the stillness of the forest floor and the cool feel of the ground. It doesn't try, as Ophion did, to be above the natural law. So, at the risk of sounding morbid, I'm accepting decline—accepting that I'm not above the natural law. I'd just like to give thanks for being part of creation and show it by continuing to rest." She planted the tip of her walking stick firmly on the floor and sat down.

Each artist had found a talisman which revealed and affirmed her new direction. Some revelations were sweeter than expected, while others were bittersweet, but all bore the good flavor of truth.

Now it was my turn to speak. "Like most of you, I walked with no particular aim. What caught my attention was this hanging moss," I said gesturing to the pale green tufts spread across the altar. "They grow in wispy clumps on tree branches, and hang down like old seamen's beards—or wild women's hair. They must have fallen during the storm, and they'll probably die soon, because to survive they have to be attached to a source of nourishment, like Adelle's stick. That's when I realized the tufts are like children. Their survival depends upon a nourishing source. I've been working with kids at risk—kids with no such attachment to sustain them. I've been depressed because these kids need so much more than our system provides.

"When I put the tufts on the shrine, I placed the underside down, hiding the spots where they were torn from the tree. Then I realized we do the same to children at risk. We try not to see their wounds. My job all winter, has been to get on the witness stand and tell their stories—revealing their wounds. This has been the hardest work I've ever done. It requires tremendous commitment. I'm just beginning to understand how this, too, is an important branch of storytelling—not a deviation from the art, but part of it. I hope for more commitment to see me through. You can see I've gone back to the altar and turned the moss belly up, exposing the wound."

Julie picked up her recorder and played a closing tune. Marcia scat sang and coaxed us to do the same. The spirit got into Adelle's feet. She took Ginny by the hand and they swooped about like the sylph and the dancing bear. We sang and danced until it grew dark and time for me to drive home.

Many unmet challenges lay before us, so, why did we feel so complete? Perhaps hearing Eurynome's feats, and hearing our own stories, we'd gained a more solid footing from which to move forth. One thing was sure: We'd wake up inspired the next day, eager to heed new muses, and serve the old ones with renewed hearts. I thanked the group for laying bare their life stories so we could immerse ourselves in the live theater of creation. After affectionate goodbyes, I was back on the road. The route seemed shorter and safer coming home. In a few hours, my husband would say, "I told you so," about the muse.

And what about the months to come? Did we remain inspired and fulfill our hopes? Well, I for one, called on the muse each time

I swore in on the witness stand. From that time forward superior court judges followed my recommendations to the letter. Within the next year Ann's stage sets won her a national award, and a new line of whimsical mugs appeared under Marcia's label at Nordstrom.

Ginny wrote to update me on the rest of the group. Julie had signed a recording contract with an avant-garde producer in London. *Love Apples on My Tree* was the title cut of her first CD. Louise had recently celebrated the birth of her first grandson, whom she cradled in her arms while watching Adelle polka with Fred Heaney at the Salmonfest. Ginny mounted and framed her bird wings and got a couple of poems published in an island anthology. But what she really wanted me to know was that each morning, rain or shine, she went to the edge of the ravine, opened her arms to the sea, and danced like a goddess stirring primal forces to life.

5

What a
Woman Is

Myth is the song of the imagination inspired by the energies of the body.

—Joseph Campbell

Hormones

I walked through the door of the teen residence center to lead Tuesday night story group. The familiar smell of fried chops wafted from the kitchen, but a strange quiet filled the hall where raucous teenage voices usually echoed. Silence in the house made me uneasy. It followed calamity, concealed smoldering conflicts, and preceded uproars. I hoped for a smooth evening, but knew better than to expect it. If emotions didn't erupt during dinner, they'd likely explode in group.

The girls lived at the residence center because their home lives had gone awry. What was best in them was badly wounded and scabbed over with ugly defenses. If they didn't get serious help now, they'd become troubled young women, dangerous to themselves, and maybe to others.

The staff hoped to help them outgrow stormy childhoods and root themselves solidly in adult life. This was no easy task. In her first few months, a girl would typically act out family traumas, trying to pull the staff into hurtful battles and stubborn stalemates. But after a year or two, most of the girls let go of destructive routines to find more creative ways to cope. At that stage, a girl became a role model for new residents, demonstrating that their stay there had a purpose: to strengthen and cultivate what was best in them. That winter we were grateful to have one such role model in the house, a seventeen-year-old African American named Nita.

Nita had come to us wearing a studied "tough-girl" guise, and understandably so: Since she was ten, her father had been in prison for violent crimes, and her mother had several younger children by men who tended to treat her roughly, and then drop out of the picture. By age eleven, Nita stood taller than her petite mother. With Dad gone, it seemed only right to try and fill his shoes as the family protector. This wasn't easy in a neighborhood ruled by gangs. For Nita, shielding Mama and the babies meant imitating Dad—staring people down, sticking out her jaw, tossing back her head, and puffing up the broad shoulders and imposing chest she'd inherited from his side of the family. She set out to earn a "rep" on the block by "talking mean," making threats, and occasionally proving she meant business by roughing up kids who messed with her siblings.

But the fact was, she had no real heart for bullying. After a few months at the center she'd happily stopped shoving and hitting altogether. The more we got to know her, the more she stood out as exemplary, making the best of school, her job, and life at the center. Unlike most of the girls' parents, Nita's worked with us and not against us. They'd each begun their own soul-work and they viewed her stay at the center as a chance for Nita to heal. Mom's visits and Dad's letters encouraged just that.

At the dinner table that evening, Nita's seat was empty. It seemed odd, for she never missed a meal, especially chops and gravy.

I sat across from Kate, my story group assistant. She was a full-time staffer with her finger on the pulse of the house. It amazed me how much sense Kate could make of the girls' testy moods, unruly conduct, and strained silences. We always met before group so she could fill me in on house news. Then we'd plan group according to the predominant theme among the girls that week. Whether it was rape, rivalry, or self-esteem, my job was to come up with a story that opened doors for exploration and learning. Neither I nor the staff had ever before seen anything quite like our ritual evolve. Though it was unusual, the administration stood behind it one hundred per cent, because it was the only therapy group run by an "outsider" that had withstood the test of time. It was less threatening to the girls than traditional group therapies. Their fascination with stories expanded their tolerance for talking about painful themes.

We'd tried different formats over the years and finally settled into a routine that worked. It started with dinner. On Tuesdays, the girls set a place for me and I joined them as a way for us to "hang out" together. This enabled them to warm up to me a little before we stepped into story work. It also gave me a chance to acclimate myself to the unpredictable emotional weather, whiff the general mood, and note any oddities before starting group. That night as always, we made chit-chat as we passed steaming platters family style.

"Where's Nita?" I asked Kate.

"She's late getting back from the doctor," Kate said, offering no more. That was my cue that it was confidential, not a cold or flu. Suddenly the chop on my plate didn't look so great. In the past year we'd dealt with pregnancies, AIDS, overdoses, and attempted suicides. I hoped this particular silence wasn't pregnant with tragedy. Kate read my mind and said, "Not to worry. It isn't life threatening."

Shelly, the girl on my left, looked at Kate, and then at me, her eyes growing wide enough to pop. She couldn't hold her tongue long enough to swallow. "It's hormones!" she blurted, ripping the strained silence wide open. Out of her mouth flew half-chewed chunks of food.

Jessica, to my right, snorted in kind. Milk shot out her nose and mouth, "It's *hormones!* Get it? *Whore moans! Like, 'ahhh, ahhh, oohhh . . . Harder, Baby, harder.'"* she howled, throwing her head back, clutching her ribs. The gut force of her laughter spewed a mouthful across the table, splattering Suzanne's angora sweater. Their grotesque display started a chain reaction. Rene's bulemic gag reflex kicked in and she rushed out of the room to barf. Suzanne, covered

in milk and little dabs of green—probably half-chewed peas—
demanded Jessica pay her on the spot for dry cleaning. Waves of
nausea, indignation, rage, and hysteria rolled in both directions
down the table. All five staff members had to pull a tight rein to get
the girls settled down for the rest of dinner. I can't tell you how
relieved I was to leave the table. I envied the cook, alone in the
kitchen, peacefully gnawing her chop.

Kate and I met in the remodeled closet we called a consultation
room. "Which chair do you want, the wobbly one or the broken
one?" I asked. (We shared a long-standing perturbation at the
underfunding of youth agencies.) "And remind me next time to lay
off the inquiries at dinnertime, will you?"

"I should have forewarned you," she said. "You walked in on a
bomb waiting to go off. We've never dealt with a hormone problem
before, not since I've been here anyway. We don't know if it's strictly
medical, or psychological, and as you saw, the girls come unglued
about it. It's dead silence, or total eruption with no middle ground.
So we haven't figured out how we're going to discuss it."

That made perfect sense to me. There probably wasn't one of us
under that roof—staff, girls, storyteller, or cook—who wouldn't, at
some point in life, get anxious about hormones.

"Nita's periods have been sporadic since she started at age
eleven," Kate said. "She gets cramps and spotting, but no real flow.
She's had tests and x-rays, but they've never found any actual cause
for it. This week it's all come up again. That's what the commotion
was about. We found out she's got quite a bit of facial hair, and she's
mortified about everyone knowing."

"Now how in the world did she keep that hidden around here? I
mean, with privacy practically nonexistent, and razors prudently
rationed, and all."

"The secrecy is what's sad," Kate said. "Before dawn every morning, Nita's been creeping into the bathroom with razors, tweezers,
and a flashlight. That's where all her spending money goes! She
saves up, and when she goes on pass, she buys razors, batteries,
and special creams. She's got a whole suitcase full of hair removal
stuff."

"Good God! Imagine her getting up at that hour every day. Put that together with how hard she works at Dairy Queen to earn a few bucks, and the picture breaks your heart. It also explains why she's always broke when we take the girls shopping."

"Exactly," Kate said. "It explains a lot of little things, and it's been going on the whole time she's been here. Jessica got up early Monday morning and stumbled in on her. They scared each other half to death. Nita broke down crying. She was so mortified I took her aside and we had a long talk about it. She poured her heart out. She feels badly about the facial hair and the fact that she has no real menstrual flow. She thinks it means she's not a real woman. Nancy took her to see Dr. Matock. They ran more tests and still found no organic cause. The doc says it's possible her flow got blocked up at the onset of menses due to emotional instability or trauma, and she had plenty of both at the time. That's when Dad went to prison and Mom was hospitalized for another miscarriage."

"Yeah, and when she first came here, remember how often she said boys were lucky because they didn't have periods?"

"She also said she was never going to get pregnant, because it led to nothing but trouble and pain."

"So if we entertain Doc's theory, we might take it a step further and say, basically, it wasn't safe to be female. With Dad gone, Nita had to be macho to take his place."

"Right. She had to have balls to protect the family and had to put her ovaries on hold, because functional ovaries might lead her into the same trap Mom was in—pregnant, broke, beat-up, and alone with six kids. So anyway, Doc talked about trying a minute dose of hormones to see if it boosts her cycle. He sent her to a specialist today, to get a second opinion. Nita was real hopeful about it."

"This all makes a lot of sense. Nita's at a crossroad. She's re-evaluating femininity. Before it seemed deplorable, so she rejected her budding womanhood; but now it's looking better, so she wants help bringing it forth. Her attitude shift makes total sense. Her mom's getting stronger and building a better life. And here at the center, Nita's got a broad spectrum of female role models. Look at us. We're a multi-ethnic staff of intelligent, beautiful, skilled, professional women." I winked at Kate who was always ready for comic relief,

"We probably make femaleness look like a veritable piece of cake, don't you think?"

Kate nodded, "Right on! Hysteria, corns, Mydol, hair spray, varicose veins, low end of the pay scale . . . and talk about broad spectrum, I'm broading all the time," she said patting her hips. We both felt beat from a full day's work, but a little sarcasm perked us up no end. In truth, we loved hashing over whatever happened to be stewing among the girls. Story group themes came together like specialty soups, based on the available stock, staples, and seasonings of the day. On this particular night we had a lot to work with: fresh turmoil, Nita's desire for change, Doc Matock's down-home insight, Kate's meaty observations, and my storytelling. It was my job to act as a wise grandmother would—to come up with a fitting story—one that would nourish Nita, and provide a context for healing. But as often is the case, the story hadn't yet come to me. Kate and I were close to the wire. I closed my eyes and pictured Nita, hoping the right tale would bubble to the surface.

In a recent story group, the others had fallen silent as Nita spoke in a near whisper. "I hadda walk Mama to the store cause she was scared to go alone at night, and I was too young to buy her wine. It was kinda dark at the bus stop and a old lady says to me, 'Excuse me sir, do you know the time?' I kep' walkin' and Mama says, 'Nita, help the lady. You gotta watch on.' Nobody around but me and Mama. I felt bad cause the old lady thought I was a man. After that I asked Mama, 'Do I look like a man?' Mama said, 'No, baby, you just a big girl, besides, it's dark and that old lady can't see.'

"I feel bad at school too, cause girls in gym class say I'm like a guy. I wanna be more ladylike cause I wanna ask this one boy Gerry to the Sadie Hawkins dance, but I don't want him and his friends to say I'm like a guy. I don't wanna be no Miss Priss, like that frat girl Whitley on TV. I wanna be still sorta outrageous like Tina Turner. Or ladylike, but strong, like Jackie Joyner."

Clearly, it was my job to tell a story which would give Nita permission to be both "ladylike" and strong, like her favorite singer and athlete. The tale should affirm her African roots, as well as her female essence. It should welcome her into the society of womanhood. A popular African tale came to mind. Sobonfu Somé, a

West African teacher and a dear friend of mine, had explained the
subtle meanings of the tale's myriad variations. Now I prayed my
tired memory could recollect one for Nita's sake.

Through the narrow window of our closet. Kate and I had a
view of the parking lot. We saw van headlights pierce the fog outside. It was Nancy, bringing Nita back from the doctor. When they
passed under the floodlight on the way to the door, we could see
crumpled Dairy Queen bags in hand. That meant Nita was fed and
ready for group. It also meant she hadn't been too upset to stop by
her workplace for food.

Kate yawned ferociously, telegraphing her exhaustion from a
long day. "Tell me you're not brain-dead," she pleaded.

"Okay," I nodded, "Remember that wonderful African tale we
worked with a couple of years ago, about a girl who's both strong
and beautiful? That story's pertinent to Nita, because the heroine is
also a protector, and the story's about her courage through the difficult passage into womanhood."

With that said, there was no need for further discussion. Kate
and I had been doing group together for years. Planning group meant
identifying the theme of the day and selecting a fitting story. The
rest had become an ingrained ritual that varied little. Kate rang the
bell and rounded up the girls while I arranged the group room. I
moved the sofa, fluffed pillows, and softened the lights, as if ready-
ing my living room for guests. The fact was, I was the visitor. The
center was their home. But it's important to arrange a room for
stories: dimming harsh lights to a softer glow, drawing seats in toward the hearth, clearing away distractions.

Evoking the mythic requires subtle attention to the surround-
ings. Our ancestral storytellers knew better than to compete with
noise, food, or bright lights. The African story would evoke mythic
presences: the virtuous heroine, the river hag, and the river monster. These beings are disinclined toward fluorescent lights and plastic chairs. They're much more likely to join us in the half-light where
candles flicker and shadows dance. Stories require their mystique,
and it's the teller's duty to guard it. Nighttime, gathering together
time, fireside or hearthside: These are the times and places for story,
and the settings most conducive to the mythic imagination.

Adolescence also has a mystique of its own, and the girls made it their business to guard it. They didn't just enter the room. They tried new walks, overstated gestures, emitted sighs, exuded auras, brooded silences, unleashed moods. They strutted, trudged, stomped, and crept into the room. One posture begged, "Notice me!" while another said, "Look at me and you die!"

Rounding them up took Kate a good five minutes. The first arrivals were antsy, impatient, eager to start. Several asked to *brag* first. *Bragging* was our opening ritual, each girl's opportunity to announce prideful accomplishments, small pleasures, and the week's good fortune. Brags helped start group on a positive note, which wasn't easy with girls who saw life as hell, families as torture, and themselves as the cause of other people's pain. Gathering around the hearth, talking about their talents and blessings didn't come naturally, but over time, most of them came to relish the chance to display their gems for admiration.

But there were always those who couldn't pull it off. That night, Shannon was stuck in an old round of self-hate. She tried to make it a team sport, "You all hate me!" she screamed. "None of you care about me! I don't have any fucking brags! How could I, stuck in this jail? . . . Erica can go ahead and tell the dumb story, but I'm not listening!" Sometimes when a girl couldn't brag for herself, others in the group could. At such times, they bragged for her, and she basked in their praise. But Shannon was so steeped in self-loathing, that praise hurt. It brought forth too many hunger pangs for what had always been missing. She was like a starving child who'd have to sip weak broth before she'd be strong enough to digest real food. Listening on the sly while pretending not to need us was about all she could take.

As latecomers filed in, and the brags wound down, the girls prodded, "What's the story?" "What's it about?" "What kind of story is it?" "What nationality?" These questions were also part of our ritual. The cataloging gave them a gratifying foothold in the story. Nita came through the door just in the nick of time. I held off answering until I knew she could hear.

"I'm hoping to tell an African story," I said with deliberate emphasis on *African*. Nothing awakened their souls like the mention of ancestral roots. They were forever begging me to tell tales from their particular ethnicity. Since they saw family heritage as a disaster, the notion of coming from a larger family moved them deeply. It was my job to unearth the tales their grandmothers would tell if lost traditions had remained intact. Celebrating ancestry through lore became a matter of esteem—affirming their origins—making each girl a heroine for a night.

The three African American girls beamed. It was their night. Nicki smiled and said, "My ancestors were African."

Nita plunked down beside her and piped up, "Of course they were! Did you think they were Swedish?" She seemed full of moxie for a girl whose best-kept secret was out on the table.

Nicki snapped back to prove she was heritage-wise and nobody's fool, "Coulda been from Brazil or Haiti."

But Nita got the last word, "They all from Africa, girl! Haiti, Brazil, Cuba, Jamaica, Costa Rica: They all from Africa." It was settled.

"Sorry I was late," Nita went on, "but, can I tell my brag before the story?" Kate gave her the go-ahead. She spoke softly, almost whispering, "Dr. Matock sent me to a special lady's doctor, I guess you call her. And I'm real happy cause she's real nice and she's helping me with a problem I have." Nita spoke without raising her eyes. Kate shot me a subtle glance, sharing my surprise that Nita addressed her theme head on. "She explained something to me. Lotta girls have facial hair." Again I felt Kate's surprise, but we avoided checking each other's eyes. "And it's a girl's prerogative if she wants to let it show, or get rid of it, or whatever she wants. So, I'm happy, cause if I don't want to shave, I can have hormone pills or 'lectrolysis that won't chafe my face." Nita smiled like it was Christmas. There wasn't a distraction in the room. The other girls kept their eyes averted, and tried to look casual, but their ears hadn't missed a word. A mixture of fear, awe, sympathy, and respect filled the silence. It'd be a long time before *hormones* were the butt of in-house jokes.

"Tell the story," somebody said.

Nita was off the hook for the moment, and I was on. I hadn't told the chosen tale for over two years. How could I be sure it would surface on call? Like everyone else, the storyteller lives in a state of constant amnesia. Just because you knew a tale at one time, there's no guarantee it will always come back to you. I knew dozens of tales by heart and if pressed, could have roughly summarized several more. But knowledge once held at the fingertips, can easily fall out of reach like a lost book. I needed a moment to focus on retrieving the tale from the dusty shelves of my memory. Luckily Kate had a few announcements to make. While she talked, I closed my eyes and tuned inward.

Our ancestral storytellers saw memory as a sacred function. They believed memory endured like a mountain, yet flowed ever onward like a great river. The memory goddess was said to imprint the soul by placing her indelible mark on the storyteller's heart and senses. This explained memory's link to odors, textures, images, sounds, rhythms, and strong emotions. Numbers can be learned by rote, but stories must be learned by heart. To awaken her memory of a tale, the teller must picture the first scene, smell its landscape, and hear the first word. This is how we prime the well of memory, coaxing the first scene out of the rock. First it trickles, then begins to flow down the mountainside forming a stream, gradually gathering the momentum of a river. But I was tired and the riverbed was still dry.

Kate wrapped up the announcements. The girls adjusted their pillows and nestled into their seats. They nagged me, just the way I like them to. That too, was part of our ritual. They listened better when they had to work to get a story. "C'mon! Are we having a story tonight or what?"

I still didn't have a solid enough footing in the story to tell it with confidence. "I hope we're having a story," I said, "but I forgot how to get hold of it. What are the instructions from Sobonfu?" Sobonfu had coached me on the ways of storytelling in her village, and had encouraged me to share them with the girls. They'd never met her face to face, but they loved her nonetheless because her methods held great delight. Nicki said, "Take your basket to the land of the ancestors and see if they'll lend us a story." I often teased that if we didn't ask politely, the ancestors would put a recipe in the basket instead of a story, and we'd have to spend the evening making crocodile stew. I looked around the room at the girls and settled my eye on Nita. "Nita," I said, "would you like to do the asking?"

"Okay," she said grinning. "Please, Honorable Ancestors, put a good one in Erica's basket so we won't get bored and fall asleep or have to cook stew."

Retrieval: Plunging Deeply

I closed my eyes and pictured Sobonfu's radiant face. Then I saw her grandmother, a consummate elder storyteller. I held my basket and prayed for a story for Nita. Luckily, when I peered inside, the first scene was there. I saw African women standing at the river's edge. I heard flies buzz, felt gritty wet sand on my feet and velvety brown water at my ankles. I smelled the yeasty sweet river. I now felt confident the story wanted to be told. Word-pictures began to surface, trickling up from memory, falling forth from my lips.

There was once a village alongside a great river in Africa. The water rolled along the sand each day as it had the day before, the year before, the century before, and all the time before that which no one even bothered to count. And all that time, people lived in the village. And all that time, when girls reached a certain age—the age when nature began to work changes in their bodies—their elders gave them a gift. The gift stood for female beauty, and with it came certain powers, status, and responsibilities. The gift was a belt, with beautiful stones and shells, and each girl wore hers to protect the generative powers within her body. No girl received hers until womanhood came upon her from the inside out.

One girl's elders gave her a fine belt with golden amber, red bloodstone, and hundreds of coral beads sewn together in a swirl, like river water 'round a rock. It comforted the girl to feel it 'round her waist in the morning when she filled her urn at the river's edge. She wore her belt so proudly, and it looked so beautiful encircling her hips, that all the people who saw her turned their heads

to take a second look. Looking at her made them notice all the beauty around them: the trees, the river, the sky, and the distant mountains.

This story had endless variations depending on the time and purpose of the telling. Sobonfu said, "You don't wear the same dress each day, well, the story doesn't either." That day the point was to enhance Nita's wardrobe, and the belt was no mere accessory. It carried the power of the mountains and the never-ending flow of the river. It protected Jackie Joyner's power-source as she leapt hurdles. It was the outrageous fringe shimmying at Tina Turner's hips as she sang.

Other village girls were jealous of her belt. When the girl walked by, one whispered, "She thinks she's better than us." The jealous girls decided to trick her. The next morning they gathered in the center of the village. A clever one called out, "Oh, did you hear the wise woman's prediction? I'm so frightened!"
"No," said the girl with the belt, "I didn't hear. What did the wise woman predict?"
"She said the river god is angry and the river will flood its banks! All of us will be washed away and drowned, unless we girls throw our belts to the river god as gifts. That alone will save the village."
"Is it true?" asked the girl.
The others nodded, "Yes, it's true!"
"Then we must go at once!" said the girl with the belt. She ran to the river. The other girls ran too. She unhooked her belt. The other girls unhooked theirs. The girl hurled her fine belt far out into the middle of the river. Then the other girls laughed. They had only pretended to hurl their belts. Now they put them back on and walked back to the village.
Being fooled like that made her eyes sting with tears. She wanted to get her belt back. She took a deep breath and dove into the river, swimming further and further into the dark water until she came to the deepest spot.

Our heroine was willing to sacrifice her belt when she believed it would protect the village. Nita, too, was a courageous protector, willingly sacrificing aspects of femaleness when she believed it would help protect the family. Now came the time for both heroines to retrieve what was lost. Nita, too had leapt into the river—going to doctors, learning about hormones, talking about it in group. She'd plunge again and again before the issue was resolved.

The River Hag

There at the depths of the river, the girl saw the river hag with green slimy hair undulating all around her. The river hag was covered with sores. The sores oozed slime, and in the slime small snails crawled, and worms burrowed.

"Greetings, Grandmother," the girl said respectfully. "Have you seen my belt?"

"Belt?" asked the river hag in a loud, raspy voice. "Did you say belt?"

"Yes," said the girl and she told the whole story of how she'd been tricked.

"I can help you," said the river hag, "but first, you help me. Lick clean my sores."

The girl was wise enough to know she was speaking to a river spirit in hag form, so she took the hag's hand, and licked the slime from the sore on her wrist. Then she licked clean all the sores on the hag's arms. Then her back, and so on until all the sores were clean, and the river hag was happy.

The point of the river hag was not to force the girls to revel in morbidity, but to tell them in no uncertain terms, that old wounds must be tended before the radiant belt can be restored. Now that her secret was out, Nita had begun to lick clean the sores of her bruised female identity. In doing so, she was bound to taste her mother's uncleansed wound, and perhaps her grandmother's, for there was no telling how long the female branch of the family had been ailing.

Like our heroine, Nita would have to overcome squeamishness. She'd have to accept certain physical realities if her menses started flowing as she hoped. In sex ed class she learned that nutrient-rich menstrual blood had the power to give life, but she also noted that discarded menstrual pads smelled like "something dead dragged outta the river." Her nose read the paradoxical news of the natural world. Fertility's next of kin is a black sheep called decay.

Hidden in the river hag scene is the knowledge that the passage toward womanhood links us not only to beauty and generativity, but also to the mysterious depths, the very source where the river of life is inextricably linked to decay and death. Our ancestors understood this, so much so, that whether Aztec or Persian, they worshipped the cycle of life, death, and rebirth, all in one goddess, the Great Mother. Her fruitful womb was also the tomb where the dead were digested and regenerated to continue the cycle.

The river hag is a vestige of the revered African river goddess. She teaches what schooling does not: that the passage to womanhood is a powerful step from which we must not shrink, but it also takes us one step nearer to old age, decline, and death. Sobonfu says this teaches a young woman to respect elders because in them she sees her future self. The ancestors felt it imperative to impart this knowledge to young women. That's why their stories convey the full spectrum of what it means to be a woman.

The girl heard a loud slurping sound coming from upstream. She felt the river floor shuddering beneath her feet. Slithering toward them was the river monster ...

The river hag said, "Hide beneath my hair." The girl did just that. The river monster slithered up to the hag and said, "I smell a human being! I want to eat it for my breakfast!" The river hag pointed downstream and said. "She went that way." Luckily the river monster moved on in search of lunch. After he was gone, the hag gave the girl a belt more beautiful and more laden with powerful gems than the one she'd had before. She thanked the hag, put the new belt 'round her waist, and swam back to shore. She dried herself in the sun and then went back to the village to complete her daily chores.

When the jealous girls saw her new belt they asked, "Where did you get that belt?" She told them about the hag at the bottom of the river.

All the jealous girls ran to the river and hurled their belts far out to the middle. Then they dove in and swam deeper and deeper until they met the slimy hag. "Give me a belt!" they cried. The hag told them they must help her first. But when she told them to lick clean her sores, they said, "FORGET IT!"

Just then the river monster came back upstream. He smelled lots of human flesh and was by now very hungry. The river hag warned the girls. They swam as fast as they could to get away but were never heard from again. As for the girl with the special belt, she never again fetched water from the river without thanking the river spirit in all her forms. She lived to a ripe old age and became a medicine woman. People came from far and wide to seek her advice. When the time came, she taught her granddaughters that the strength and beauty of woman-hood grow from the inside out. And that is the end of the tale. Thank you Ancestors for lending it to us. Now we give it back.

Jealous Girls

"Thank you, Ancestors!" the girls said clapping their hands, as was our custom. I scanned their faces in order to read Nita's without singling her out. She wore a knowing smile as if the tale had brought her a personal message.

"Round-robin?" Suzanne asked.

"Yes," I answered, "round-robin." This meant everyone would have a chance to make a personal comment.

Suzanne wanted to start. "Lots of girls at school are jealous of me," she whined petulantly, "because they'll never have my hair-style and clothes. I'm really used to people being jealous. And I don't care if they hate me because I know why. They just wish they had my looks, that's all." There were myriad reasons for Suzanne's superficial self-image, but that's not where we were headed that night. I glanced Nita's way to see if she was ready to speak yet, but she avoided my eyes.

Kim wanted to go next. She launched into a hateful diatribe against her mother and sisters. They were bitches who hated her because she was beautiful and got more attention. Kim's tone was crass, and it echoed Suzanne's focus on surface appearance. The story spoke of inner beauty, and yet there we were, right back in the covergirl/pin-up mentality, where beauty equals slim young blondes, waif-like poses, and pouty lips. Kim and Suzanne set a stiff cosmetic code in the house, which many of the younger girls tried to emulate. For all of them, but especially for Nita, we needed an expanded standard of beauty.

"What kind of beauty are you talking about Kim?" I asked, "an outside shell, or something that shines from the inside out?"

"Well the story is about the inside kind," Kim said with a shrug as if we were out of her league. She looked around to see if anyone was going to help her. Luckily, Nita's hand popped up. She said, "I'll speak about that cause that's my problem." Kim looked relieved to be off the hook.

"I won't name names," Nita said, "but I get jealous of some of them girls at school who wear short skirts and flirt with guys. I'm not talkin' about none of you girls, here. You're all mostly good friends of mine. But I get mad when guys pay attention to girls like that—girls who just hang around the mall and buy stuff with money from their folks. They don't respect no elders, and yet they got tons of belts to wear, know what I'm sayin'? I usta intimidate some of them girls. But I'm trying to make a change. I wanna get over my old 'intimidation tactics' like the school counselor calls it. But when I get jealous like that, I just get mean, like I don't know no other way."

"Is it fair to say, Nita, that there are two parts at work?" I asked, "One as courageous and kind as the belt girl, and one that can be mean like the jealous girls?"

"Yep, that about says it," Nita grinned.

"In the story, the meanness washes down the river. Who knows what happened to the jealous girls? It's the belt girl who goes back to the village and puts down roots. Which is taking root in your life?"

"You mean like, the kind part or the mean part? The kind part, for sure. It's going that way more and more. That's the way it's gotta keep on, too, if I wanna make my sports goals and go to the dance and all.

"See, I guess everyone knows I'm sprung on this guy, Gerry. I feel all soft when he's around, and I don't wanna hide my inside beauty any more. I wanna have my inside beauty show like the belt girl."

"Nita, I think it's working. Right now, for instance, " I looked around at the others and added, "I'm probably not the only one to notice."

Several voices piped up. "Yeah, it shows." "Heck, yeah, all the time."

"That's what I really want," she said smiling. "I don't want to go all sissy and quit track or nothin', but I wanna be more ladylike 'cause I don't wanna be all dressed up at the dance and have Gerry's friends say I look outa place."

Testing the Water

The hormone thing would be worked out later, and so would her worry over the facial hair, but at this moment, among her peers, Nita bared her soul to reveal her most immediate fear: that of a possible wisecrack at a fragile moment. She was testing the water, but she wasn't going to plunge into serious dance plans until she felt some assurance of safety. She'd outgrown the old intimidation tactics, but what new shield would take their place? I didn't know the answer, but I knew how to respect the question. I knew how to wade along the edge of it, watching the water for clues. From previous talks I'd learned Gerry was an excellent candidate for Nita's first date. There was no reason to suspect treacherous waters there. His good intentions didn't form a complete shield, but they strengthened the potential safety of the first date.

"You don't want to be embarrassed," I said, just to let Nita know I was still wading beside her. "As I see it, Nita, you have two things in your favor." That statement drew all the girls' attention like fish to a fly. Nita wasn't the only one worrying about the dance.

"First off, you know Gerry respects you. No doubt he sees your inner beauty." Her eyes grew wide, she held her breath and nodded stiffly. "His respect, that's one big thing in your favor. And he's no dummy, either. Is he the type to respect someone who doesn't deserve it?"

She looked to the group. "No!" "No way, not Gerry," chimed those who knew him. Nita took that in and smiled.

"What's the other thing?" she asked, her eyes pinned to mine.

"The other thing you already named yourself. You have friends here, people who love and respect you. Perhaps their love is like an invisible belt, one that gives you strength and self-respect." I waded out a little deeper, and hoped there were no jagged rocks. "Some of your friends will be at the dance. I don't know for sure, but it seems to me they might be the types who'd stick up for you if anyone said anything rude." Again, the girls nailed the bait. They found calls to loyalty irresistible.

Kim made a fist and said, "Yeah, if that pig Dwayne says anything, I'll kill him, Nita. You have my word."

Shannon hollered, "We'll torch their lockers!"

"I'll put hot sauce in their jockstraps!" Jessica yelled.

We teetered on the old familiar verge of chaos. Kate gave me one of her, *How-you-gonna-get-out-of-this-one?* looks. She had no intention of rescuing me. I had to think fast. "Quiet!" I yelled. "Quiet!" The girls weren't used to me yelling and they hushed more out of surprise than obedience. "The loyalty is excellent." I said, "But you have to express that appropriately."

"Bla, bla, bla," said Christine. "You're just like staff."

"Hey!" I said. "We're talking here about supporting Nita. She wants to let her inner beauty show at the dance. She wants to feel ladylike and she's trying to get away from intimidation tactics!" I turned to Nita to get the focus back to her, "Is that right, Nita? Is that what you mean by ladylike?" Some of my feminist friends might balk at my repetition of Nita's phrase, "ladylike," but she used it in a positive sense, and echoing it was more respectful than substituting a word of my choice in its place.

"I don't want to pour hot sauce on no jocks, if that's what you mean," she said grinning.

"Okay then, peanut butter, get it, *penis* butter?!" Jessica whooped, whirling hysterically away from the point once again.

That was it. Kate had had enough. "Jessica, one more outburst like that and you're out of group for the rest of the night."

"They did it, too," Jessica pouted, settling back into her seat. "Okay, I'll shut up, but I don't think its fair. Kim called Dwayne a pig."

"Look," I said, "the loyalty and enthusiasm are great. But this point about being ladylike is important too. Aren't there any ladylike ways to stick up for a friend?"

"See, that's what *I* want to know," Nita said. We had six minutes before group ended, and in that time I wanted to respond to her question, or at least try. To drop the tough-girl guise, and embrace the softer side of womanhood, Nita would have to feel safe. To release her hold on the protector role, she'd have to feel protected. Staff helped her feel safe at the center, but they couldn't follow her to the dance. I was wary about putting the other girls in the protector role, but if they couldn't stick up for her, who could? Nita needed to learn that no woman is an island, sufficient unto herself. She needed to learn the type of strength one gains from relying on trusted others. Among the girls, as in families, individual healing requires group support.

I took a breath and plunged head first into deeper waters. "What we're talking about here, is how to stick up for a friend without attacking like a gang of vandals." I looked each of the girls in the eye. None of them had the level of sophistication I was talking about, not even Nita. They'd had assertiveness training, and could distinguish assertiveness from hostile aggression, but when the heat was on, the timid ones hid, and the fighters lashed out. I knew the role model in this instance would have to be Kate.

"Kate," I said, "say you had a friend like Nita, and you overheard mean remarks about her. What would you do?"

"Hmmm," Kate said. "Well, I guess I'd say something to stick up for my friend. Like I might say, 'Hey! You don't really know Nita but I do, and I can tell you straight up, she's a fine person. That's all there is to it."

"I like that," I said. "It's strong, without getting overly hostile." I turned to Nita, "How would you feel with a friend sticking up for you like that?"

"I'd feel good," Nita nodded approvingly.

"Do you think that's ladylike enough for a dance?"

"Yep. See that's what I'm talking about, but that's hard for me 'cause I'm used to intimidation tactics."

"What about your friends here? How would you feel if one of them stood up for you that way?"

"I would feel very happy as long as they didn't embarrass me with no hot sauce," Nita grinned.

Jessica piped up, "Kate can I please say something now? It's not about hot sauce. It's totally appropriate." Kate nodded. Jessica said, "I'm not going to the dance, but if I was, I' d say something appropriate to stick up for Nita."

Kate encouraged, "Well, okay, Jessica, what would you say?"

"Like, say Dwayne said something really gross like . . . " Kate raised a finger in warning. Jessica caught herself, "Well, just say somebody made a comment that wasn't appropriate. Then I'd say, 'Hey, Nita's my friend and she looks good in a dress. What's a matter—are you jealous?'" She checked Kate to see if she'd won any approval and Kate nodded. Nita nodded too.

"Some of your friends will be there, won't they, Nita?" I asked. She nodded again, "Yeah. Nicki, Charmaine, and Shelly."

"I wonder if they might support you at the dance," I urged, looking their way. Charmaine spoke up, "I wouldn't let some creep get away with raggin' on Nita." Nicki and Shelly felt the same way. They agreed to meet with Kate before bedtime, to start planning how they might support Nita at the dance, appropriately, of course.

"It's nearly time to go," I said. "Thanks for a good group. Nita, you're brave to face things head on. I'd say you're as courageous as the belt girl, plunging right into the river. Going to a dance is one of many plunges you're taking this year. There's no guarantee you won't meet the river monster, but with support from others, you have every reason to believe in yourself and follow your hopes, just like the belt girl." Nita beamed and looked around to make sure everyone heard.

"Okay, group's over, " I announced. "You ladies can go." Some-times group ended with a rush of sweatshirts and hairstyles racing out the door. That night, the girls just sat. They asked for another story. They asked why I had to leave—why we couldn't have a slum-ber party. Kate and I had to peel them out of their chairs in order to get back to our closet to debrief.

Weeks later Nita did go to the dance with Gerry. They looked big, sweet, and shy in the photos she showed at brag time. It was the first of a few outings with him, none of which ended in humili-ation.

In the months to come Nita's hormone supplements needed a bit of adjusting. But her menses finally flowed to her satisfaction and for the facial hair she chose electrolysis. After a year Doc Matock stopped the hormone supplement altogether. He'd been right. A little boost did the trick. After that Nita's blood flowed with the moon, of its own accord.

She continued to bring a gentle openness to group and set a supportive tone for others trying to make changes. She channeled her fierceness into athletics, gaining the admiration of her team. She won several track awards and her coach helped her seek col-lege scholarships. I went to her last high school track meet and saw her scathing glare unnerve the competition. It delighted me no end to see her intimidation tactics put to good use. She shook her well-formed limbs, looking as confident as Tina Turner and as focused as Jackie Joyner. Nita had found her own way to weave *sweet* to-gether with *tough*. She gave the word *ladylike* new meaning, and taught us all something about what a woman is.

— 6 —

Spin Gold!

A story reveals its gifts only to those who enter it . . . The key to learning from a story is to find a doorway to its interior.

—Michael Meade

To hear soul's speech . . . one must relax the limbs as if in love, as if asleep, as if in death. This state is the essential condition to see and hear the cares and concerns of the soul.

—Russell Lockhart

The Boastful Father and the Coerced Daughter

Over the phone Faye described herself as a fifty-six-year-old academic. Erudition rang through her savvy inquiries about my work. Meeting new people on the phone, I'm used to the sometimes jarring incongruities between voice and visage. But when we met face-to-face two weeks later, I saw Faye's finesse was consistent throughout. Slender, with a contemporary hairstyle and understated jewelry, she could easily have passed for a woman ten years younger. She had the gift of knowing her own good looks well enough to

114

feature them without getting in their way. It was only after we'd talked for half an hour that the aura of exhaustion settled around her. She'd been ill for a year with a lingering "flu" that was finally diagnosed as Chronic Fatigue Syndrome.

I knew what Faye was going through. Eight years before I'd been struck down by the illness, myself, and was still recovering.

"Childbirth and menopause were a breeze compared to this!" Faye said dramatically. "I've always rolled with the punches. I never thought I'd be in therapy, but this is dreadful, and I'm not coping well at all."

She had persistent swollen glands, light-headedness forgetfulness, aches, and exhaustion. "I went from doctor to doctor getting more humiliated as I went. They all said the symptoms were psychosomatic, due to depression or stress, which is a polite way of saying, 'You're neurotic, lady.' My father was a doctor and if he were alive today, I know he'd call it 'malingering': putting off recovery to get attention or avoid work. That infuriates me. I hate being treated like a fake! Thank God, I finally found a specialist who recognized CFS."

Faye had read every book available on the disease. "It's chronic, debilitating, and there's no known treatment except rest." she lamented. "Worse yet, there's no guarantee rest will do any good.

"Indulge me while I enumerate the damages. My social life is defunct. I've cut back on classes. I can't possibly ask for disability compensation, because I look fine. I'm not in a wheel chair, or stuck to an oxygen tank, so people think there's nothing wrong. But my sick leave and vacation time are all used up. I'm too dizzy to stand up and lecture. I can't even read students' papers without my mind hazing over. It's like having a head full of cotton! I should have published much more poetry by now. This sets me back even further.

"I don't know who I am any more. Teaching, writing, lecturing; I am my work. I've juggled family and profession all my life. I had my babies while in graduate school. Everyone said, 'Faye, take a year off.' But I said, 'I can do it,' and I did. Cross-country skiing, I was always the one out ahead, making tracks. Now I can't even bring up the rear. My family doesn't understand. They can't accept that I'm not the sparkling Faye, who used to inspire everyone. I'm turning into a tired old woman!"

Faye's exuberance worked against her. I wanted to say, "Faye, slow down. Don't wear yourself out. Conserve." Instead I asked, "Have you learned to conserve?"

"I suppose not," she replied. "I'm always under pressure. I had a dream about it which I'd like to discuss. But first I want to make sure you're not a Freudian." She fussed nervously with the buttons on her sleeve. "I've studied enough psychology to know Freudians would read all sorts of things into this dream: penis envy, Electra complex, or God knows what other humiliating notion. Let's be frank from the start. I've had it with humiliating diagnoses, so, if you're thinking *penis envy*, let's get it on the table now." Faye wilted into the couch. "Sorry to be so glib," she moaned.

She'd reached the end of her short supply of exuberance. She now looked more like a forlorn child than an able professor. Her resentment of doctors made sense to me. I remembered all too well my own debilitation and how it was met with patronizing pats on the shoulder, and the suggestion that my symptoms of CFS were all in my head. At that moment, seeing Faye fade before my eyes, I nearly fell into a whirl of painful memories. Working with her, I'd have to ride an edge where my own CFS was part of my education, not an abyss of commiseration to fall into each time we met. Faye's sad eyes searched mine as if to divine whether I would coldly probe her dream, or listen with compassion.

"Faye," I ventured, "I'll listen to your dream with sympathetic ears, and try not to dice it up with a Freudian scalpel."

Her eyes brightened. "Well, *scalpel* is the operative word," she said. "The dream is about surgery." Somehow, the word scalpel had transmigrated from Faye's yet untold dream to my lips. This peculiar occurrence happens often when working in the imaginal realm of story and dream. I took it as a sign that the muse of intuition was present and actively carrying sparks between us at lightning speed. I asked Faye to close her eyes, allow herself to reenter the dream, and tell it in the present tense.

"I'm in my late teens. My father is frail and elderly but very excited. He goes to a faculty meeting at the medical school where he got his degree. He tells them I'm a gifted surgeon and have already performed successful heart transplants. He says it with great pride. The faculty seem stern and reserved, but impressed nonetheless. They discuss it and conclude they'd like me to do a transplant while their students observe. My father tells me to prepare for surgery. He makes me put on a mask and surgical gloves and won't listen when I say I know nothing about medicine. I feel terrible because I don't want to disappoint him or make him look like a fool, but I'm completely on the spot and it terrifies me.

"I woke up in a cold sweat with tears running down my face. My husband, Bill, had never seen me so upset. I've never broken down and cried like that. He insisted I see somebody."

Faye buried her face in a pillow and broke down again. Here was a woman whose work and reputation preceded her. I'd long admired her essays, poems, and radio readings, and respected her as a role model for aspiring women. I'd been flattered when she'd called. And now, here she was unloading untold distress, as she'd never done before. Her body jolted violently with each sob, until I thought she would break. I suddenly felt desperately useless, as if watching from a window to see a child stumble into heavy traffic. My own recovery from CFS was still tenuous. My stamina was limited and I didn't yet feel strong. No one had been able to help me when I'd been in Faye's shoes. How in the world was I going to help her?

Two or three minutes passed. Head down, Faye shivered and shook like a high strung pony in distress. I kept trying to breathe and steady myself. I pictured my back resting against the trunk of a sturdy cedar. For the moment Faye needed to unload, but she'd soon look to me for some sort of solace or wisdom. What could I offer? My knowledge of CFS only pointed to the grim fact that she wouldn't swiftly recover. She'd probably never be the same, and might remain too sick to work for a very long time. All I could do was acknowledge her suffering. That was it. Her biggest complaint was that she suffered, and no one believed she suffered. I believed. Furthermore, I understood the extent of her pain. Her identity rested upon her role as a leader, a top performer in her field. Being sick was like being nobody.

Emily Dickinson's words ran through my head, "My business is circumference." Suddenly a broader image struck my mind's eye, that of a cedar grove. I sat with my back against one of the trees, guarding the circumference, while Faye sat in the center. "My business is circumference." That phrase gave me the perspective I needed. I wasn't an angel who could come into the center of Faye's life and relieve her suffering. I was the guardian of the circumference in which her story would unfold. My job was to provide the forlorn girl and the weary woman with a safe place to grieve, and to get to know the other players in Faye's dream—the boastful father and the stern instructors. These were the figures who characterized her inner life and made Faye's illness uniquely her own, distinct from mine and anyone else's. The secrets of Faye's healing would lie with them.

As Faye wept I recalled the fairy tale, *Rumpelstiltskin.** It bore a striking resemblance to her dream. Both began with a father falsely boasting of a daughter's unique skill. In each case the boasts led men of rank to expect miracles. Faye and the young heroine were both coerced to produce far more than they could deliver. *Rumplestiltskin* would provide a useful mirror, thanks to the grandmothers of Germany, who must have crafted and preserved the tale to aid women pressured by outrageous paternal demands. Lucky for us, Faye's dream led to the healing waters where dreams converge with the larger river of lore. Another poet, Hilda Doolittle, had explored these waters with great dedication and gained inspiration and insight. I'd hold off mentioning it, however, as H.D.'s dreamwork guide had been Sigmund Freud, himself. I didn't want to rock the boat by bringing up that touchy name again.

Faye's sobs slowly subsided. When she finally spoke her voice was softer, not in volume but in timbre, as if resonating from a deeper part of her body. She said, "Where do we go from here?"

"Let's take the dream as a guide," I said. "First off, would you say it looks forward to a new solution, or back toward an old wound?"

"It goes way back," Faye said, mopping smeared mascara from her face. "I think the old wound with my father plays a role in my

*See my retelling of the Grimms' fairy tale, *Rumpelstiltskin,* in the appendix, p. 260.

illness, but I don't want to just hash over old problems. I prefer taking the bull by the horns, so, could you suggest some homework?"

"Yes," I said, "read *Rumpelstiltskin.*"

"*Rumpelstiltskin!* Oh, that takes me back. I haven't read it since I was a girl. It'll take me five minutes to read it, then what?" Even with Chronic Fatigue, Faye pushed for a full load of homework.

"Highlight the parts you identify with, and write a paragraph about them if you've got the energy. Otherwise just bring it in and we can talk about it next week."

"Okay," she said, as she wrote out a check to pay for the session. "As a girl, my favorite part of *Rumpelstiltskin* was the end, when the heroine outsmarts the little man. I've always wanted to teach folklore, but we already have a folklorist at the university. Maybe someday, I'll teach that course. We'll see." Fairy tales usually give rise to wistful thoughts of youth, but Faye remembered *Rumpelstiltskin* and thought of expanding her course load. She truly fit the CFS profile of the overachieving woman.

The following week, Faye started the session as she had before, a bit keyed up. Eagerly, she outlined parallels between the tale and her dream. "The miller wants to impress the king," she said. "That's like Dad in the dream, wanting to impress the faculty. The miller falsely boasts his daughter can spin straw into gold. Again, it's like the dream. Dad boasts I can perform surgery, when of course, I can't. In the dream the faculty want to see me do heart transplants, just like the king wants Ms. Miller to spin gold. He locks her into a room full of straw and commands her to perform a miracle. He threatens death if she fails. Just like me under the spotlight in the operating room—unbelievable pressure, impossible expectations, deadly anxiety."

"Like your life right now," I offered.

"Yes, like my life. Expectations making me crazy with anxiety. I know I can't change the fatigue, but if I could just get the anxiety under control I'd be happy."

I suggested the dream and the story would help us understand the anxiety, and that perhaps understanding it would help us loosen its grip on her. Faye tensed her jaw and pressed her eyebrows together, cleaving her forehead with a deep groove right down the center, as if brain strain would birth a useful analysis. But we needed the sort of understanding that James Hillman gains from "befriending" rather than from analyzing a dream. "Let's hold off analyzing for the moment," I said. "Try getting comfortable. See if you can relax." Hearing this, the groove down the center of her forehead grew deeper. Analysis was easy for Faye, relaxation was hard. I spoke softly as if gentling a high strung pony, and suggested she take her time to find a comfortable posture in which to relax, breathe gently, and be aware of the energy flowing through her body. Most diehard achievers resist relaxation and Faye was no different. "But I don't want to waste my session today," she protested. "Shouldn't I be working on the problem?"

"Well," I said, hoping to bypass resistance, "many scientists have had breakthroughs during restful moments." Luckily this intrigued her. She closed her eyes and rested her neck on a pillow. It took a few minutes before the strain dropped from her face, but eventually she relaxed and grew keenly aware of the flow of energy through her body. Now she could focus her full attention on the dream and what it had to teach her. I asked which part of the dream called to her most vividly.

"The beginning," she said. "My father has a painful grip on my wrist. He looks old and feeble but his grip is so tenacious, it's creepy. He's convinced I'm some kind of surgical wizard he can show off. I can't imagine a more difficult spot than the one he's put me in."

"Stay with it if you can," I said, "and see what else comes. Maybe another image, or a memory."

"A memory," she said, "of when I was a kid. Dad used to tell my uncles I'd follow in his footsteps in medicine. He was oblivious to the fact I never wanted that. He used to embarrass me at family gatherings by saying I'd be a great surgeon some day. My older brother was a big disappointment, but I was supposed to make Dad proud." Faye's lips tightened and big tears ran down her face. She choked her words out with great strain, "I got straight A's in language and literature. I won a scholarship. I wanted Dad to be proud, but he said literature was a waste of time." Once again, Faye, the erudite professor allowed the forlorn girl's tears to flow from deep within. Like the miller's daughter she was all too familiar with the pain of being pressured to do things not in her nature, things which didn't make sense or ring true to reality.

The miller's daughter did a great deal of weeping, but Faye hadn't wept at all as a young woman. She'd been too busy pushing herself. But now her old sorrow flowed into the new like a river flooding its banks. She worried that weeping was a waste of time, a nonproductive way to spend our sessions. I had to reassure her to the contrary. Grief was now her ally, and sorrow her teacher. All these years she'd denied her sorrow. Now she needed to taste it fully. There were times she couldn't distinguish the source of her tears. Were they "valid" tears of grief over her mother's untimely death, or were they "petty" tears of self pity? I told her not to worry about categorizing her tears.

For the high-achieving woman the hardest part of having CFS is reducing her demands on herself. Typically, she denies her frailties and accentuates her capabilities. Only after grieving the past and fully accepting her illness in the present, can she embrace reality and begin to shape a future, based not on what she thinks she should do, but on what she truly can do. It would be no different for Faye.

Over the next few weeks, she took a close look at old family patterns which had shaped her drivenness. For generations the young adults in the family had been expected to dispose of their hearts' desires and "transplant" paternal dictates in their place. This had been true for both Faye and her father.

He'd failed to fulfill his father's wish that he become a wealthy doctor. His younger brothers had put him through medical school with what they could scrimp from their mining wages. He'd been expected to open a clinic, and once established, put his siblings through college. As the book-smart oldest son, he was supposed to have been the taproot on whom family fruition relied. But as it turned out, Faye's father was more comfortable with books than with people. He used gin to ease workday anxieties. He never managed to build a full-time practice, and could barely support his children, let alone send his siblings to college. They never escaped the mines, and he never escaped the shackles of this failure, though for years he fantasized Faye would release him by achieving greatness in medicine.

"Dad was painfully shy when sober," Faye recalled, "but when he drank he became a magnanimous fool. He bragged and lavished praise for all the wrong reasons. When Granddad lay dying, Dad told him I was in medical school. I never even applied to medical school! He sat there and lied 'til the bitter end. Nothing else mattered in those last moments except impressing Granddad."

On a different occasion she recalled, "The shame was, Dad couldn't take pride in my real accomplishments. He said literature was a 'pastime,' a 'self-serving amusement.' Nothing was good enough. If I helped mother can pears he'd say, 'Saturday you better help Aunt Emma. She's got pears to can too.' I won every honor available at my high school, but it was never enough. If I got an A it should have been an A+."

"Your dad was like the miller with the false boasting," I said, "but he was also like the king, always demanding more gold."

"He sure was," she said, "and a greedy king at that."

The Greedy King

Over the next few weeks Faye began to realize her adolescence had been overshadowed by patterns associated with the greedy king. "I was eleven when Mom died. Before that, Dad basically ignored me. After that he reached out to me, or clutched at me is a better way to put it. I remember him saying no one but Mom had ever really loved him. I wanted to prove I loved him, but no amount of effort on my part would suffice. Mother had put him on a pedestal. In her mind, his being a doctor was the world's greatest achievement. She overlooked a lot. She never criticized him for drinking or being in trouble with the IRS. Being idolized by her sort of glued him together. After she died he became obsessively demanding with me. Nothing I could do was ever enough."

I pointed out that towards herself, Faye carried on the greedy king tradition. Nothing she could do was ever enough. She agreed and we enumerated the ways. She expected herself to recover from CFS faster and more fully than other patients. While ill, she still expected herself to maintain a fully active work life and family life, despite her doctor advising her otherwise. Now it was she alone who expected herself to spin gold. She fully understood how this exacerbated her fatigue, but like a powerful addiction, her gold-spinning was a hard habit to break.

The Thanksgiving holiday was a perfect example. Instead of asking others to take charge, she took the whole feast upon her-self—planning, cooking, and entertaining as usual. But after stand-ing several hours in the hot kitchen, she fainted. "Last week when I left here, I fully intended to go with the low-stress potluck plan, as you and I discussed, but when the holiday rolled around, it just seemed that anything but one of my turkey dinners would fall short, and since we were having guests and family over, I just had to put on the Ritz. Bill and my daughter, Charlotte, offered to make the turkey. But every step of the way I let them know I didn't want any-thing to be different this year."

"Things are different this year, Faye. You're ill," I said, irked at her for not following through on the low-stress plan.

"I just don't want to be defeated by this disease . . . It would be the first Thanksgiving I didn't dazzle."

"Who do you have to dazzle?" I asked.

"It's not really about dazzling someone in particular, it's more a matter of not admitting defeat."

"And anything less than dazzle is defeat?"

"Yes, that's right," she said crossing her arms over her chest.

"By whose standards?" I asked, aware that my rapid-fire ques-tions might sound a bit aggressive.

"By my father's standards, or his father's standards, but I've ab-sorbed them, so they're obviously mine, too," she said loudly, fend-ing me off with a scowl.

I spoke softly so she couldn't reject my words out of hand, "These standards are destructive, Faye. They're stronger than common sense, stronger than your desire to heal yourself, and stronger than your willingness to stick to doctor's orders. I'd say the greedy king runs the show. There's no question about it."

"I know, I know," she said rolling her eyes, "but knowing doesn't change it."

"So, you're locked into this pattern as firmly as the miller's daughter is locked in the room full of straw."

"It feels that way," she nodded. Faye and Ms. Miller were backed into corners with no way out and life-threatening forces at hand. Ms. Miller would be killed if she failed to spin gold. Faye was driving herself toward collapse. Her illness accentuated her mortality more than she cared to admit. It must have been dawning on her as we spoke because tears filled her eyes.

"It's serious, isn't it?" she said.

"You're asking me?" I returned. "You're the one who wound up flat on the floor. That experience should tell you about serious."

Faye swallowed a sob to speak, "Well, when I collapsed, I must have hit my head on the stove, because I've still got a terrible goose egg." She rubbed her head. "When l came to, everyone was standing over me and I was looking up from the sofa."

"It must have been frightening," I said.

"Honestly, Erica, it was embarrassing. I'm used to lecturing to hundreds, but to be fussed over while flat on my back, that's another story. Bill called the doctor of course, though I felt awful about disturbing him on Thanksgiving. He said I had to stay off my feet for the rest of the weekend, and he warned me about complications developing if I don't take better care of myself. I thought the dinner would go down the tubes, but our guests were charming about setting the table, and my daughter and son-in-law took over in the kitchen. They were all so kind, it humbled me. All in all we had a lovely meal."

"Amazing!" I said with a grin.

Faye frowned, "What do you mean?"

"How much this resembles *Rumpelstiltskin!*" I said. "When Ms. Miller gives up, when she collapses, that's when the little man comes to help. When you faint, when you collapse, then all the family and friends flurry around to help. You didn't have to dazzle them . . . There's something to learn from what you're telling me, Faye."

"I know," she said. "It's that relying on the family is sweeter than spinning gold. The lesson is obvious, but it's a hard one for me to learn." Faye's illness had forced her into territory achievers often avoid, that of reliance upon others. We talked about fainting as an expression of vulnerability, a cry for help. As long as Faye kept up the facade of self-sufficiency, her family gave her a wide berth, but when her distress showed, they moved in to help. The challenge before her was to learn to ask for help.

Queenship

That winter Faye attempted to rest more, to drive herself less, to monitor the greedy king's demands, be more mindful of her health, and practice asking for help. Her family understood this, and Bill teased, "You don't have to faint, Faye, to get my help. Just ask." Bill was good to his word, and if Faye didn't get help, more often than not, it was because she didn't feel up to asking.

Unfortunately, the light that Thanksgiving shed on Faye's internal drama was not enough to daunt her compulsive ways. The greedy king held sway in her psyche, and in his eyes, rest was not only nonproductive, it meant one of five things: weakness, failure, incompetence, laziness, or death. Every time Faye lay down to rest she felt guilty of the first four, and afraid of the fifth. We combated this with writing assignments which, as Faye put it, "suit my twisted mind. They make me feel productive about exploring my compulsion to produce!" She was to lie down and write in her journal about the anxieties that came up. More often than not, she'd doze off after a paragraph or two. We laughed at the irony of this psychic bargaining, but it worked. Jung recommended bargaining with difficult aspects of the psyche rather than fighting them outright. Faye said, "The greedy king is stronger than I am, so the best strategy is a good bargaining position." She wrote poetry about the pride-sick father and the greedy king. Especially apt was her poem on Ms. Miller's marriage to the king. She wrote:

THE PRICE OF QUEENSHIP

What choice had I
But try to redeem father's pride?
I never refused demands to spin gold,
But strove to prove my highest mettle.

What choice had I?
My girlish dreams eclipsed
By golden dream of perfection,
High attainment on command.

What choice had I,
Sovereign Fiend, but to give my hand
At the cost of my heart?
Either way I die.
What choice had I?

Faye wrote in her journal, "For better or worse, my father gave me away to the groom of high attainment. There was no joy in the union, only a singular goal: academic perfection. I willingly married the king and took his commands to heart. When I got a 3.8 on an exam, I hated myself. I literally wanted to die. Only the gold, the perfect score, was acceptable. I sacrificed my heart's desires for it. I gave up my social life, sports, dance. That's how I see the heart transplant in my dream. My heart's desires cut away to be replaced by Dad's scheme."

But there was sorting to do here. Granted, Faye's father had pressured her unmercifully, and this had injured her ability to play and relax, but something in it had suited her. Dad's scheme had forced her to narrow her scope to academics, which led to the discovery of her greatest joy, her true calling, literature. She was one of those people who strove to fulfill parental dictates without losing track of her own destiny. We talked about the very real pain of coercion. But alongside it, we couldn't dismiss the fact her father had honestly recognized her brilliant mind and her inclinations toward discipline. In his twisted way he'd helped her find the niche which was truly hers, the life of a scholar.

This bore an irony similar to that of the fate of the miller's daughter. In marrying the greedy king she became queen. And who's to say this was not her rightful destiny? Faye belonged in the world of literature. There she was a queen, a grand dame with clout, who was in the position to bestow blessings upon striving students and influence the academic world for the better. She was happy with this position, and even though her father had been madly coercive, his actions hadn't deterred her from her rightful destiny, and may even have spurred her towards it.

Her marriage to the greedy king held mixed blessings. To follow Hillman's advice and "befriend" the king would require acknowledging the benefits, as well as the wounds. Upon examination, Faye saw how her compulsion to achieve had yielded meaningful rewards. It had assured success and status in her rightful domain. If she hadn't fallen ill, the greedy king might never have surfaced as a problem at all. She was clear on one thing, she wouldn't want to relive life without her drivenness. For hadn't her gold spinning won her an honored position, numerous degrees, awards, and medals, all of which indicated a certain queenship she didn't want to live without? "I just wish it held more real joy," she sighed.

"More real joy," I echoed. "Does the real joy lie elsewhere?"

"Joy seems eons away," she answered. She stared out the window at sea gulls drifting by as if they might remind her. "Poetry is a great joy," she said slowly, "Sappho, Emily Dickinson, William Carlos Williams, Marianne Moore, Carl Sandberg, Maya Angelou, Denise Levertov. Great fiction and theater . . . Jane Austin, D. H. Lawrence, Tennessee Williams, Shakespeare." Her tongue slowly savored each beloved name. "My kids, Dylan and Charlotte, who've become lovely adults. And Charlotte's kids, Ashley and Zack." Tears came to the corners of her eyes. "Being called Grandma, now that's a joy . . . Enthusiastic students. Skiing, and hiking wilderness trails with Bill. Oh," she said raising her eyebrows, "making love with Bill while listening to Chopin, especially on a Sunday morning . . . Baking bread. I make wonderful sourdough from my own starter. Drinking wine with my best friend Clara, especially when we read Sappho and Emily Dickinson aloud." She grinned, and punctuated her last line with a self-satisfied nod, then added, "That's my definition of joy, and if I could hold onto those, my life would be worth living."

The Child She Holds Dear

We were now looking at things valued beyond gold, beyond honors, and achievement. The queen found life worth living when she gave birth and became a mother. I believed Faye mothered the things she loved: her kids, her grandkids, her students, her marriage, her art, and her friendships. When I pointed out that illness jeopardized her ability to mother these things, her tears welled immediately, letting me know we were in the right ballpark.

"Are you saying I'm at a new place in the story, the mothering place?" Faye asked.

"It seems that way," I nodded. "These tears seem different."

"Yes, that's right. These tears are different," she said. "They're not the forlorn girl's tears. They belong to another part of me."

"More like the distressed queen, about to lose her child?"

Faye nodded. "This part of the story perplexes me, though," she said. "The little man, who helps the queen so generously at first, now turns on her and demands her child. He's a tricky fellow. First he works for a mere pittance, spinning rooms full of gold in exchange for her necklace and ring. Then on the third night, when she's run out of jewelry, he asks for her firstborn. She'll be killed if she doesn't agree, and if she does, she'll become queen. She has no choice. In desperation she agrees. But somewhere in there the little man turns from a redeeming figure to a greedy one, claiming for himself the child she holds dear." A deep vertical trench formed, dividing Faye's forehead in two. "At first he's a magical elf who hears her cry, and cheerfully works all night to save her. Then he becomes a little demon holding her to a pledge made under duress."

"Which part do you relate to," I asked, "elf, or demon?"

"Elf," she said.

I, too saw a lot of elfishness in Faye's ability to juggle several tasks at once. I guided her to focus on the little man, "befriending" him by getting under his skin, as if getting into character for a play. She closed her eyes and zeroed in on the part of the story where the little man seemed most vivid. Soon the contented half-smile of the imaginative realm softened her face. She described the first time the little man appeared out of nowhere and stood before the forlorn girl and her pile of straw. I asked her to describe him in the first person.

"I'm brown and crusty as a beechnut," she said sprightly. "My joints are gnarled, but abler limbs you'll never find . . . I'm fit and skilled like no other. I do all my own brewing and all my own baking. I know the secrets of the earth and forest. My knowledge holds magic power. I draw my stamina from the earth itself, and delight in all tasks. A mountain of work is child's play to me." Faye's embodiment of the little man required no rehearsal, and charmed me as much as a dramatized tale from Radio Reader. I asked her to notice how his attitude was akin to her own.

"I know this rough and ready attitude. It's the sort of spirit that's freed in me after ten at night when the dog is quiet, Bill has gone to bed, and I'm alone in the library with the computer. A delightful arrogance possesses me. I become completely facile. All the ideas, sources, references, and vocabulary are at my fingertips. I really do transform a chaotic pile of scraps into gold. Rather than exhaustion, I feel exhilarated writing into the wee hours. It energizes me, and I draw on reserves which seem inaccessible to others. People have always said, 'Faye, how do you do it?' I can't explain it, except as a kind of possession, a *rush*, as my students used to say. But the little man is very much my ally, I can tell you that."

Her union with the little man brought her tremendous vibrancy. She looked pumped like an athlete claiming victory. It was exciting, but also a little manic. I was concerned that the amount of adrenaline coursing through her body would inevitably lead to a collapse the likes of the one on Thanksgiving. Better here, in the office, than in the car on the way home, I thought, and began urging her to look at the downside of the little man, the part she called "a little demon."

"I can't relate to the demon," she said.

"Can't, or don't want to?" I pushed.

"Can't," she answered defensively.

"Well, then," I said, groping for another route, "how about letting the elf take its course. Imagine you leave the office feeling elfin, what then?"

Faye grinned. Her eyes still closed, moved rapidly under her lids as if she were dreaming. "Imagine whatever I want?"

"Yep."

"Okay, first thing I do is get on the elevator and see if I have my credit card. I do. Next, I think of doctor's orders to go lie down after my appointment. I dismiss that thought at once, and plan a shopping spree. Bill and I already agreed to keep our Christmas low-budget, but I put that out of my mind, too, and head for the stereo store. Dylan has been raving about these new laser disc players. I go to the salesman and he helps me pick one out for Dylan. Now I have to get something big for Charlotte. She and her family haven't had a vacation in years, so on impulse, I go to the airlines and get them tickets to Fiji, which they can use any time in the coming year. Now I feel like going over to Clara's for a glass of wine before I go home." (Wine was also against doctor's orders.)

"How do you feel doing these things?"

"Great!" she said, "except for knowing Bill will be furious."

"And how about your joints and muscles, how do they feel?"

"Achey, I guess, but they'd feel that way even if I'd gone home to rest, so what does it matter?"

"It matters that the elf energy starts out as an ally, but somewhere along the way it turns on you and becomes a health hazard."

Faye stiffened and sat silently for thirty seconds. Finally she said, "You're saying that's what happened on Thanksgiving. My elf energy turned on me and became a hazard."

"Yes. Getting all hyped to do a dazzling feast led to a crash. The elf wasn't your ally when you collapsed and hit your head."

Faye opened her eyes and glared at me. "The hard thing about this," she said angrily, "is that the elf has been my ally all my life. Getting *hyped*, as you say, is how I get my best work done. It's my creative spark. I can't get anything done without it."

"There are other ways to get things done, Faye."

"And what's wrong with my way?" she challenged.

I replied, "Well, what's wrong with it is . . . It's a bit manic, and bad for your health."

"Manic? Manic! Call it what you like!" She yelped defensively, jumping to her feet. "It's my *joie de vivre!* Without it I'd just as soon shrivel up and die! You have no idea what I'm dealing with here. You've probably never been sick a day in your life. And as for your insulting diagnosis, you may be perfectly accurate, but as far as I'm concerned, you can stuff it! I won't be diagnosed." She grabbed her bag, gloves, and coat, and grasped the chaotic bundle to her chest.

We still had ten minutes to go, but Faye stormed out the door and slammed it on her scarf. She opened it again to grab the scarf. "Damn, damn, damn," she mumbled, bending down to retrieve it. Her keys fell out of her purse, and she made a growling noise as she again bent to the floor to snatch them up.

"Faye," I said in a somewhat conciliatory tone, "may I ask one thing before you go?"

"What!?" she snarled.

"Where are you headed, exactly?" I asked.

With her teeth bared she said, "I am going exactly and precisely, home to lie down and take my bloody nap! Are you happy?"

"Relieved," I said, "I'm relieved."

I'd fallen into the unfortunate trap of using a tactless diagnostic term, the very thing which had turned her off doctors, the thing she'd warned me about when we'd first met. It was a mistake on my part, one made out of frustration, and only time would tell whether or not we could make good use of my blunder.

Mothering

More than once during the course of our work, Faye insisted she held sacred her fond memories of her mother, and refused to "dredge them up." She said they had no bearing on current problems. I felt they might, and yet she cleverly evaded the topic. The visit after she'd stormed out of the office, she apologized for being touchy and explosive. I accepted her apology and admitted to impatience and a hasty choice of words. After the air felt clear, our discussion took a lucky turn in which Faye herself brought up the subject of her mother.

"So last week, Erica, when you said there were other ways to get things done besides the elfin approach, what did you mean?"

"Well," I said, "an alternative approach is that of the queen as mother. As mother, she finds within herself a powerfully protective voice. Previously her weeping consisted of inarticulate sobs. Now, with a child to protect, she makes strong verbal protests, and the little man takes note."

"Hmmm," she said, "my mother was rather inarticulate, but when it came to me, she usually spoke up. If Dad tried to harass me about chores she'd say, 'Harvey, she's only a girl. Let her be.'"

"So, around your mom, you weren't under pressure?"

"Not at all. Mom was mellow. We had fruit trees and she used to can peaches, plums, and applesauce. It was great. I loved helping her because we'd chat or listen to the radio. She never got on me about how much I was getting done. She let me dawdle. Around Mom I could relax."

"There's your answer, Faye. Your mother's example. She got things done didn't she? Canning, housekeeping, child rearing, gardening, etc.?"

"Oh, yes, she did all that quite competently," Faye nodded.

"That's a good way to get things done," I encouraged, "the motherly way, patient, consistent, protective, not rushed or, excuse the word, *manic.* "I raised my eyebrows and paused to see if the term was still offensive.

Faye grinned, "Oh, it's okay. I looked it up. It's an old Greek word referring to an elevation of spirit. I don't have any beef with that," she said. "And as for patience, I learned to be patient with my kids, because that's the only way to get on with little ones, but being patient with myself is another story, entirely. How would you suggest I go about it?"

"Let's try conjuring the memory of canning with your mother."

Faye closed her eyes and reminisced, "I'd be sitting at the table, swinging my legs, listening to a tune on the radio. Mom and I would hum or sing along. She'd ask me to wipe the jars, or place peaches in a jar. The kitchen would be full of steam from the canning tub. We'd have the wood stove fired up, so it would be super warm, but nice. The windows would be wide open and if we were lucky a cool breeze would come through. If not, we'd go outside every hour or so, and splash ourselves with cool water from the well. It was always peaceful."

"That's a perfect memory to work with," I said. "You can conjure that memory as a means to calm yourself when you're keyed up, or as a way to wind down before a nap."

This suggestion worked for Faye. She conjured the memory on a regular basis, reacquainting herself with the calm which had come naturally to her mother, and which had so pleasantly colored her early years. This helped her to rest, which led to a decrease in some of her more problematic symptoms, including headaches and "brain-fog."

The Faithful Messenger

Unfortunately, Faye wasn't out of the woods yet. After maintaining a plateau of improved health for some months, she was asked to speak as part of a prestigious lecture series at an Ivy League university. She impulsively agreed. "They've asked me to speak on Emily Dickinson, and if I have to say no to my favorite topic, then I might as well shrivel up and die!"

Her doctor said she could give it a try. I urged her not to throw caution to the wind, but she'd already set her course and plunged in, preparing an ambitious lecture. She stayed up into the wee hours, two consecutive nights, despite Bill's admonitions. There was no stopping her fervor. Her elfin enthusiasm took over and she crafted a powerful talk, but the high it provided didn't sustain her. After the lecture Faye said, "I'm usually a great speaker because I don't read. I extemporize, and get a lively rapport going with my audience. But I was exhausted from the flight, and didn't sleep well in the hotel. My head ached throughout the lecture, my mind stayed foggy, and my voice wavered. I was definitely the forlorn girl, given too great a task. I didn't manage to spin gold, and my delivery certainly wasn't queenly." There wasn't a hint of self-pity in Faye's voice as she gave me this matter-of-fact account of the situation.

She went on to say, "I've been doing a lot of thinking. What happened with this lecture is an example of what we talked about the day I stormed out on you. I think I'm finally ready to accept it now. The elfin energy is no longer my ally. It pumped me up when I first started writing the lecture. For a couple days I felt like my old self again, crafty, invincible, and yes, *manic*. But halfway into the project it turned on me. Adrenaline carried me only so far, and then I crashed. I had no reserves to complete the task. I prepared a brilliant talk and gave a mediocre one. And now, it will take two weeks of rest to recover. The day I stormed out you said, 'There are other ways to get things done besides going manic.' The next week we devised the mother memories to help me rest. I seem to have that down. But now I need something else—not the manic elf—and not the calm mother. I need something achievement-oriented to help me follow through without burning out. Do you see what I'm driving at?"

"Absolutely," I nodded, closing my eyes. I pictured the final segment of *Rumpelstiltskin*. "Remember how the queen follows through?" I asked.

"She outwits the elf by guessing his name."

"Yes. And the way she goes about it is important. She gets a new ally to help."

Faye shot me one of her perplexed frowns. "What new ally?"

"Don't you remember the queen's faithful messenger?"

"Vaguely," she squinted. "Isn't he the one who overhears the little man singing, '*Today I brew, tomorrow I bake, the next day the queen's child I'll take. My name is Rumpelstiltskin, but luckily nobody knows it.*'?"

"Yes," I replied. "The queen employs that trusty fellow to help her, and he comes through when she needs him. He functions quite differently than the coercive father, the greedy king, or the manic elf."

"Differently in what way?" she quizzed.

"No false claims, no gold spinning, no heavy demands, just reliable service, within reasonable limits."

"What sort of limits?" Faye grabbed for her pen and began scribbling notes.

"Well," I said, "they have three days to guess the elf's name. The queen stays up all night wracking her brains, but her messenger doesn't get so ruffled. He seems thorough, but rather plodding, and systematic. He's never described as frantic, and he doesn't work all night."

Faye chuckled. "That's the opposite of my all-nighters. You know who fits this description? Bill. He's a systematic plodder who doesn't get ruffled, and refuses to work past five. But he's a technician by temperament and by trade. I'm an artist. Artists can't function that way."

"They can if their health depends on it," I said, resisting the urge to tell her that illness had forced me to learn the value of plodding.

"Plodding just sounds hum-drum to me," Faye said. "I mean, anyone could be a messenger. There's no real imagination required."

"Maybe not," I argued gently, "but there's a great value to the sort of service he provides. He does things the king and the little man can't do."

"Like what?" she asked.

"He gives attentive service at a fair price, not a life-or-death fee. It's her first partnership based on truly workable terms. He doesn't lie about her skills, or threaten her life, or demand her child. And she doesn't expect him to stay up all night, working frantically to bail her out. It may be a bit mundane, but in the long run this relationship could sustain her, where the others drain her dry. Who knows, in the long run, maybe this kind of partnership yields more truly creative work." This bit of wisdom had come out so neatly I wondered why it hadn't occurred to me ages before.

By the look on Faye's face I could see it was making an impression, but her eyes were full of questions. "In theory that sounds fine," she said, "but artists are typically manic. They work all night, they forget to eat, they become enraptured with the muse."

I handed her a post card from my desk drawer, a portrait of Georgia O'Keeffe, which featured her beautiful weather-worn face and hands. "This artist painted prolifically, well into her nineties," I told Faye. "She thrived on a sensible work rhythm, balancing exuberance and rest. She ate three nutritious meals a day, and come evening, she rested. She didn't need to make herself sick in order to find her muse. On the contrary, she kept herself fit for the muse."

"I've got a feeling you're right, Erica. The frail, tormented artist is a romantic stereotype. There are plenty of fine writers who take good care of themselves. I've just never had any as role models, and at my age it's not easy to find a whole new way of working. How am I going to learn the ways of the messenger?"

"You said yourself Bill functions that way. Why don't you study his style and see if it could translate to your own work."

Faye smiled. "Bill is one-of-a-kind. His dad is eighty-two and still farming. He's never pressured Bill, and Bill's never had the need to prove himself to anyone. I've always envied him that. We're going to the farm on Saturday to help thin onions and carrots. Believe me, we'll have three good meals, and I'll get a good dose of messenger-style company with those two."

During our next visit, Faye reported her observations of the faithful messenger. "On Saturday I was quite charmed by Bill and his dad. They spend a lot of time chatting about the vegetable patch, soil conditions, insects, gophers, crows, the best technique for thinning, etc. Their conversation was pleasingly witty, and it was relaxing to work at their no-pressure pace. But I had less patience for this style when it showed itself during the work week. Bill came home early Monday when the air conditioning went out in his office. I was surprised at his nonchalance. I myself, would never dream of quitting early for such a minor reason. He said he couldn't concentrate while he was uncomfortable, and it made more sense to call it a day. I could see his point, and yet I found myself getting annoyed that he would give comfort so much priority.

"I knew enough to let it go, but we still had a fight later that week on a similar topic. He said he'd read that some Chronic Fatiguers have won disability pay, and suggested we look into it. I hit the roof. I sounded just like my father, too. I told him, no way was I going to stoop that low, while I'm still more competent than half my colleagues! Bill didn't get ruffled. He just said disability means an impairment in functioning that could happen to any sick person, and there was no need to be defensive about it.

"After I cooled down I realized he was just trying to help, and in fact he was right. Bill and I sat down and plodded through our medical records and insurance forms. It was a real lesson in the faithful messenger approach. We're not going to pursue it with a dogged fervor, but we're going to meet with the insurance rep and go through the procedures one step at a time." This turned out to be one of the most effective steps Faye took in coping with her illness. Over the next two months she and Bill managed to arrange a leave of absence from teaching, with disability compensation. Though she'd expected resistance at every turn, all parties agreed amicably.

During her leave of absence the faithful messenger came alive in Faye's imagination, and though he lacked artistic flair, he became her favorite character alongside the queen. "The two of them together have great potential," she said. "The queen is a source of inspiration, while the messenger has the follow-through to bring her vision into being." Faye carried this rapport within herself like a secret love, and grew accustomed to the comfort it evoked. She opened her imaginative ear to his guidance and advice. She wrote his words in her journal, engaging in what Jung called a "colloquy with the friend of the soul." With the help of the faithful messenger, she learned to set moderate goals. She took to handwriting her journals while lying down, rather than sitting at the computer. She collected no-fuss recipes and made simpler meals. She made a pact with herself not to go to the computer at all after five, and she stuck to it.

Naming the Little Man

But the manic little elf still roamed the forest and could pop up at any time. For example, she started out one morning reading and resting as her doctor prescribed. Then an idea shot through her head: "I should revise my filing system today." Even though she'd long since given up coffee, this thought surged through her like a double espresso. Before she could stop herself, she was in the library, tearing through her massive files. Hours later, Bill came home for lunch and found her frantically shuffling papers. He urged her to stop for the day and go back to it tomorrow, but that evening when he got home from work, he found her feverish and exhausted. She'd accomplished the reorganization, but at the expense of her health. "Bill gets so angry," she said shaking her head. "He says I'm obsessed."

"Is that a fair assessment?" I asked.

"You know it is," Faye replied. "I just wish I could catch it sooner. I was halfway through the file job before it dawned on me how manic I was."

"Catch it sooner," I repeated her words. "To do that would be to name the little man before he takes the upper hand."

"How does that work?" Faye asked.

"Well, I'm imagining it like this," I said. "The thought, 'gee, maybe I'll redo the files,' comes into your head. Instead of jumping up and acting on it, you recognize it and name it for what it is."

Faye's eyes gleamed. "You mean name it as a rambunctious, hasty, overzealous, whim from the elfin side of my personality?"

"Exactly and precisely," I said, recycling one of her phrases.

"I suppose once I name it I've got a better chance of tempering it," she said, "a better chance of going in a more moderate direction."

"Exactly and precisely," I said grinning. Faye was one of the most psychologically clever people I'd ever worked with. She grasped metaphor and had a knack for putting it to use. I'd never remarked about it to her. Because she was such an achiever, I hadn't wanted to imply she should strive to impress me. But at that moment I couldn't resist. "You're one smart woman, Faye," I said.

She grinned, and bobbed her head, "Thanks, I know."

In the weeks to come, she "befriended" the little man through inner dialogues. Marie-Louise von Franz teaches women to educate troubling inner males through imaginal give-and-take conversations. When the elf showed himself in the form of a manic impulse, Faye learned to catch him right away, to sit down and "converse" with him in her journal. First, she'd hear and write out all his entreaties to act manic. Then she'd "talk sense" to him, explaining why his urges had to be modified and rechanneled. These conversations helped Faye's common sense to gain the upper hand.

Over the months that followed, Faye delved into her poetry, and a stronger poetic voice emerged, one of greater clarity and immediacy. For the first time her writing departed from the hallowed halls of academe and gained some real street-smarts. She started writing about local environmental and political issues, and dedicated poems to living people, rather than dead poets as she had in the past.

The university accepted her proposal that she resume teaching half-time the following year to see how it went. That year she also felt ready to manage her drama without my help. On our final visit Faye said the difficult players were still active in her psyche. She read from her journal, "I doubt I can banish the pride-sick father, the forlorn daughter, the greedy king, or the troublesome aspects of little man. And I doubt I can ever completely avoid the troubles that go with them. But, I've got a powerful ally close at hand. With the help of the faithful messenger, I can manage these others and take better care of myself."

"Faye," I said, "may I make a good-bye request?"

"I'm pleased you have something in mind," she said.

"When we first met, you said the end of *Rumpelstiltskin* was your favorite part. Could we give some attention to the end of the story and all that you love about it?"

"Mmmm," Faye nodded as if sipping something that hit the spot. She closed her eyes. Her breath grew deeper and steadier. By the look of smoothness that came to her face, I knew she'd arrived at place of powerful remembering. "At the end of the story," she began softly, "the queen is fully in charge—so much so, that she can afford to play a game with the little man. She could name the little rascal right out, and be done with him, but she doesn't. She takes charge of the timing. She draws out the game, exercising her power. Being allowed four guesses, she play's with him, knowing full well she'll win in the end. She teases, 'Perhaps your name is Tom? Well then, are you Dick? Or might you be called Harry?' She lets the little man think he has the upper hand, right up until the end. But then at the last minute, she bests him, by naming, 'Rumpelstiltskin.' He's so startled and upset, so exasperated, he's consumed by his own frenzy." Faye smiled. "Finally, I've arrived at a place where I can speak directly to the elfin spirit. It used to possess me, but now I'm in charge of the timing." She opened her eyes and said, "May I make a request?"

"Sure," I said.

"I'd like to know whether you knew all along the faithful messenger would be my 'friend of the soul,' to use Jung's phrase." Faye's eyebrows perched inquisitively upon her forehead.

"No, to be honest," I said, "I didn't. I didn't know how nicely your alliance with him would serve until we stumbled upon it."

"I thought so," she said. "So what do you call that, luck, or intuition?"

"How about lucky intuition?" I chuckled. "We stumbled upon him at the right moment, just the way he stumbled upon the elf at the right moment. Maybe it's luck. Maybe it's intuition. Maybe it's a gift from the muse."

7

Mom and the Nuns

We often tune into a myth because it amplifies what we are doing.

—Jean Shinoda Bolen

Stories go to work on you like arrows.

—Benson Lewis

Talking to the Dead

"Do you make house calls?" she rasped into the receiver. "The reason I ask is that I'm laid up with a broken foot—shattered in six places. I can't drive."

"First off, Bonnie, tell me what sort of problem you need help with."

"Isolation, I guess. I've never lived alone before and it's getting to me. I'm all cooped up and I'm smoking too much. The home care nurse says I need therapy."

I hadn't made a house call in years. "Hmm," I said. "Where do you live?" It turned out Bonnie lived in the woods on the far bluff of an island that wasn't easy to get to. Normally I'd suggest a local counselor, but I'd been meaning to go there anyway, since an old friend had moved there and she'd been badgering me to visit. Bonnie offered to pay my ferry fare, so I thought I'd make clever use of a day by visiting my friend and putting in an hour's work to boot.

On the appointed morning I was grateful to be out before dawn, wiping the steam from my windshield. Sunrise ferry departures to unfamiliar destinations have a way of portending adventure. I felt sorry for commuters heading for offices and factories. The sun split the clouds just over the Cascades making Mt. Rainier look like God's own mound of peach sorbet. The sky overhead was hazy, but the sun was blazing strongly enough to burn it off by noon. On the western horizon the Olympics shone chilly blue. It was one of those crisp Northwest days that make you feel clear-minded and eager.

I found my way to Bonnie's cabin, down a long, steep two-track full of potholes deeper than my sedan's axle was high. Ferns and blackberry stalks grabbed at the car from both sides, and on my left, the mushy bank dropped off severely. It would be easy to lose a car down that ravine. It would get swallowed by eight-foot ferns and two-pound banana slugs. Suddenly my clever adventure seemed foolhardy. If I turned up missing, no one would know where to search. I wondered what had possessed me to do a house call.

When Bonnie's place finally came into view, I'd have taken it for abandoned except for the trail of chimney smoke snaking up through the trees. The roof sagged under a wet rug of moss. Bracken fronds sprouted out of the cracks in the foundation, raising their hairy fists, as if staking claim to the place. Lichens and mushrooms populated the cracks between shingles. It looked as if the forest's determination to eat the cabin had far surpassed Bonnie's interest in saving it. Mud pressed against the uphill side of the cabin, and up the slope, more mud sat ready to slide with the next heavy rain. Another good slide could push the whole cabin down the hill. Bonnie needed more than therapy, she needed a retaining wall, a home inspector, and a repair crew.

"I told you it was rustic!" she whooped with a crane-like laugh which disintegrated into smoker's cough. She sat half-submerged in an ancient overstuffed chair with her foot and huge cast propped up on an ottoman heaped with pillows. "This place is a pit," she said. "That's a story in itself. I never intended to live here. See, my aunt died, and left it to me. I was going to fix it up and sell it. Get a decent place in Seattle or Portland. Then I broke the foot chopping wood. Whole damn woodpile fell on top of me. I'm lucky to be alive!"

The cabin's dank staleness was compounded by ascending braids of smoke from Bonnie's Marlboro. "I never had therapy before. I guess I could start with personal demographics," she said nervously, "I'm forty-four, single, and I make a decent living with the help of *Babe.*" She nodded toward the computer in the corner surrounded by chaotic piles of astrological books and charts. "I do charts— mostly mail-order these days. I heard you use Tarot cards and my- thology, so I figured you wouldn't be spooked by the charts." She stubbed out a butt and blew smoke to one side in an effort to shield me.

"Anyway, l didn't call you here about astrology, or the damn foot. I called cause there's some weird shit going on, and I need to talk to someone. Now I take it from the paperwork you sent, that all our discussions are confidential?"

I nodded, "Yes, with the exception of violence. If you or some- one you know is in danger, I won't keep that under my hat."

"I understand," she said fishing the last Marlboro from its pack. "This isn't about physical harm, but it is about life and death. What do you think about talking to the dead? Do you think it's crazy?"

"That depends," I said. "It can be crazy. It can also be healing."

"So you wouldn't take me for schizophrenic . . . You wouldn't figure I should be locked in the back wards?"

"Probably not. Why don't you tell me what's troubling you? If I can't help you, then I'll try to find someone who can."

"Yeah," she said releasing a fat cloud of smoke. "Okay, up until last fall, I'd never lived alone." Bonnie bit her lip as her eyes teared up. "I'll go back to the beginning, so you get the picture. Our dad died young. My sister, Jane, and I were raised by our mother and two aunts. They owned a couple of farms east of the mountains. After Dad died, the farms got run down. So Mom, Velma, and Millie sold the land, and bought a few rental homes in Seattle." Bonnie coughed and cleared her throat. "Is this what I'm supposed to do? I'm supposed to tell you my story from the beginning?"

"Sure," I said, wanting to encourage her. "That's a fine place to start."

"They always wanted a vacation cabin, so they bought this place. That was back in the sixties. This was our summer home. It was in good shape then. Hard to believe, huh?"

I smiled and she went on with her story, "Back then was our heyday. My sister drove around in a Mustang, picking up boys. I went along a few times. Mom and the nuns . . . that's what we called our maiden aunts, the nuns . . . they fixed up this place. They were really sturdy country women, those three. I thought they'd never die." At this Bonnie's eyes teared again and she wept quietly.

Trying to subdue her tears, she sniffed hard and swallowed. Weeping plugged her passages and made it harder to smoke, talk, and breathe. But her story had a will of its own and pushed to come out.

"Anyway, Mom got sick first. She had a long, slow struggle with cancer, starting in seventy-five. My sister, Jane, got pregnant, and married, in that order. I was engaged to a fisherman named Hank, but my wedding got postponed on account of Mom needing me. To make a long story short, about the time Mom died, Millie got sick. That was in eighty-two. Of course, Hank had given up on me by then.

"With Millie, it was just like with Mom—first the breast, then the lung, then the liver. It took about six years. By then, I'd spent the better part of my adult years nursing old ladies. Not that I resented it—it's just that, without realizing it, I turned into a second generation nun. Millie and Velma called me their angel, because I prayed a lot. That's what got me through it, I think, prayer and these," she said waving her pack of Marlboros.

She sucked hard on the one she had lit, "They say bad luck comes in three's. Well, Velma got uterine cancer just before Millie died. It's a good thing my business was booming by then, because we'd already sold off all the real estate to pay Mom's and Millie's bills. There wasn't anything else to draw on. We never could get health insurance. With Velma, it was right out of my pocket." She looked at me, "Is this all right? Me rattling on this way, I mean. This is what you do in therapy isn't it?"

I nodded.

She went on, "Three cancer deaths in one family—we knew it wasn't coincidence, of course. The same thing happened to other farm families down wind of the nuclear plant. We never got any compensation, though. We gave up trying. I'm not very good at holding my ground, and I had my hands full doing the bedside care. Hank wanted me to sue. But that isn't my way. He used to get so mad. He said my problem was trying to solve practical problems with esoteric solutions.

"Anyway, Velma needed me by her side. She didn't want me to waste my time with litigation. A compensation check wouldn't do her much good with one foot in the grave. But she wanted some way to repay me for my trouble. So she left me this place. She refused to sell it. Stubborn 'til the end, she saved it for me, whether I wanted it or not."

Bonnie gave a half-hearted laugh, blew her nose, and grabbed a fresh pack of smokes. "Jane and I had her cremated last fall. Afterwards, we went out and got drunk. We loved them with all our hearts, but it was a relief after they'd all died. That may sound cruel, but I was forty-three and had never had a life of my own. Janie said it was time for me to start living . . . to travel . . . maybe meet a guy . . . whatever. But," she said taking an extra long drag, "easier said than done." She looked at me for a moment, then switched topics to ask, "So what's your sun sign?"

Her question caught me by surprise. She had every right to ask about my background and credentials, I just wasn't used to the zodiac being part of that. But given Bonnie's tradition, it was her fundamental criterion for selecting a therapist. "Gemini," I said, "sun and moon in Gemini."

"Oh," she said, "Double Gemini. Of course, I should have guessed. You're deductive and intuitive and very empathic, right? So, I'd say you've got several planets in Cancer."

I nodded, impressed at her ability to read my astrological chart simply by looking at my face and hearing me say a few words. But she wasn't my counselor, I was supposed to be hers. I aimed the lens right back at her. "So, Bonnie, is it fair to say you're afraid to leave the cabin, and you're afraid to stay?"

She nodded, and looked at me expectantly.

I didn't want to waste my time and her money on too many house calls, so I went directly for the heart of it. "So, let's see if I've got the picture . . . If you leave the cabin, you face the unknown. That's scary. But if you stay, you might talk to ghosts 'til the cabin falls in—or you die of lung cancer. And that's scary, too, is that right?"

"Bingo," she nodded blowing out smoke.

"Okay," I said, "are you ready to fill me in on the ghost situation?"

"Before we get into it, can I ask you a few questions, you know, to see if you're right for the job?"

"Fair enough," I nodded.

"First off, do you believe in the afterlife?" she quizzed.

"Yes."

"Do you believe in reincarnation?"

"Yes," I said, "I think of it this way: The dead body decays, giving nutrients back to the earth. Through those nutrients, life continues in a new form. So after death, why wouldn't the soul continue in a new form?"

"Okay, then, do you believe in communication with dead ancestors?"

"Yes. Like most people on this earth, I believe ancestors offer strength, guidance, and protection."

"Well, wait a minute, then," she said, "what don't you believe in?"

"Hmm," I said, surprised by her question, "Well, I don't believe in absolute knowledge, or pure science. I believe the mysteries outweigh the facts. So when experience points towards the mysteries, I'm inclined to be watchful. If what I see affirms the mysteries, I'm inclined to believe."

"Very philosophical," she said. "You must have Sagittarius rising."

"You're right," I said, flabbergasted at her intuitive skill.

"Yep," she nodded, "You're in the right line of work: A spiritual detective. That's good. What about your mid-heaven?"

"Virgo, if I remember right," I apologized. "I'm not much of an astrologer."

"Virgo," she savored. "Uh huh, I can see that. Persistent, good on details . . . Sort of a *Columbo of the soul.*"

At that we both cracked up laughing. I didn't tell her I loved Columbo, but I told her I fancied myself a good investigator. Bonnie squinted at me with her head cocked as if to divine the rest. "You're determined," she said. "I can see that. Is your Mars in Capricorn, then?"

"Bingo," I replied, borrowing her phrase, succumbing to her expert hunches. We both laughed. In twenty minutes, she'd read me more deftly than I'd read her. Like Columbo, I'd have to keep plodding before my understanding would overtake the basic chaos of the case.

"I think you can help me, Erica," she said more seriously. "As you put it, my experience 'points toward the mysteries.'" She reached for her tobacco.

"So," I said, "we've got half an hour left. Are you ready to tell me what the ghosts have been up to?"

"Ready as I'll never be," she winked and lit up. Then she attempted to change the subject back to my chart, "That Virgo midheaven is real organized about time. Do you always think that way: a half hour for this or that?"

"You're avoiding the subject, Bonnie."

"Damn," she said, "I've been known to do that. That's part of the problem. It's a combination of my Gemini sun and Aquarius rising. I jump from one cloud to the next." She pressed the palms of her hands to her forehead as if gathering her thoughts and then began. "Okay, sometimes it's like they're right here with me, all the time. At other times they drift away, but no matter what, Velma shows up several times a day. Mom shows up several times a week, and Millie wanders around outside most of the time." She peered over the upper rim of her glasses to see how I'd handle this news.

"Do you see them, hear them, or what?" I asked.

"Okay," she said. "Here's an example: I'll be sitting here doing a chart, and I'll think to myself, 'Look at that north node.' And all of a sudden I hear Velma. It's not the same as hearing your voice. I don't hear her with my ears, really. It sounds the same as when you remember a past conversation, only it's not a memory because it's happening now. I can also *feel* them, but I don't *see* them, thank God. Does that sound nuts?"

"Not necessarily," I said.

"What's really weird about it," Bonnie went on, "is that Velma now knows astrology. She's picked up tons of information, in fact. I asked her how she suddenly knows so much about astrology. She says she's always known a lot and dying brought back things she'd forgotten in life."

I'd seen something like this before. It was with an astute palm reader who confessed she really knew nothing about reading the lines on the hand. She simply held her clients' hands and passed on cues she heard from her mother who'd died decades earlier.

"Velma's voice is helpful, then?" I asked.

"Yes, it's helpful, all right. Her tips are right on the money. And it's not like she tries to pester me. She doesn't. She just chimes in with a fresh insight, and then hangs around the room for a while. She won't explain a single thing about the afterlife, though. She says the living are supposed to learn about life and couldn't comprehend the afterlife, even if it could be explained in words, which it can't. But she did say that most people's best ideas come from their ancestors, they just don't realize it." I wasn't sure where to go with this. Did it matter where the Velma voice was coming from? Whether Bonnie was getting messages from a dead ancestor or from her unconscious psyche, she was getting information of considerable accuracy and value, if the impromptu reading she'd just done for me was indicative. It didn't sound as if the spirits of Mom and the nuns tried to detain Bonnie from getting on with life. In fact, Velma urged her to focus less on the beyond and more on the here and now. Judging from the condition of the cabin, and Bonnie's description of how her mind flitted from cloud to cloud, I certainly agreed. But I wanted to make sure the spirits weren't trying to haunt the cabin or hold Bonnie back from life.

She couldn't say exactly what was holding her back from life, but she felt truly immobilized. The spirits took the edge off her loneliness and made it easy to stay in the cabin, while the foot injury provided a convenient excuse to hide out. She felt her success in mail order astrology was another convenience which kept her isolated and immobilized. "I think about traveling, and meeting a guy, but l never do anything about it. It scares me how complacent I am. I'm afraid twenty years from now, if I live that long," she said holding up her culprit tobacco, "I'll wonder what happened to my life! I'll wonder how the hell I sat in this chair thinking grand thoughts and never carried out a single one. Like Janie says, I traverse the universe in my mind, but in actuality, I don't budge an inch."

At that point, I couldn't say whether the problem was based on the particulars of her situation or the particulars of her personality or a combination of the two. Bonnie believed in the astrology of fate. She believed her personality fit her life circumstances like a glove because of celestial influences at the moment of birth. Modern psychology also looks to the past. Psychologists scour the emotional constellations of infancy to chart the causes of adult suffering. Experience had taught me that sometimes the past cries out for our attention, because the soul remains wrongfully snagged there. Sometimes, going back is the only way to free it. But at other times, the soul yearns to move forward and its movement is hindered by fixations on the past. I asked about Bonnie's early years on the farm to try and determine whether her soul was snagged there or whether she was simply paralyzed before the precipice of change.

With a doting mother and two adoring aunts, she'd had more nurturance than most youngsters. But in her second week of life, her mother suffered a breast infection which disrupted nursing. They tried every available infant formula, but none of them would stay down, and Bonnie underwent a frantic ordeal of near starvation. Finally after eight days, breast feeding resumed, and she began to thrive. The family believed this tentative start in life explained Bonnie's preoccupation with the spirit. They were respectful of her mystical inclinations, though they didn't share them.

Family life had always been important to her. While they were growing up, her sister, Jane, tended to be feisty and rebellious, sometimes engaging Bonnie in teenage adventures. But for the most part Bonnie had been a home-body whose greatest pleasure came from reading about metaphysics and helping others. "It's my Pisces moon," she said, as if explaining the obvious. Her father died of a heart attack when she was twelve. This was by far the most painful event of childhood, but she was allowed to grieve, and felt supported by her mother and aunts throughout.

Mysticism, grief, compassion, and the care of others characterized her life. She may have been caught by the familiarity of these, but more than that, she was paralyzed by the sheer strangeness of the freedom and possibility that lay ahead. She now desired things which did not come easily to a somewhat eccentric middle-aged woman, particularly one who'd been living like a nun. Experience had taught her much about sacrifice, love, patience, and spirit, but very little about the adventures of socializing, flirting, and travel. She understood loss and hardship and knew what it required of her, but she knew little of how to court good luck and gain. Metaphysical musing lifted her out from under the burdens of this world, but it hadn't taught her to seize the day.

Her cast wouldn't come off for another two weeks, so we agreed to two more house calls. If we went on from there, she'd have to come to my office in the city, which would be interesting. She thrived on high levels of nicotine. In my nonsmoking office building, she'd have to contend with its absence.

Grounded Eagles

Bonnie phoned the day before the second house call. "Erica, you won't believe what's happened here. This morning I heard stomping in the bushes, like a really big critter was running around outside. I got my crutches and went out. There was a huge bald eagle running up and down outside the cabin. Man, have you ever seen one up close? They're bigger than a turkey! This guy has arms bigger than mine and his talons are way bigger than my hands. He scared the shit out of me! His beak is so big he could take your hand off in one bite. I didn't dare get any closer than five yards or so, and he wasn't exactly eager to get any closer to me, either.

"Anyhow, his wing was broken, and he was obviously stranded here against his will, so I called Fish and Wildlife figuring they'd come get him, but they can't. They say it happens to eagles a lot. Believe it or not, they get attacked in flight by crows and seagulls.

The smaller birds harass them and dive-bomb their wings. Once they lose two or three wing feathers, they literally can't fly. So, I've got company up here. They say it could be months, or even years before he flies again!"

"That's amazing, Bonnie, amazing," I said thinking to myself that it required something as startling as a surprise visit from a grounded eagle to get Bonnie out of her chair.

"Yeah, now I'll have to get up twice a day. Once to pee, and once to feed my eagle. But I have to ask you a favor. Could you stop by the ShopRite on your way here and pick up some liver? That's what he likes best, liver."

"I'd be honored, Bonnie. But just so it's understood between us . . . when you get a boyfriend up there, he'll have to get his own groceries."

"Fair enough," she chuckled, "I just hope he'll have functional limbs, and an appetite for something besides liver." The humor between us was a lucky bonus that made the house calls more appealing. I had an easy time liking Bonnie and she had an easy time liking me. That night I made sure to check into the local lore on eagles. That was lucky, too. I found a pertinent Yakima tale called *Coyote and Eagle Visit the Land of the Dead.* Stories have a way of availing themselves at the right moment. Now all I had to do was watch for an opening to tell it.

When I arrived at her place the next day, Bonnie hobbled to the door, grinning. She whispered that we should stand quietly near the woodpile and toss the liver toward the big cedar tree. I handed her the package, and she frowned saying, "Oh, chicken livers, I guess I should have told you, he prefers beef." The eagle had only been in her care for two days and she'd already become a stickler for his preferences. This must have been the kind of care she provided for her mother and aunts. But in this case, I wasn't about to go back to the store. The eagle would have to settle for chicken livers.

Bonnie tore them into juicy hunks and flung the first piece. It landed on a salmon berry bush and dangled there for a minute. Then suddenly "Thunder Thighs," as she called him, came bounding out from behind the cedar. He gave us a stern look and then turned his head, snatched the liver, tossed it back, and swallowed it down with one gulp. He looked to me as if he liked chicken liver just fine. He was undoubtedly the most impressive creature I'd seen in ages. I'd watched eagles hunt and soar above the beach near my home. I'd seen them swoop past with salmon in their claws, and once I'd even seen one with a cat in its grip, but I'd never seen one walking on the ground. Soaring, it's the grand wingspan that impresses the eye, but grounded, this eagle's heft and powerful legs left me breathless. His head was pure white, and his beak and feet were as yellow as daffodils.

When the liver was gone, Bonnie and I forced ourselves to go inside. After all, she was paying me by the hour.

"So, guess what!" she said proudly.

I sniffed the air. It was definitely fresher than the week before. "You've cut down on smoking?" I said.

"Yep! The time goes by quicker with an eagle around. I'm back down to less than two packs a day now, like I was before Velma died."

"That's great, Bonnie. You know what they say about Smoke and Eagle? They both perform a similar function."

"You're kidding, what?"

"They both soar to great heights. In myth and religion they both serve as messengers, carrying human prayers upward to the great spirit."

"That's lofty," she said. "I thought you'd say my smoking stemmed from insecurity, or a perverse death wish."

"Well, there's the rub," I said. "Sacred substances are easily misused. Tobacco used to be reserved for ritual occasions only."

"Right," Bonnie nodded, "I just did a chart for an alcoholic who euphemistically refers to booze as 'holy communion.'" Again Bonnie played the trickster and made me laugh.

"But back to Eagle and Smoke," I said. "There's one important difference between the two, and it's why I figure your grounded eagle is a good omen."

"Okay, Columbo, lets hear it."

"All right," I said. "Smoke goes up and doesn't come back, but Eagle soars around, communes with Great Spirit, and then returns to Earth. He carries messages both ways. When you want to know what Great Spirit feels, ask Eagle."

"Like astrology," Bonnie said. "Astrologers bring people messages from the stars, tidings from above, if you will. We're like eagles. We bring people messages from the great spirit."

"Messages they can put to use in life," I added.

"Yeah, if only *I* could put them to use in *my* life."

"The cabin seems to be a retreat for grounded eagles." I said eyeing the cast which sat like a centerpiece between us.

"How 'bout that?" Bonnie pondered, "Me and Thunder Thighs . . . A couple of grounded eagles."

"I wonder, Bonnie, if there's something useful about being grounded right now?"

"I don't know," Bonnie said. "I've never gone in for that Zen stuff. *Chop wood, carry water, God is in the details,* etc. That's how I broke my foot, tending to mundane details."

"Come on, you're an expert in the Zen stuff of caring for loved ones. Even now the task of caring for Thunder Thighs suddenly gives meaning to your life and brings you out of depression."

That's true," she concurred, "but it all sounds so burdensome, doesn't it?"

"It sounds conflicted, ambivalent, split, maybe."

"It's just that part of me has great visions," Bonnie confessed, "but making them real is another thing. I'm easily defeated. I make excuses."

"Do you want to hear a local story about Eagle?" I asked.

"Yeah," Bonnie nodded adjusting her pillows.

"It's called *Coyote and Eagle Visit the Land of the Dead.* It's a story from the Yakima tribe, near your birthplace."

Coyote's sister died and joined Eagle's wife in the land of the dead. Coyote and Eagle hated mourning and wanted their loved ones back. Coyote suggested they wait 'til spring and make a trip to the land of the dead. He figured they could stuff the spirits into a basket and tote them back to the land of the living. Coyote wanted to make it a rule that the dead would always come back in spring, just as the leaves return to the trees.

Eagle didn't want to wait 'til spring. He wanted his wife back right away. So they set out, Eagle flying

above—Coyote walking below. After many days they came to the shore. At the other side of the water they saw spirit houses. They called out for the spirits to ferry them across, but no one answered. "What a waste of time," Eagle said. "There's no one here."

But Coyote knew spirits rest by day and come out at night. After sunset Coyote began singing. His song was heard by spirit men. They ferried across the water for Coyote and Eagle and returned with them to the island of the spirits. When they landed the spirit men warned, "Don't look at anything. Keep your eyes closed. This is a sacred place."

"We are hungry and cold," said Eagle and Coyote. They were taken to a beautiful lodge. They heard drumming and dancing, and couldn't help but look around. Moonlight alone lit the large room. Everywhere spirits were dressed in beautiful ceremonial robes decorated with elks' teeth and shells. Their faces were brightly painted and they wore feathers in their hair. Even though the spirits were former friends and loved ones, they ignored Eagle and Coyote and went about their business.

The next night, Coyote and Eagle carried out their plan to kidnap the spirits. First, Coyote swallowed the moon, making it so dark even the spirits couldn't see. Eagle grabbed the spirits and stuffed them into a basket, closing the lid tightly. Coyote hoisted the basket to his shoulder. Then they headed for the land of the living— Eagle flying above and Coyote walking below.

After traveling a long distance, they heard noises from the basket. "Let us out!" said the spirits. "This ride is much too bumpy and we are crowded in here." The spirits were turning back into people so the basket got heavier and heavier. Coyote wanted to let them out, but Eagle said it was too soon.

A while later Coyote could endure the weight no longer. He let them out of the basket. They turned back into spirits and fled swiftly back to the land of the dead.

**At first Eagle scolded, then he took heart. "In the spring
we shall try again," he said.**

**"No," said Coyote, "I am tired. Let the dead stay in
the land of the dead." If he had listened to Eagle, and
left them in the basket, the dead would come back each
spring as the flowers and leaves do. Instead, they remain in their own place. Now Eagle is the only one strong
enough to soar to the land of the dead, but even Eagle
can never bring them back to the land of the living.**

"Just like Orpheus," Bonnie mused. "You're never supposed to
look at the dead. I guess it's like Velma said, it's just not right for
the living to see the afterlife. We're supposed to learn about *life.*"

"That's important for you, isn't it Bonnie?"

"Obviously," she said, stretching her casted leg in frustration.
"Believe me, I'm tired of studying death and dying!" She threw me
an angry look. "I don't need to bring back the dead, wherever they
are!" She groped her pocket for a cigarette, lit up, took a full drag,
and sighed as she let it out.

Suddenly she was pacified. All the emotional tension disappeared. She put her head back and rattled on about her Pisces moon,
her Gemini sun, and Aquarius ascendant and how she probably
wasn't meant to have a mate or any significant foundation for herself, as these things didn't really matter. Her talk became more and
more lofty and abstract. I was surprised at how long she went on,
and yet it was so compelling, that by the time she'd finished her
cigarette, she'd almost enlisted me into sharing her "nothing really
matters" attitude. My hunch that she needed grounding suddenly
jelled into a conviction.

"Bonnie," I said, "a few minutes ago you got emotional about
your situation. Then you lit up and soared into a metaphysical
cloud."

She grinned, "Sorry, Columbo. That drives people crazy, I know.
That's my Aquarius rising. I start to see patterns, you know, ever-
widening circles and stuff. It's like I see ultimate truth, you know,
Eagle's point of view, and all relative truths lose importance."

"Life is made of relative truths," I said. "Eagle's message comes
back to Earth, to be enacted *here*, remember?"

"I know," she said sadly. "Ultimate truth provides no solid materials for building a life. I can spiral out there with awesome visions, but I always wind up right back here where the pain is. Janie can't comprehend ultimate truth. She accepts relative truth, and when you compare her life to mine, it's obvious that relative truth is the most useful of the two." She thumped the cast against the pillows, sighed, and reached for a smoke.

"Wait," I said. "Hold on a moment. That was the same little sequence as the last time you lit up."

"Huh?"

"Your face gets flushed with emotion, your leg gets tense, makes a little kick, then you sigh and grab the cigarettes."

"I don't want to feel those emotions," she said.

"What if they have something to teach you?" I asked.

"Those emotions have been there a long time," she said holding her lighter tightly in one hand and her pack of cigs in the other. Both hands shook and her face grew purplish.

"They'll probably stay in there a lot longer if you keep dissipating them with the smoking," I said, hoping my words didn't come out cruelly.

"Well, what do you suggest?" she asked, loosening her grip on the smoking gear.

"You could try breathing gently, and taking note of the feelings in your body."

"Okay," she said, settling back a bit, putting the smokes into her pocket. "Is this the part of therapy where you feel worse now in order to feel better later?"

"That's what we're aiming for," I nodded.

She looked at me for some kind of guidance.

"Let's just take a few minutes to focus inside," I said.

"All right," she said anxiously, still looking for help.

"You could close your eyes if that seems right," I said. "See if it's possible to relax and be in your body. Take however much time you need. Let's make a bit of room to study whatever feelings come up."

After a minute or so, Bonnie noticed a weird sensation in the casted leg. It felt extremely heavy. I asked her to study the feeling. Soon she said it felt so heavy, she might never move it again. The weight seemed unendurable. It reminded her of Coyote collapsing under the weight of the kidnapped spirits. I was delighted that Coyote had come back to her. This meant her psyche had taken to the story as yeast takes to a good starter dough. I hoped that now the story would continue to germinate within her psyche and would give rise to something of substance—perhaps a nourishing bit of relative truth she could put to immediate use.

She soon noticed the rest of her body. In contrast to the heavy leg, it felt as if it might float away. The sensations frightened her. When she studied the fear it seemed to be generated over the mounting sensation that the two parts were separating. It felt as if the leg would sink into the earth and the rest would ascend toward the sky. "I want to scream!" she said. "I want a cigarette!"

"See if it's possible to stay with this a moment longer," I urged.

"Damn it! I can't," she said opening her eyes. "Isn't that terrible. I'm going to have to go at this a little at a time." She fumbled to light a Marlboro, and relaxed immediately on the first drag. She saw me looking at her inquisitively. "Relief," she said, as if to explain her sudden change from distress to ease.

"What happened to the two parts?" I asked.

She closed her eyes again, "It's amazing," she said. "My leg feels lighter." She continued focusing in this way and began to feel a sense of movement in her legs, a stride, almost a lope, as if she were walking along on a trail. "It reminds me of Coyote walking along with Eagle flying above," she said. "Staying connected feels much better than splitting apart." For two or three minutes she enjoyed the feeling of two close companions following the same path, one earthbound, the other airborne. Intermittent drags on her cigarette seemed to help keep them from splitting apart. I asked her if the companions were inclined to communicate. After a moment a faint smile appeared on her lips. She said Coyote called out to his friend, "Stay close!" And Eagle called back, "Don't worry! I won't let you out of my sight!" The communication pleased Bonnie a great deal. Then she stopped to light another cigarette. It seemed her bloodstream required constant doses of nicotine.

It was nearly time for me to go. Bonnie had had such pleasure with her images, that I hesitated to dull them through interpretation, and yet some grounding of their meaning was necessary. I asked, "Is there part of you that gets heavy and gives up, and part of you that floats off and doesn't care?" She nodded. I asked what she'd like to do for each.

"Well, the heavy part could use some lightness, and more mobility. And the lofty part needs to stay closer to the earth, more involved."

"Do cigarettes help?"

"No," Bonnie said sadly. "They just postpone the pain. If they were helping, I wouldn't need you, would I, Columbo?" She asked for an assignment to put these images to work.

"During the course of the week, pay attention to the two parts," I suggested. "Keep an eagle-eye on them. When you feel so heavy you want to collapse and give up, watch what you do. When your thoughts get so lofty that nothing seems to matter, watch that too. Study how these dynamics work."

"Okay," she nodded, grabbing her pencil to make notes, "Keep an eagle-eye on both parts, see how they work. But once I've studied them, isn't there something I can do?"

"Well, you could do like Coyote does," I said, "release the load."

"Yeah, but how do I do that, exactly?"

"I can't say, exactly, Bonnie. If I tried, you'd just have to amend my answer later anyway. You'll find the way."

"But what about the lofty part, what do I do when it soars off?"

"Do like Coyote does in your vision," I said. "Call it back."

"Call it back," she echoed, "of course."

Clarissa Pinkola Estes regards story as medicine. The teller can only hope that useful ingredients in the medicine will take effect. But each person metabolizes a story differently, so there's no predicting which ingredients will help once it gets into the blood. That day started a long-term helping relationship among Coyote, Eagle, and Bonnie, one that was full of rich results beyond my expectations. The story worked its way into her like an arrow, causing her to become intrigued and hopeful about mobilizing and grounding her energies. In the months and years to come Coyote and Eagle helped to guide and empower her in building a new life. But as she herself had predicted earlier, things got worse before they got better. The old defenses of giving up and drifting off were her primary methods of avoiding pain. If she truly managed to keep an eagle-eye on the whole process, pain would be close at hand. I didn't see any way around it, and I forewarned her this might be the case.

Final Resting Places

The following week the cabin was so thick with smoke my eyes began watering immediately. I was sick of the smell of stale smoke which clung to my clothes and hair each time I left Bonnie's. Luckily, this was the last house call.

"I've had a lousy week!" Bonnie barked the minute I stepped through the door. "Thunder Thighs nearly choked to death on a goddamn piece of liver."

Her face was blotched from crying. "The only friend I've got on the face of this earth, and he nearly dies, Like a goddamn old lady!" Her whole body convulsed with the rage of grief. Her casted leg jostled back and forth until an avalanche of pillows fell to the floor. She pounded the heel of her cast against the ottoman.

"Look at the psychotic shape I'm in," she said shaking her head. "Look at me. I quit smoking for two fucking days, Erica, two fucking days! I thought, 'I'm gonna beat this thing. I'm going to stay right here and figure out my life.' Each time my mind started to lift off, I'd call it back to the here and now. I did mundane stuff—my nephews' scrapbook, see?" she said holding up the scrapbook as tangible proof of her effort. She shook her head as if it were all too much for her, "Then the fucker gets a piece of liver caught in his throat, and I lose it!"

Her voice tightened suddenly, shooting shrill sarcasm into the air. "For twenty years I've run a terminal ward! Why should it be any different now? I'm like a death sentence. No one survives my care. Hank was smart to get out. You and Thunder Thighs better beware, my affection puts you on God's hit list." She shook her head and shoulders as if to shake off unbearable thoughts and emotions. "Am I talking crazy, or what? I know better, but I feel cursed. Do you understand what I'm saying?"

I nodded. Of course I understood. Caring for a suffering loved one, being unable to alleviate their agony and humiliation, is one of the more painful experiences of human life. Bonnie had spent her twenties and thirties in this pain, and had done so unbegrudgingly. But how does the human heart, which longs for justice, comprehend such unjust odds? Surely a curse makes more sense to the heart, than the notion of random misfortune.

Bonnie didn't wait for me to speak. Her voice softened and she looked me in the eye. "He's fine now, Erica, but I swear, when he started choking, I freaked out. It was spooky how much he looked like an old woman in distress. It was like reliving scenes I'd rather forget. My mind flooded with old mistakes I'd made—forgetting to mash Millie's food—letting Velma fall asleep with her head tipped back so she nearly choked on her false teeth. I screwed up a few times, not because I didn't know what to do, but because I was too goddamned exhausted to think straight."

Bonnie hugged her good knee to her chest and bawled without holding back. As she wept, I could see something slowly release its grip on her body. Once again, the wounded eagle had stirred her to the core, playing a central role in her healing.

A few minutes later, when she was through weeping, she looked more relaxed than usual. Her skin glowed and her eyes were soft. It was evident that changes were taking place inside, and though the exact nature of those changes wasn't yet clear, I could see they were changes for the good. She'd refrained from smoking for over twenty minutes. The cathartic release of intense weeping freed a softer essence so that she looked younger and seemed more hopeful. The active grieving cleansed her system, and was an important step forward, but I knew more was needed to get Bonnie out of her entrenched isolation.

She wanted to get on with her life, but like Eagle and Coyote, some part of her was still distracted by the dead. Cremating her loved ones hadn't put an end to their presence in her life. On the contrary, she said it had been easier to close the door and get a little privacy before they'd died. Now that they were spirits, Mom and the nuns seemed to have round-the-clock access to Bonnie. Perhaps like Eagle and Coyote, she would have to first move toward the land of the dead in order to gain resolve about fully joining the living.

Halloween was approaching. I thought of All Hallows Eve and the Day of the Dead. This was a traditional time for families to enter the cemetery and honor dead loved ones, not to bring them back, but to commune with them, one day out of the year. I'd seen the holiday celebrated in Central America. It allowed villagers to actively acknowledge the indisputable fact of death, while at the same time providing them with a means of relating to departed ancestors. Built into the celebration was a deep respect for the separation between this world and the next. An all-night vigil took place on the ancestral grave, which, one night a year, became the gateway between the land of the living and the land of the dead.

Perhaps Bonnie could benefit from the idea of approaching the dead at such a gateway, on the appointed night, rather than passively receiving them in her home night or day. To broach the subject, I asked if they had a family grave, a place where their ashes rested. Her answer startled me at first, and then seemed so obvious I was appalled at myself for not having asked sooner.

It turned out that Bonnie still kept their ashes locked in a safe right there in the cabin. Mom and the nuns had not yet reached their final resting place. Their remains were cooped up in the now derelict cabin they had once worked so diligently to maintain. I wondered if Bonnie kept them there out of attachment, out of a desire to punish them, out of simple negligence, or a combination of these. No wonder she felt immobilized. Like Coyote, she'd collapsed under the weight of the spirits she held hostage. I wondered if it was an insult to the departed to have the cabin falling down around their remains. I tried not to overreact, and sought a neutral tone of voice with which to ask Bonnie if she had plans for the ashes.

"Oh, yeah," she nodded. "That was part of what I wanted to do last summer, but I never got around to it. Mom wanted to have her ashes released into the stream, you know so she could flow out to the sea as her final resting place. Velma and Millie wanted to have their ashes scattered over the place here, Millie on the garden, or what used to be a garden, and Velma in the woods under the big cedar."

"Where Thunder Thighs hangs out?" I asked.

"Yeah," Bonnie said smiling, "right there."

"Well, what's stopping you from following through this fall?"

"I guess I could do it this fall. It just seems like I should fix the place up first, and maybe wait until spring when it looks a little fresher around here. It's got to be right, you know, I want to say some prayers and have a little ceremony with Jane. I already started to write a prayer for the occasion," she said scanning her heaps of papers. She reached into the middle of an unruly pile and pulled out a dog-eared sheet of purple paper. "It's just that I can't seem to get it finished," she said passing me the sheet.

I began reading. It was obvious why she couldn't get it finished. It was an attempt to describe the meaning of life, death, and the afterlife in esoteric jargon. Each sentence got loftier than the last until there was no way to decipher it, unless you happened to be God or you had a Ph.D. in metaphysics.

"What if you kept it simple, Bonnie?" I asked. "What if you limited it to a simpler theme?"

"Simpler? Like what?"

I perused the purple sheet for the one coherent line which had caught me. "Like this theme here," I said pointing to the middle of the page, "where you simply state your wish that their souls find peace."

"Well," she said, reaching for her first cigarette of the session, "I'd still have to pick out ceremonial urns for their ashes and roto-till the garden. I couldn't very well dump Millie's ashes in the weeds." She lit up a Marlboro and sat back as if to think it over.

"So," I said slowly, "you'd rather put it off for now and think about doing it in the spring?"

"God!" she exclaimed, looking at the ceiling, "That sounds terrible. It sounds abysmal. It's not what I want at all. Let me write this down." She grabbed for a pad and pencil as though writing down a concept so foreign she was bound to forget it. "Okay, what you're saying is, I could do the ritual this fall if I keep it simple. What did you say it could be about?" she asked searching the purple sheet.

"Second paragraph, first line," I said. "Where you express good wishes for their souls in the hereafter."

"Okay," she said, "I'm writing that down. My wish for their souls? Is that all? Like what I hope for them in the afterlife?"

I nodded.

"God," she said, "I'm glad I hired Columbo. Your Mars in Capricorn is really straightforward. That must save you a lot of time."

I mentioned that All Hallows Eve was two weeks away and that traditionally speaking, it would be a fine time to approach the ancestors, provided she didn't try to kidnap them like Coyote and Eagle. Bonnie looked at me as if I'd caused her head to swim. I wondered if I was pushing her into deep water. Perhaps she needed more time. But before I could slow things down, she was on the phone to Jane to see if she would help. At one point Bonnie held the phone two feet from her ear because Jane spoke so loudly. I could hear her voice through the receiver, "Thank God! Bonnie, I was afraid you'd keep those ashes forever!"

A week later Bonnie came to the office for the first time. Her huge cast had been traded in for a small wrap which allowed her to drive, though she was still on crutches. She looked brighter and better dressed than during the house calls, and she said she felt confident about getting through the hour without smoking because she'd already gone several mornings without a single cigarette. She explained her secret: "You see, Erica, Thunder Thighs is getting very tame. He sits on the woodpile where he can watch me through the window. I swear he thinks I'm his wife, or his mother, I'm not sure which, but he likes to keep tabs on me. So we chat back and forth. Mostly it's me talking and him giving me the eagle-eye, but every time I want a smoke, I chat with him instead and it helps. After two o'clock or so, he goes off on his own and I give in and smoke. But I'm proud of myself for going most of the day smoke free. Even if I smoke steadily after that, I stay under a pack a day, which is big progress for me."

She and Jane had planned a simple ritual and Jane's two teenage sons had decided to participate. Bonnie wanted me to hear the words they'd written to be spoken upon release of the ashes to their resting places. "We plan to scatter the ashes in the order they each died, Mom's first, Millie's second, and Velma's third. That way we go from the stream, to the garden, to the cedar tree. It's all

very poetic. We include all four elements: water, earth, air, and fire."
She launched into a rather elaborate description of the elements
and their symbolic meanings. It got harder and harder to follow,
but she caught herself, "Damn, there I go! Metaphysical meander-
ing again. Let me just read the damn thing. The first one is for
Mom," she said as her face flushed with emotion. "This is the prayer
we'll say while scattering Mom's ashes downstream: *"Nadine Marie,
lover of the sand and sea, born under the sign of Leo, you were a
loving sister, wife, and mother. We grieve your loss with sad hearts.
We hope the land of the dead holds you as gently and lovingly as you
held us. We pray your soul flows over time as freely as water in the
riverbed. We promise to accept your passing and not try to bring you
back. We hope you can look down upon your grandsons and smile.
We love you always, and in our loving, aspire to emulate what was
best in you, your sweet kindness."*

I was impressed with the beauty and simplicity Bonnie and Jane
had achieved in their writing. Bonnie said she'd hired someone to
come to the cabin and till up the old garden plot. She went on to
read the words they planned to say while spreading Millie's ashes
on the freshly tilled soil. *"Milicent Ann, lover of earth and growing
things, born under the sign of Taurus, you were a skilled gardener and
a wonderful cook. We miss you and the joy you brought to family
gatherings. May the winter rains carry your ashes deep into the soil
where they can nourish spring flowers. We pray that your soul is ever-
renewed, like a garden in the spring. We love you always, and in our
loving, aspire to be like what was best in you, your generosity."*

Bonnie felt proud of herself, and with each reading her emotion
grew fuller. By the time she got to Velma, she wept. *"Velma Jane,
lover of words, born under the sign of Libra, you were a wonderful
teller of jokes, and a woman of wisdom. You are greatly missed, for no
one could tell it like it is, quite like you. May your soul reach deeply
into the earth like the roots of the great cedar, and may your spirit
reach to the sky like its topmost branch. We love you always, and in
our loving, aspire to emulate what was best in you, your stubborn
passion."*

I couldn't put my finger on what was motivating Bonnie, but
we'd done something right. She was now striding, loping along the

path, where before she'd been paralyzed. Perhaps just planning to release the ashes was like releasing the spirits of the dead. Her load was suddenly lighter. She spent the rest of the session telling me about all her "progress." She'd raked the driveway, gotten the garden tilled, and scattered wildflower seeds on the soil. She'd resumed her old hobby of reading novels, and all week, she'd managed to smoke less than one pack per day.

Her next appointment fell two days after All Hallows Eve. She came through the door smiling, eager to tell about the ritual. "Jane and the boys stayed overnight the night before, which was a trip in itself, just to clean out the guest rooms and make up the beds. The boys got up in the morning and I gave them machetes to clear the path to the stream, 'cause it was overgrown, just like everything else around there. They were real enthused and marked the path with candles and stones. It was beautiful.

"We read about All Saints Day and talked over how we wanted to do the ceremony. The boys really wanted to wait until dusk and do it all by candlelight in the dark. At first I wasn't so keen on that, with my foot still gimpy, but they talked me into it. I was going to print up the prayers we wrote in really big type so we could read them in the dark, but Jake, my oldest nephew, said, 'We've got all day Aunt Bonnie, let's learn them by heart.' I thought that was terrific.

"The day went by really fast. We rigged up a little hoist to carry the urns. The boys attached torches to each end so it was very dramatic. And of course, we memorized our prayers. Josh, my younger nephew, figured out a little harmonica riff to go with each prayer. Those boys are incredible. We were all really into it and we spontaneously decided to fast until we'd finished. I made a pumpkin pie and some raspberry scones, using Millie's recipes. We decided to have a little wake after the ritual, with cider and treats. Jane's husband and mother-in-law came for that part.

"Anyhow, at dusk, it cleared up and the moon came out. It was the perfect All Saints Eve. It took about five minutes to walk to the stream. We took our time and walked in single file. I was in front, leading the way, gimp and all. Josh was next, holding the front of the hoist. He looked quite stunning with the torch flaming behind him. Jake held up the rear of the hoist, with the rear torch right in front of his face. We're lucky we didn't start a forest fire, now that I think of it. And of course, Janie brought up the rear. She had a little bell she rang slowly to keep us walking in rhythm. An owl was hooting in the ravine below.

"By the time we got to the top of the waterfall, we were in a different state of mind. I was speechless. I took Mom's urn, and pulled the cork. I got dizzy and nauseous. Maybe it was from fasting. But something inside me panicked. I realized we were really doing it. We were dispersing her ashes to their final resting place. There was no going back, no changing our minds. Keeping her ashes in the safe had been a way to keep her spirit with me. Now I had to release both to the water, which was flowing away from me. That was intense. I felt terrified that I'd never get her back. Josh took hold of me, like he thought I was going to jump.

"Finally I thought to myself, 'This is it, I have to set her free.' That's a hard moment, Erica, that's all I can say. She died twelve years ago. You'd think I'd have accepted it by then, but suddenly, there was a whole new wave of sorrow. Well, Josh nudged me to lift the urn. I raised it up and tipped it sideways. The ash poured out slowly and fell down in front of the waterfall like a little cloud of smoke, except it traveled down instead of up. All of a sudden, the owl soared out of its tree and swooped toward the waterfall, right through the cloud of ashes. We all saw it. We were startled and terrified, but at the same time, it was like an old friend of Mom's coming to welcome her." Bonnie began weeping as she spoke. "I knew at that moment, that we were doing exactly what we should be doing, and I was happy. I felt like that owl came to pay its respects and greet Mom's soul.

"We were so stunned by the owl, we had trouble starting our prayer. It found another perch further upstream, and started hooting again. Finally Jake got us saying the prayer in unison. We watched the water glisten in the moonlight, and it seemed like Mom was now made of an incredible combination of things: moonlight, owl wings, and water. We all felt that. Josh played his harmonica and the owl kept hooting like it was calling back to him.

"We turned around. Janie was leading us back to the cabin, and I was bringing up the rear. I kept thinking 'Whenever I need you, Mom, I'll know where to find you.' That stream will always be sacred to me, now.

"We went to the garden next. It was hilarious, because Thunder Thighs got riled up. He ran up and down the length of the garden like he was a patrol cop and it was his beat. We didn't worry about it being irreverent, because Millie always liked animals, and she was always good natured about critters and kids acting up. Josh played a mellow riff on the harmonica, and that settled him down. Then we each took a small handful of ashes. It was so silky in our hands. We sprinkled it around the garden. It was like sprinkling fairy dust. We said our prayer in unison and watched the moonlight on each other's faces. It was beautiful.

"Then we went to the cedar tree. Thunder Thighs got real territorial when we invaded his area. For a few minutes I was afraid he was going to charge the boys because he'd never met them before. It seemed like we might have to skip that part of the ritual. I motioned for the boys to move away, but they held their ground. Then Josh started playing again and Thunder Thighs got mesmerized by the harmonica. When he settled down we said our prayer in unison and sprinkled Velma's ashes around the trunk of the tree. Thunder Thighs looked the other way like he was sulking. I thought to myself, 'If I ever get stuck on a chart, I'll come out here and get Velma's opinion.'

"When it was over, we all felt good. There was something so right about the four of us blood descendants doing it together. David and his mom arrived right on time and we dug into our goodies. By then we were in the mood for a little celebration and cutting up, so it was good to have them join us.

"I'll tell you what was the strangest part though, Erica. It was going back into the cabin after the ritual. We'd cleaned and organized the day before, and we'd gotten rid of a whole truckload of junk. They'd been saying the place seemed so much more open and spacious, but for some reason it hadn't hit me yet. But after the ceremony, going back inside, was like entering a new place—neat, organized, and clean. It was like visiting someone else and wishing my place looked like theirs, only this was my place. I felt completely at ease for the first time in years. I can't explain it, except to say Mom, Millie, and Velma were finally at rest, and everything seemed lighter. I guess I'd been feeling the weight of their presence without realizing it. I've felt different ever since. Nothing spectacular, but I feel freer to get mobilized."

Saying Good-bye to Smoke

After that, the ancestral spirits no longer hung around the cabin. Bonnie connected with them by visiting the stream, the garden, and the cedar tree. Her release of their captured souls caused a meaningful shift in her spiritual practice. Visiting them in their chosen resting places, she sought the guidance of their down-to-earth wisdom which focused more on practical matters and less on the "ever widening circles" of eternity. In her prayer and meditation, the relative truths of everyday life gained an important place alongside her pursuit of ultimate truth. Bonnie was now able to think and plan more clearly. She formulated goals: to make friendships, meet men, restore the cabin, and at least entertain the idea of quitting smoking. She felt she needed help in attaining her goals and decided to continue therapy.

Over the next four years she progressed toward these goals. But no matter which of her goals came near completion, when things got tough, the old split returned. Part of her collapsed by the roadside like an overburdened Coyote, while another part sought the solace of lofty detachment. The collapsed side saw the goal as unattainable, while the soaring eagle saw the goal as insignificant in the overall scheme of things. Several times, this split widened, creating a void in which futility took over.

At these low points, Bonnie had to face the fact that in forty-some years, she'd never learned how to set and attain a goal that had to do with her wishes for herself. She'd excelled at responding to the needs of others, but was a complete novice at following through on her own goals. This was a loss which had to be grieved several times through the course of Bonnie's therapy. Once she'd grieved the sorrow, we were always able to return to the image of

Coyote and Eagle traveling the same road, staying in touch. This image of the two friends became her touchstone for the inner cooperation she needed to accomplish her goals, but it also became a symbol for her desire to have a mate with whom she could share her life.

Along the way, she decided to make the cabin her permanent home. It became important for her to separate her home life from her workspace so she could distinguish between the office and the living room, work and leisure. She designed an addition, a separate area for her astrology business. She hired a reputable crew to refurbish the cabin, and after many months of hemming and hawing, she became romantically involved with the senior carpenter, Nate. Nate was a fifty-six-year-old widower with grown kids, a kind man and a good match for Bonnie. Nate loved the island. He owned a sailboat and loved to sail around the Sound, something she'd always longed to do. Nate was well respected in the community, and brought Bonnie into his wide circle of friends. Social functions terrified her at first, but once she got her feet wet, she found them easier than she'd anticipated.

She knew it was ideal. She knew Jane was right in saying she should hold onto Nate because men like that don't come along every day. But she was also terrified to change old routines, and most of all, she was insecure about having sex after nearly twenty years celibacy. But once she finally scraped together the abandon to take the plunge, she discovered she relished sex more at mid-life than she had as a young woman.

Eighteen months later, Nate told Bonnie it was time to get married. Basically, Bonnie agreed, but there were a few kinks to be worked out. He wanted to live at his farmhouse and rent out the cabin. "He makes it sound great," Bonnie explained. "He wants to build me a separate office out back where I'll have a view of the mountain. He says we'll put in a fax machine, a separate phone line, and we'll update *Babe,* my old computer. All that sounds wonderful, but I can't picture renters at the cabin."

Bonnie sorted carefully through all the threads that kept her attached to the cabin. After a few weeks tossing around ideas, she concluded, "The cabin is my spiritual home. I've got history there, and the remains of my ancestors. Thunder Thighs is nesting nearby with his brood, and I don't want noisy renters disturbing them. Besides, I want my nephews to have access to the cabin. It's their second home." Bonnie's position was clear. She made efforts to solidify her conviction and prepared to state her wishes to Nate. Her greatest hope was that her head-strong man would yield to her wishes regarding the cabin. She was willing to live together in the farmhouse, but wanted the cabin to remain her workplace, and a weekend getaway for her family and for Nate's. Never before had she so firmly asserted her own wishes, and she lost sleep fretting over how it might backfire.

To Bonnie's amazement and great joy, Nate accepted the idea, particularly since she proposed the cabin as a special catalyst for getting their two families together. The trial run was a summer barbecue where Jane, David, and their sons met Nate's son and daughter and their spouses. "It was a little nuts," Bonnie said, "but all in all it went well." Bonnie and Nate took the opportunity to officially announce their plans for a September wedding. To their delight, everyone in both families approved.

After the wedding, Bonnie seemed content with all but one aspect of her life, her smoking. "When it only affected me, it wasn't that big a deal," she explained. "But now, Nate has to put up with filthy ashtrays and my bad breath." It bothered her deeply that her habit encroached upon Nate, even though his only concern was for her health. When it came to quitting, her old split came into play and sabotaged her efforts. One part was easily defeated, while the other transcended all concern with philosophical explanations to justify smoking. At one point she even convinced herself that her smoking was a form of prayer to the great spirit and would therefore have no detrimental effect on her lungs.

By that time I'd grasped the rudiments of her zodiac enough to poke holes in her lofty theories. She got used to hearing me say, "Bonnie, that sounds like your Aquarius ascendant blowing hot air again." Once I suggested she confine her use of smoke to burning incense during prayer. This practice can actually help spiritually inclined people form a more conscious relationship to smoke. For some, it even helps them cut down on cigarettes or quit altogether.

But Bonnie hated the idea, because she knew it would reveal her smoking for what it was: a hazardous addiction.

So much of Bonnie's life had healed, and grown, but the old split prevailed when it came to quitting smoking. Time and time again she tried to quit, but her craving to suck in smoke was as powerful as an infant's instinct to suckle. We traced this oral fixation back to her starvation as an infant, but rediscovering the old terror did not help her quit. I often wondered if she would simply wind up being one of those people who learns to accept a compromising vice.

When she actually did quit cold turkey one weekend, her motive seemed so typical of Bonnie, I wondered why I hadn't seen it coming. Nate's son and daughter-in-law brought their new baby along for a weekend sailing trip on the boat. It was a very special occasion, being that this was the first grandchild. It was also the first time Bonnie had been confined with a nursing mother and her infant. She made sure to smoke up on deck at all times, so as not to contaminate the air around them. Several things about this bothered her. "What hurt the most," she told me later, "was wanting to bond with them during that special time, and having this filthy habit drag me into isolation every half hour. I thought, 'This addiction is stronger than my family bonds. That's scary.' So I decided, 'There's no time like the present. It's going to be hard, no matter when I quit. So, now's as good a time as any.'"

The Short Fuse and the Broken Feather

After three or four months, Bonnie looked great. Her pallor had brightened, and her eyes glistened. Her hair seemed to have more body, and she'd gained weight which was good, because she'd always been a bit thin. She'd survived the sleepy, grumpy stages and was now beginning to enjoy being a nonsmoker. She felt content with all aspects of her life. She was happily married, she'd formed a couple of meaningful friendships, and she now regularly embarked upon travel adventures. We began talking about her therapy coming to a natural close.

The following week she said, "Nate told me to work on my short fuse before I end therapy. He says I've been getting huffy a lot, now that I've stopped smoking." Examining Nate's complaint, Bonnie said he had a point. It seemed things bothered her more than they used to. She cited a particular incident when Nate's daughter called about five in the afternoon asking to borrow something. Without checking with Bonnie, Nate invited her and her husband to dinner. Neither Bonnie nor Nate had grocery shopped in several days, and the 'fridge was literally bare, but Nate seemed oblivious to that. When Bonnie pointed it out, he told her it would be easy to throw something together.

"That upset me," Bonnie explained, "I hollered, 'If it's so easy, then you won't need my help!' I slammed the door and went out to weed the garden. Nate made grilled cheese sandwiches and tomato soup, and it was actually pretty good. Later on when I calmed down, I told him that's not my style. When company comes, I like to have a little more notice so we can serve a decent meal."

Further discussion revealed that when Bonnie was smoking she'd been less brusque and more flexible. It didn't take long for her to recall that she used to light up the minute she was upset. "When you inhale that smoke," she explained, "it's so satisfying it sort of pacifies you. When you blow it out and it dissipates above your head, you get the feeling that whatever's eating you doesn't really matter that much in the grand scheme of things."

Was she saying that smoking was her way of repressing anger, or acquiring patience? Probably a little of each. Patience with Nate would help a great deal, but repressing her anger would undermine the marriage in the long run. I didn't want to reject what was worthwhile in her description—the patience. Subtract the smoke, and it resembled the most basic anger management technique of all: Breathe deeply and remember, "This too, shall pass." In a good love relationship, it's important to recognize one's anger, but not to hurl it suddenly at the spouse.

It didn't take Columbo to see that what Nate needed at the crucial moment was for Bonnie to apply a bit of patience. He'd said he could live with their differences, but he wished she wouldn't get so huffy when their differences came up. He didn't mind her position on dinner guests, but he wished she'd have been more light-hearted about telling him.

The question in my mind was: Now that Bonnie's old friend, Smoke, was gone, where was the patience going to come from? I asked her that in so many words. She closed her eyes in silence for a moment. What came to her were the old friends, Coyote and Eagle. She recalled how they curbed each other's rashness at key junctures in the story. "When they get to the river, Eagle's upset. He says it's all a waste of time. That's like me going off on Nate and storming out the door. If I could be like Coyote, and say to myself, 'Just wait, be patient, it will work out,' I'd be a lot better off."

Bonnie's answer seemed complete unto itself. She needed nothing from me other than encouragement to put it into practice. After another eight weeks, she and Nate felt confident that they could amicably talk through minor conflicts.

Bonnie's therapy was completed. On the day of our final visit, she arrived with a gift in hand. If she'd given it to me at some earlier stage of our work, it wouldn't have been right. I would have taken it as a sign that in her isolation she saw me as a substitute friend. But now she had a circle of friends who would see her through life. A certain type of love had grown between us, and giving and receiving the gift was an expression of that love. On my side it was the love that gets awakened when you see someone through deep changes. It was a love of my work, but it was also an appreciation for what was best in Bonnie, and a sense of gratitude for the things she'd taught me. On her side, I suppose it was the love felt toward one who'd held the lamp while she'd groped toward her new life, one who'd called her back when she flew too far aloft.

We didn't say all this. She just blushed and handed me a large envelope. I blushed and took it. Inside was an oversized handmade card with a crude watercolor of a soaring eagle on the front. I opened the card and a large feather slipped out and fell to the floor. When I knelt down to pick it up, I saw it was bent in two. I felt very badly, thinking Bonnie had given me a cherished eagle feather, and I'd clumsily broken it before I could even thank her. When she understood my chagrin, she said, "Erica, it was already broken. You'll understand when you read the card."

I realized it was all right, and went on to read the message.

Dear Erica,

I asked Bonnie to pass this feather on to you. I thought you should have one of my broken feathers, since you helped me and Bonnie get used to living with our feet stuck on planet earth.

Love, from your friend,
Thunder Thighs

P.S. I soar in ever widening circles, but I always come back to roost. If you ever come visit, bring BEEF liver.

I chuckled and Bonnie whooped her crane-like laugh. But it didn't disintegrate into smoker's cough. It just filled the room and rang off the walls. She stomped her foot and slapped her thighs. We both cracked up.

8

A Piece
of Fat

We dream in metaphor, and at our deepest levels we dialogue in
metaphor, and through metaphor we can achieve fundamental
understanding.

—Lee Wallas

Stories show a path, shine a light on our way, teach us how to see,
remind us of the greatest of human possibilities.

—Christina Feldman and Jack Kornfield

"Hello," said the voice at the other end of a poor connection, "I
know you, but you don't know me. My name's Monica Raven. I'm
calling from the reservation. The way I know you is, I was in the
courtroom in 1986, when you testified against Joe Masters. That
took guts, you know. You helped my cousin Trina get her kids back.
You remember Trina Sedgewick?"

"Sure I remember Trina, and I remember you, too, Monica. I
went to a ceremony a couple of years ago and you told a story. I
never forgot that. I'm a storyteller, too."

"No kidding. That explains something. You were real sharp han-
dling Trina's case. We probably never told you how much we all

appreciated that. Joe's a very intimidating guy. But that's water under the bridge. Trina and the kids are fine. Now I'm the one who needs help."

"Monica, I'm honored you remembered me, but my contract with the reservation ended years ago."

"I know. I was hoping we could work out a trade. I fish salmon and hunt deer." She sounded like she had all the time in the world and planned not to hang up 'till I agreed.

"What kind of help are you looking for?"

"Well, the new principal at the school is trying to force my daughter to class every day. She's got a thing against me. She's mad 'cause I was chosen for council and she wasn't. Everybody else at school respects fishing and hunting days. But this new principal goes digging for rules to work against me. I need my daughter's help, and she's got to learn the trade. Working with me is the real education she needs, Erica. Can't you see that?"

Sure I could see. Monica wasn't alone with this problem. The schools were supposed to help tribal kids, but in some cases they actually interfered with the learning of vital skills and responsibilities. If there was a neutral bone in my body at that moment, I couldn't find it. She'd buttered me up with flattery, and made me recall good times on the reservation. I thought of my dad's dental practice back home on the great lakes, and his many trades with tribal folks—venison for a filling, salmon for a bite adjustment.

"Look, Monica, this isn't really a therapy issue, and I couldn't be your therapist, anyhow, because of mutual acquaintances, but I'd be happy to meet as fellow storytellers and chat about it." We settled on the term "consultation" as a way to describe our meeting. She insisted on trading meat for my advice.

She brought me a king salmon that was too big for the minifridge at work. We had to walk down to the market, and get some dry ice from one of her fish vendors. The sky was intense blue. We had a clear view of the sharp-edged mountains across the sound. Monica's deft brown hands grasped the heavy catch as if born to do so, and the handsome vendors spoke to her with familiar respect. We ordered burnt-tasting lattes from the coffee roaster and sat down to talk in the park.

"So here's the deal, Erica. If Roberta Storm—that's the new principal—would just get off my back, my daughter and I could keep working with the school as we always have. She can read, add, and subtract—no problem. She's got a basic idea of history. What she really needs is to learn to be self-sufficient, like me. I can't do this forever, and she's going to have to take over some day."

"So Roberta Storm is enforcing rules which previous administrators have ignored?"

"Ignored for good reason, yeah."

"And you think she's doing it to get back at you—for what—some jealousy she feels toward you?"

"Right. Now we're getting down to it. It goes way back, starting I guess, with a pow-wow in the seventies when I won a dance contest she thought she should have won. She left the reservation to go to college and who-knows-what for twelve-or-so-years, but she's back now, and wants on the tribal council right away. I miss a few meetings because of hunting and fishing, so she proposes to the council that she take my place. That's not how things work. She thinks education and parliamentary procedure should give her the edge, and she's pissed off at me because the council didn't bump me."

"Normally, wouldn't you go to the elders with something like this?"

"Yeah, but that's a problem in this case because they want to welcome her back. They want me to welcome her back, too, and they want to stay real neutral. What I need is someone to help me with a battle strategy. That's why I called you. I heard Joe Masters threaten to run you off the road and slit your throat. You spoke up anyway. That's the kind of help I need."

The salmon suddenly seemed way too big. A mercenary fee. I now saw what was on Monica's mind. She'd been present when my court testimony had turned the tide for Trina's case. In her mind that meant I was some kind of warrior woman who could go around setting wrong things right. This just wasn't so. I backtracked and tried to explain the difference between a court battle and a battle between a parent and an administrator.

"Well then, maybe I should hire a lawyer and go to court," Monica said.

"Oh boy," I said. "You think you're losing time and money now, Monica, believe me, a court battle over this could disrupt several fishing seasons."

"Damn!" she said, licking the latte foam from her finger. "Well what do you suggest?"

Being in the company of a fellow storyteller put me in an intuitive mood. That meant my mind wasn't spurred along a rational course to answer her question. Instead, it lumbered around like a big bear on the prowl, sniffing after familiar scents, so that when my words came out, they appeared to have nothing whatsoever to do with Monica's question. "Remember that story you told at the ceremony?" I asked.

"*Coyote and Crow,* sure I do. Why'd you bring that up?"

"It keeps coming to mind. Isn't that the story where Coyote's hungry as usual, and he sees Crow has a tasty piece of fat?"

"Right," Monica nodded. "Naturally, Coyote starts plotting how to get the piece of fat, but what's that got to do with Roberta Storm?"

"Well," I said, "somebody's hungry, and somebody else has a nice piece of fat."

"Oh, yeah," Monica said, "sure. Roberta's mad because the way she sees it, I've got a piece of fat she wants."

"Being on the council," I said.

"Yeah, being on the council. And that old dance trophy, that's an old piece of fat she hasn't forgotten."

"So, like Coyote, she's trying to use her clout and her wiles to get your tasty piece of fat for herself."

"Right," Monica said, "only it's more complicated, because I want a piece of fat she's got."

"Permission to take your daughter out of class."

"Exactly," she said. We sat there nodding at each other, two storytellers momentarily satisfied because we'd come up with the perfect metaphor. But soon enough, we'd have to face the real bugaboo that lay before us—what to do about the problem. A strategy was called for.

"Basically, Monica," I said, "you need to get that piece of fat from the crow's mouth, and it's going to take a Coyote-style plan to do it."

"Yeah," she said, "Coyote uses flattery on Crow. He says, 'Oh, Wise Chief, I've heard you have the most splendid song. Let me hear you sing!' Crow is so pleased to be called Chief, he starts singing and the piece of fat falls out of his mouth, right into Coyote's hands."

"Do you think flattery would work with Roberta Storm?" I didn't tell Monica how effectively her flattery had worked on me, although I was thinking it.

"You know, I think it just might," she replied. "Roberta sure wants to feel important. Ever since she's been back on the rez, she's been trying to get others to make a big deal over her, and nobody does."

"Well, if you were going to use a bit of flattery on her, what would be the arena for it?"

"You mean like the school or the council?" she asked. I nodded and Monica retreated into herself for a moment to think it over. "Actually," she said, "there's a third arena—church. We've been doing some good things for the youth, including storytelling, sex-ed, and abuse prevention. Roberta comes to all the meetings and makes suggestions galore. She wants to be on the advisory board, but we haven't invited her. It would be a good arena to put my flattery to work, because she sure couldn't do any harm on the board, and she actually has some good ideas. I could butter her up and make her feel real important."

"If you did that for her," I said, "you figure she might get flexible with school rules for you?"

That's exactly what Monica hoped for. In the week before the next meeting, she thought a lot about how to do it. About how to ease away from this antagonistic tussle with Roberta and ease into a mutual backscratching thing. She thought about the kinds of things Roberta would like to hear, and she thought about how and when she might say them. She figured if she handled it right, Roberta might drop a tasty piece of fat into her lap. She didn't expect things would come together in one fell swoop, but that's exactly what happened. The next time we met, Monica said it was to celebrate. She brought a couple of venison steaks and said they were for my husband and me to grill up some night when the kids were away. It was raining, so we sat in the back of a cafe overlooking the gloom and ordered tea.

"Here's what happened," she began. "At the meeting I suggested that the church coordinate with the school because they have access to materials and know-how that the church lacks. *Materials and know-how,* that was my key phrase to get Roberta's attention, and it worked. She spoke up about the specifics of the materials and know-how she herself personally has to offer. I took it from there and started speaking as her advocate, telling the board how much we could benefit from her input as a liaison person between us and the school. I put in a good word for her personally, pointing out her accomplishments on and off the rez. You could see her head spin, but she wasn't about to pass up the chance to look important, no matter who was blowing her horn, even me. After the meeting she thanked me for the support. She was still smiling like she'd just swallowed something good. So I told her I thought she might help me. I said it was a real shame that my daughter's classroom attendance interfered with her tribal education.

"So, here's what she said. You won't believe this! She said some of the other schools have it set up so kids can get credit for skills training outside of class. She said she'd see what she could do to help my daughter get school credit for learning to fish and hunt. Isn't that the damnedest thing?" Monica said tilting backwards in her chair 'til I was afraid she'd fall over.

"What a brilliant idea!" I exclaimed. "She's not so bad after all, then, that Roberta Storm."

"No," said Monica. "No. The fact is, she's a hell of a good woman. No wonder we butted heads. She's as strong as I am."

"Like Coyote and Crow," I added.

"Yeah," Monica said, "like Coyote and Crow. When Coyote gets the fat he earns Crow's respect. They become friends in the end."

9

Call
1-800-BIG-BEAR

Everyone is a visionary if you scratch deep enough.

—William Butler Yeats

"See, I can wake up in a mood and know that I'm gonna be after one thing: to catch my husband Ted in a screw up. Like yesterday I woke up late and came downstairs. He was packing Tracy off to school. Tracy, that's our seven-year-old. Ted wanted me to notice he had everything under control, which he did. He said Tracy had a good breakfast and he'd made sure she had everything she needed for school. Then I saw he'd put the wrong kind of rubber bands on her ponytails, the kind that break the hair. I was literally pleased that he'd screwed up so I could point that out. Weird, huh?

"After work, he said he'd mow the lawn later. I went in to fix dinner, watching for rain, secretly hoping it would pour, so I could criticize him for not mowing soon enough.

"I do it to the kids, too. They come home, wipe their feet, and hang their coats, and then come in to show me their good marks. What do I do? I jump on them, for putting their bags on the table. They're getting sick of it and I don't want to live like this either."

"What was your favorite fairy tale as a child?" I asked.

"You think my favorite fairy tale says something about *me?*"

"Possibly," I replied.

"Well, it was from the Grimm Brothers. It was the one about the two sisters, *Snow White and Rose Red*."*

"Oh, yes," I said, "I can barely recall that one. Wasn't there a big lovable bear?"

"Yes," Dawn replied. "And a dwarf who kept stealing the gold behind everyone's back."

"Yes," I said. "What was it about that dwarf?"

"Well, remember the girls were eager to please, yet no matter how helpful they were, the dwarf was always cross and ungrateful." As she spoke her eyes registered more with each word that she knew she was talking about herself. "Wait a minute," she said. "My family is eager to please, yet I'm cross and ungrateful."

Thirty minutes' discussion revealed that Dawn begrudged her loved ones their small pleasures, whether little cat naps, or good grades. I got the feeling she envied them, just as the dwarf envied the bear's great wealth. I said as much and she agreed. She resented their happiness, and tried to steal it, though robbing their joy offered her no real satisfaction. Continued conversation revealed she hadn't felt so cross and ungrateful when she'd been pregnant or nursing the babies. During those times she'd felt perfectly content with herself and everyone else. She'd been useful, needed, loved, successful, and satisfied. The problem was, four kids were enough. She and Ted agreed on that. It was time to stop having babies. As the kids got older, she watched them develop satisfying interests of their own—interests having nothing whatsoever to do with her—and that hurt.

"Ted says it's a sign of good mothering that the kids are so gregarious and active outside the home. I just hate myself for resenting it."

It didn't take much history digging to learn that in her youth, Dawn hadn't been allowed or encouraged to develop her own vision. "The best I ever did was to hook up with Ted who has vision for the both of us. He and my best friend Marilyn both drag me out of the house regularly." Ted's infectious enthusiasm went a long way.

*See my retelling of the Grimms' fairy tale, *Snow White and Rose Red*, in the appendix, p. 263.

They hiked, took the kids camping, and held season tickets to the symphony. Marilyn, Dawn's pal since junior high, was a lesbian actress and political activist with a wide circle of friends and a nonstop social life. It was easy to see how Ted and Marilyn both gravitated toward Dawn. Dawn went along for the ride, agreeably supporting their visions, asserting few opinions of her own.

"I don't even know what I like!" Dawn shrieked in frustration one day. "I let Ted and Marilyn tell me what's good and what isn't." Then she asked me the question of all questions: "Erica, how do people find out what they like? I mean, how do they know?"

My heart flooded with sympathy for Dawn. This was one of the most innocent questions I'd ever heard come out of the mouth of a woman pushing fifty. I wanted to give her an answer she could get her teeth into. "You pay attention to the feeling that comes over you. The music you like is the music that makes you cry, that lifts you up and makes you feel like a new woman."

Dawn's eyes went red. Tears pooled at the edges, then rolled silently down her cheeks and chin. "I had that feeling once," she said groping her pockets for a tissue. "I was driving Peter home from baseball, and we wound up stuck at a broken stoplight. It was a really hot day and we had all the windows down. The woman in the car beside me was listening to the most wonderful tape. This music was intense and sad, but proud and joyous all the same. I didn't even mind being stuck in traffic. I asked her what it was. She held up the cassette. It was, get this, *The Gypsy Kings*. I had Pete write it down, and later I told Ted about how excited I was to get this tape. When I told him the name, he said, 'Oh yeah, those are the sons of authentic flamenco artists. They're a real sell-out the way they went electronic, and popularized traditional material.' Do you know what I did, Erica? I shrank with embarrassment. I figured it must be my unschooled sentimental ear which attracted me to the Gypsy Kings, and I never said another word about it."

"The killjoy dwarf again," I said. "You struck gold, and then let it get snatched away."

"Yes," she said, "but how do I prevent that? I mean, just because Ted makes a critical comment, that's no reason for me to drop my interest."

I went back to the story. "The bear, the sisters, and the mother—
they're all so good-natured, remember? There's something about
that full-bodied good-naturedness. The dwarf's killjoy comments
can't spoil it. The girls stay patient with the dwarf. They humor
him, and they don't take his cross words to heart."

Dawn carried this idea home. She thought about the bear's
fullbodied amiability and the girls' resilient cheer. She imagined
how she might sustain such moods even under the sting of criticism. Marilyn soon provided her with a chance to try. "Marilyn
wanted to drag me to the gay and lesbian theater for a dress rehearsal. The last time we went to a dress rehearsal it wasn't that
good, and I missed *Roseanne* on TV. So I said, 'Marilyn, let's go next
weekend if we hear it's good. But tonight, I'd rather stay home and
watch *Roseanne.*' Marilyn's not used to me being so direct about
things like that, and it pissed her off. She got real snide with me
and said, 'It's a reflection on the state of your psyche and your life,
Dawn, when you pass up live theater to lie around like a housewife
and watch sitcoms about housewives.' Normally that type of comment would have shut me down, but this time I humored her. I
was proud of myself, Erica. I thought of the robust bear, and here's
what I said. I said, 'If you want to go without me, Marilyn, that's
okay, but I'm making Kahlúa milkshakes tonight before *Roseanne,*
and I've got a big tumbler with your name on it.' And guess what.
She dropped the whole cultural snob thing and came over to watch
Roseanne."

This was a major victory. But Dawn still had a ways to go. Her
forty-seventh birthday approached. She was born on July third,
and as usual, the Fourth seemed like a perfect day for a holiday/
birthday bash. She and Ted planned an early evening barbecue
followed by fireworks viewed from their rooftop balcony.

Zack, their oldest, asked Dawn what she wanted for her birthday. She said she wanted a CD. She wanted the music she and Peter
had heard in the traffic jam some months before, the Gypsy Kings.
"The kids managed to find it at the mall," Dawn told me later.
"They wrapped it in gold paper and gave it to me at breakfast on the
third. Ted rolled his eyes and went out to mow the lawn. I put on
the Gypsy Kings and washed the insides of all the upstairs win-

dows." She went on to tell me how she'd gotten swept up in the intense rhythms and the raw soul of the vocals. The lemon-scent of the cleaner and the blinding afternoon light made her dizzy. She drew the squeegee downward in measured strokes. Beyond clean, the windows shone like diamonds and squeaked to perfection. Dawn sang out a few Gypsy phrases, "El camino, mi camino, el camino del verano. Que yo soy un vagabundo. Ya me voy por este mundo." She knew it meant something along the lines of, "The path, my path, the path of summer. I'm a vagabond. I go for this world right now."

She felt tremendous power in her arms. And deeper in her body it was as if she'd hit upon her center of gravity for the first time. She knew how to stand and how to bend over. She knew how to get up, and walk with a full bucket in her hand. She walked like a gypsy queen, moving from this new point of power, and she knew what they meant when they sang, "I go for this world right now."

The next morning Ted made breakfast. He burnt the first batch of pancakes as usual because he had the flame too high and too little oil in the pan. He looked sheepish when he saw that she noticed, but she just swaggered over in her blue robe and hugged him like he was a big, irresistible bear. That got the day off to a better start. After breakfast Ted pulled her into the shower. They were in there so long they used up all the hot water, providing the kids with a ready excuse to put off the dishes.

"We had a lot of fun getting ready for the party," Dawn went on. "He set up the grill, I did the flowers. We went out together to get the meat and ice. The boys swept the balcony while Ted and I made a huge fruit salad. Then it came time to select the music. Ted has great taste, and he's hard to argue with. He started picking out CD's and setting them in the order he wanted them played. I said, 'Be sure and put my Gypsy Kings on when it starts to get dark, will you?' He said, 'Honey, that stuff is no good for a party. We need conversation music, see? A little Gershwin, followed by a little Jelly Roll Morton. If you want vocals, we can play a little Sarah Vaughn. It's an American holiday and we've got to have American music.'

"Well, you know Erica, in the past, that kind of conversation could ruin my day. I'd get sour, forget about my music, and then nag Ted 'til bedtime with one gripe after the other. I just couldn't get caught up in that. So, again, I thought for a minute of the good-natured sisters and how they playfully tussled with the bear, messing up his fur, and all. I stood there, the way I had stood washing windows the day before. I didn't argue or fuss, I just said, 'Honey, whose birthday is it?' Ted didn't know what to say. He looked flabbergasted. He almost started to argue, but he knew he couldn't win on that one. So he said, 'How about when the fireworks start?' and I said 'that's fine with me, and that was that.'"

That summer Dawn learned how to know what she loved, not from what others told her to love, but from the feeling inside. Her love of flowers led her to a job with a local florist, which led to flower arranging, garden design, and eventually to her opening her own business. Within two years it generated impressive profits. Her calling card read:

Snow White & Rose Red

Weddings, Funerals

custom garden designs

call: 1-800-BIG-BEAR

At the end of the fairly tale, the sisters learn the bear is really a prince cursed into animal form by the envious dwarf who'd stolen his gold. Before regaining princely form, the bear smote the dwarf with one blow. This triumph satisfied Dawn's love of swift justice, but her envy and the cross, ungrateful moods which accompanied it did not die easily.

Once her business was established and the newness had worn off, she again found herself envying her children's extracurricular activities. During a bout of dissatisfaction, she traced the source of her envy to the fact she'd never had a creative outlet merely for the sake of enjoyment. She decided to try and learn from the kids, rather than just resent them. She tried joining a book club, taking a drawing class, and keeping a journal, but didn't strike gold until she got into singing, and joined an acappella group. She felt she'd been born to sing, and besides lovemaking, birthing, and nursing babies, nothing but singing could 'rouse to life the robust bear who lay hibernating in every corpuscle of her being. She learned to strengthen her voice and control her tone. She felt an almost religious inspiration in the power of the voice rising from the pelvis, building in the belly, expanding in the chest, and being honed through the throat and head. On our last visit she reiterated, "There's nothing like filling a room with the harmony of well-blended voices. For me, singing is the ultimate." She wanted to end our final session with the telling of her recent dream.

"It's just a brief scene," she said, "but it leaves me with a good feeling. I was on my way to rehearsal, and saw a fruit stand beside the road. I decided to stop and buy some sweet cherries so later I'd have something to take home to Ted and the kids. The fruit vendor turned out to be a magical little guy with a felt cap and a long pointed beard. He was really knowledgeable about plants. He sold me the sweet cherries and then insisted on giving me a potted dwarf rose. It had beautiful red buds on it. I tried to pay him, but he wouldn't hear of it."

I was deeply moved by the appearance of a generous dwarf to compliment the cranky dwarf with whom she was so familiar. I asked what the dream meant to her.

"Something about the dwarf being healed," she said. "Over the past three years, the changes I've made have freed me from the choke-hold of envy, and in its place there's now gratitude and generosity. Singing fills me with good things like sweet cherries and dwarf roses. Can't beat that." She concluded, "I don't have to always look to Ted and Marilyn because I've found my own vision." Full of fiery songs, sweet juices, and fragrant scents, Dawn's psyche fed and restored the crotchety dwarf to his more generous reputation as a knowledgeable earth spirit, a supernatural creature giving living treasures in the style of famous dwarfs the world over. This healing restored Dawn's family as well. After we'd said good-bye and she was halfway out the door, an afterthought came to her. She turned back and said, "I'll tell you the best part of all this. When I come home at night, Ted and the kids are glad to see me."

I shot this quick reply, "Must be those sweet cherries!" just as the heavy door swung closed between us.

But Dawn had heard me. Her laughter echoed through the hall until the elevator bell dinged and the doors swooshed open, like the arms of a big bear eager to receive her.

— 10 —

Like Good
Norse Witches

You do not have to walk on your knees
for a hundred miles through the desert, repenting.
You only have to let the soft animal of your body
love what it loves.

—Mary Oliver

Instead of the evil, dried out old prude . . . we know the witch to be
a strong, proud woman, wise in the ways of natural medicine.

—Luisah Teish

Trapped in the Tower

Her first words to me wavered through the phone, half question, half apology, "My name's Judith and I'm calling about counseling? I've already had quite a bit of counseling, actually, but I can't say it's helped. I'm really good at analyzing things to death without resolving anything?"

"Can I ask what needs resolving, Judith?"

"Well, I've got problems with my mother that spill over into my marriage. See, I come from a fundamentalist background. Mom

188

pounded it into me that sex is dirty and sinful. I'm thirty-eight now, so you'd think I'd be over it, but I'm not. Even though my husband, John, is really patient, I still shy away from touch. To make a long story short, he called me frigid last week. Don't get me wrong, he's not usually mean, and he promised never to say it again, but it still hurts because it hits the nail on the head. We agree something's got to change, but I don't want to go back to sex therapy. A friend gave me your article "The Healing Power of Stories." It brought up memories because when I was little I used to pretend I was Rapunzel.* Anyway, I decided to call you. Does that make any sense?"

"Sure it makes sense," I said. "You must have felt trapped and overprotected like Rapunzel."

"That's putting it mildly," Judith replied. "I used to hide upstairs in my room pretending it was the tower and Mom was the witch."

Judith went on to tell me things she'd already worked on in therapy. Throughout childhood her mother had tormented her with rantings about the devil. Satan lurked in children's souls, and in order to save Judith, Mom kept her apart from other kids and chastised her daily for sins of pride, greed, laziness, vanity, disrespect, and worst of all, sexuality. Judith's quiet father hadn't condoned the fanaticism, but he hadn't defended Judith against it, either. Hearing her story made me furious. There's nothing more insidious than the erosion of a child's selfhood under the guise of holiness. Judith and I arranged a time to meet the following week.

When she came in for her first visit I was struck by her ample womanliness. Her bulky sweater covered but didn't conceal soft, full curves, maternal and sensual, like a lusty peasant women in a Bergman film. Her blonde hair fell luxuriantly around her shoulders. Somehow I'd expected her to be frail and mousy. Now I could see how her voluptuousness would unnerve her prudish mother and at the same time make her husband yearn for touch. It wasn't long before Judith again used the word *frigid*.

"You have two kids," I noted with measured tact, "so I'm assuming this is not strictly a Platonic marriage."

She sighed and shook her head but didn't say anything.

*See my retelling of the Grimms' fairy tale, *Rapunzel*, in the appendix, p. 268.

"Okay," I said, "might I ask how frequently Rapunzel lets down her golden hair?"

Judith chuckled. "John and I have intercourse, oh, about once a month." Her voice took on the apologetic tone of a child reporting failed homework. "But that's not nearly enough for him. If he had it his way, my hair would be down every day, practically."

"A big discrepancy," I said.

"Yeah. I shy away from affection because when he talks nice to me or gives me a hug, it feels like pressure to have sex."

"And with an overbearing mother like yours, I bet you hate pressure."

"Yeah," she said.

"We know your mother's religious views on sex, but as a couple, do you and John have shared views?"

"He grew up Catholic," she said. "You know, 'sex is for procreation only.' I converted for a while when we got married, but we eventually left the church. Before the kids were born we went to India for a meditation retreat which really opened our minds. Since then we've studied Taoism, Sufism, and the Native American medicine way. You could say we're spiritually eclectic."

This seemed like the perfect opening to challenge her mother's inculcations with broader spiritual views. "Then you know that many religious tradions celebrate sexuality. Your own Norse ancestors, for instance, had great reverence for the goddess, Freya, who was quite a lover." Judith looked at me with glazed eyes so I pressed onward, trying to penetrate the fog. "Many worshipers see sex as sacred. Certainly you must have seen exquisitely sexy art in the Hindu temples of India." A heated tone had overtaken my voice. I closed my mouth to prevent a lecture from coming out.

"Sex just doesn't come to mind when I visit a temple," Judith defended.

My "eclectic" bias seemed to have catapulted prematurely. Aimed to topple the indoctrination which trapped her, it bounced off and fell to the ground with a thud, leaving the tower unscathed. I found myself in the role of the prince, wanting to free Rapunzel, but like the prince, I'd have to take things slowly. He visited her tower again and again without expecting her to venture forth. This was necessary because the witch had so thoroughly convinced her life out-side the tower was wicked. Like Rapunzel, Judith's urge to come down from the tower would have to awaken of its own accord. I'd have to avoid the snarl of trying to force freedom upon a willing prisoner. The only way to help her was to take an empathic position toward her withdrawal from sex.

"It's not just sex," Judith reflected. "It's life in general. I pull away from everything. I do my best to be a good mother. I love Curt and Cindy, but to be honest, the day-to-day chores of motherhood bore me. I started a silk-screening business in the garage, but sales lag and I don't have the gumption to drum up new business. I procras-tinate everything, and accomplish nothing."

In the weeks to come, Judith kept coming to see me, even though it seemed we accomplished nothing. I felt inadequate to help her and discussed my concern at my next consultation meeting with a group of trusted colleagues. They asked how I'd felt in the most recent session with Judith. I said in addition to feeling inadequate, I'd felt bored to distraction with her litany of complaints, and guilty for not staying engaged, but also frustrated and angry. I'd wanted to shout, "Judith! Get a life!," knowing this tack would only cast me in the role of the overbearing mother, or as Judith called it, "the witch."

The consultation group said Judith's inner struggles got projected out during the session and I was the lucky bystander who got stuck with her feelings. Upon examination, I saw what they meant. I wound up feeling all the conflicting emotions of her drama—the bored incompetence of the wife, the frustration of the husband, the pushiness of the mother, and the rage of the trapped girl—while Judith sat passively complaining. The group told me to concentrate on one thing: helping Judith take responsibility for these struggles within herself.

A few days later she sat across from me, biting her lip, squinting back tears. "I feel so guilty. John does lots of things to show he loves me, but I don't reciprocate. I don't want him to even talk nice to me because that leads to touching me. He deserves better."

"Let's take a close look at what happened last time he touched you," I said, trying to follow my colleagues' suggestion.

"That was last weekend . . . He asked if he could have a hug. I hugged him, but didn't want to kiss on the mouth, so I turned away. He asked if we could have some intimate time. Then I told him 'maybe.'"

"What did you mean by 'maybe'?" I asked.

Judith tried squeezing a grin through her tears, "Maybe means 'probably not,' and finally 'no,' after a few hours of hope on his part and dread on mine. I know I make us both miserable. I should be up-front about saying no, but I just feel guilty pushing him away all the time. He deserves someone who'll love him as a sexual person and not recoil from a kiss."

"Kissing bothers you."

"Yes. My aversion to kissing made my old therapist think I'd been sexually abused, but even under hypnosis no memories came up. If John would just hug me like the kids do, with no expectation, then that would be fine. But he kisses me on the mouth and expects me to kiss back. It's so imposing."

"Imposing," I echoed.

"Yes, he leaves me no room to breathe . . . no way to bow out gracefully. I feel so intruded upon."

"Shall we study that feeling and see what we can learn?" I asked. Judith nodded. I guided her to relax and get comfortable so she could intensify her inner awareness. Hakomi teachers call this state *mindfulness*, those who study shamanic methods call it *light trance*, others call it *focusing*. Jungians arouse such states through *active imagination*. These disciplines vivify the inner life, not as a reflection, but as an experience here and now. Like divination and meditation, these skills enable us to access deeper truths and receive guidance from a greater pool of knowledge beyond the personal. Judith's meditation training had familiarized her with such skills. She shut her eyes to close out distractions and began focusing on the problem of kissing.

"With a kiss, I can't breathe. John's desires are in my face, and I feel so pressured I can't stand it."

I urged her to pay attention to the kind of pressure she felt.

"It's like I have to submit to his needs, whether I like it or not. I resent that so much. I feel sorry for him, so I try not to show my resentment, but he picks up on it anyway. He gets real hurt and I feel bad, and wonder why I don't just give him what he wants. But then I'm afraid he'll hound me every week, and then every day, and it'll be just like living with my mother!"

"It triggers old rage," I said.

"Yes, and I feel so guilty putting that on John, when he doesn't deserve it. It hurts him when I put up a wall," she replied.

"Suppose the wall could talk, could make a statement about its purpose, what would it say?" I asked.

"It would say, 'Stay back. Don't touch,'" she said squaring her shoulders.

"Where are you in relation to the wall?" I asked.

"Behind and above it," she said, sitting up taller with a hint of confidence in her voice.

"It feels good back there?" I asked.

"Yeah," she nodded smiling.

"So, how about letting yourself bask in that feeling for a moment?"

Judith filled her chest and torso with a deep breath. A look of self contentment smoothed her normally frowning brow.

After a pause I asked, "What do you notice?"

"I feel strong back here," she said, "like I make the rules."

"What rules do you make?" I asked.

"No kissing on the mouth," she said sternly.

"Anything else?" I asked.

Shame pinched her eyes and mouth. "I want celibacy," she said like a defeated child. Her face, now slick with tears, flushed magenta.

"Judith," I said softly, "I really believe you want that."

"I do," she said, "I'm just afraid to tell John. He keeps encouraging me to heal our sex life, but I don't want that kind of pressure. I can't force myself to want it when I don't. It makes me feel like a failure."

Like John and the former therapist, I too, hoped Judith's libido would heal. But I was coming to understand that such hopes weighed on her like a millstone around her neck. Perhaps it was time for the denial to end.

"You can't force yourself to want it." I echoed her phrase.

"It's discouraging, and false, too. A year of sex therapy didn't help. Who are we kidding? John's still hoping you'll fix me and I'll suddenly become a passionate wife."

"Do you want that?" I asked.

Again shame pinched every muscle in her face. Tears rolled across deep furrows. "No, I don't want it, or look forward to it in any way. I can't stand the pressure of John hoping for it."

I felt sad for Judith and John, knowing there was no way to make them want the same thing.

In the weeks to come they had several late night discussions wherein they fully acknowledged this seeming stalemate. Separation was mentioned, but not seriously considered, as neither wanted to live without the other. They hammered out an agreement that to me seemed awkward and stressful, but they felt it was the most acceptable solution they could come up with. Judith agreed to help John masturbate twice a month which was more pleasing to him than doing it alone. John agreed not to ask for more. They both counted the days—he with eager anticipation—she with reluctant resignation. He still felt rejected and deprived, she still felt guilty, but the new rules reduced expectation and tension. I would have liked them to come up with a less stressful agreement, but my colleagues said it was a step in the right direction. To take responsibility for her own struggles, Judith had to work things out her own way.

Walls and Witches

Some weeks later, Judith complained of waking up at night with claustrophobia. She'd get up and go downstairs, open a window and sit in the dark. After the third or fourth time, she realized these episodes were preceded by a recurring dream. "The dream is pretty vague," she told me. "First I go into a room feeling relieved to have a quiet space to myself. But it's not peaceful like I expect. The room starts shrinking. The four walls get closer and closer. I look for a way out but the doors and windows are sealed. I wake up feeling really panicked, like the life's being crushed out of me. I feel this great sense of danger and have to get up."

"What sort of a room is it?" I asked.

"Just a nondescript room. The walls are a soothing peachy color, like the color of my childhood bedroom. What do you make of that?"

It seemed the bold position of direct interpretation was necessary. I chose my words carefully. "I think the dream is about your childhood defenses. Your withdrawal behind walls soothed you as a child—and provided a little peace. But as an adult, this defense is dangerous."

"Dangerous how?" Judith asked soberly.

"It's crushing your libido and stifling your inspiration."

"What do I do to change it?" she asked.

I answered her warily, "The old pattern would be for me to push for change, and for you to begin resisting it, right?"

"Yeah," she nodded with a sheepish grin. "That's the formula."

"Well then, maybe the question is this: Do you have any real desire for change?" I asked.

"I don't know about desire for change, but I feel tremendous envy lately when my friends talk about how much they love sex. I can hardly remember the times I've enjoyed it. When John comes near me, even if I want to warm up to him, I go into the automatic stonewall response."

"Part of you wants to warm up?" I asked.

"I wouldn't be here if it didn't," she answered coldly, an iciness in her voice pushing me away. I felt the kind of slap John must often have felt in reaching out to her.

"Are you in the stonewall mode with me now?"

"I guess so," she said, in a nonchalant tone while reddening in her ears spelled out fury.

"I wonder what that stone wall hopes to accomplish," I said.

She glared angrily and snapped, "It's to stop . . . it's to keep me from . . . it's to stop . . ."

"To stop what?"

"It's to stop me from envying my friends, from envying you. From getting mad, from blowing up, from doing something bad!" she blurted with a crimson flush of rage surging through her neck and face. "It's to stop me from doing something shameful or sinful. I don't know. It's to stop me from upsetting anyone. It's just to stop me!" she snarled.

"What's dangerous now, Judith," I said, "is that it stops you in all the wrong places—your love life, your mothering, your creativity. So much energy goes into sustaining this wall. No wonder you're depleted."

She looked me straight in the eye, "That's easy for you to say. No doubt you have a great mother who nurtured you every inch of the way. You probably love sex. My mother telephones me three times a day. She criticizes me nonstop and makes me feel miserable." Judith sat rooted to the couch. Her nostrils flared and she breathed heavily. A bullish tension in her shoulders and the solid way she'd set her hips captured my respect. Her frustrated inertia had finally given way to fury.

I took advantage and kept the pointed questions coming. "So tell me, does your wall protect you when your mother calls?"

"Damn it, no! I said she makes me feel miserable!"

"Well then, she still holds the key and she's still keeping you imprisoned," I said.

"What do you mean? I've got John and the kids, and my business. I left the church. I'm spiritually open-minded!"

"You're cold with John, and bored with the kids," I said. "You're neglecting your business, and you're spiritually uninspired."

"So!?" She hurled, running out of fire.

"Look, Judith," I said softly. "Of course you need to wall off your mother, but as it is, you wall yourself off from the things you need most, and she's the only one who gets through."

She put her face into her hands and sobbed, "I've got it ass backwards," she wailed. "But I really do want to make a change."

"What's the first step, then?" I asked.

She cried face down for a moment or two, producing a vast amount of tears. After soaking the front of her blouse and at least ten tissues, she shook her head and chuckled, having arrived at a place where laughter is not incompatible with tears. She hadn't forgotten my question and soon worked her way toward a reply.

"The first step is screening my phone calls," she replied, "so I'm not always subject to Mom's attacks."

Something important transpired that day. Judith's anger stirred smouldering coals deep inside. These coals grew hot enough to ignite the urge to act—an urge which had long been dormant within her. Hot flames burned through damp old defenses, and she was able to mobilize a plan. Screening calls sounds like a small measure of action, but for Judith it was a meaningful step toward change. As with Rapunzel, steps toward change would lead to deeper pain.

In the weeks to come, Judith screened out most of her mother's "witchy attacks." But this brought a deeper problem into view. "Even when I don't talk to Mom at all," she noted, "I still feel bad, like I'm a terrible daughter not to call her back, and a worthless wife not to do more for John and the kids."

She spent the bulk of one session inwardly focused on the dynamics of feeling bad, terrible, and worthless. We examined the monologue running through her head. Dominating her private thoughts was an extremely self-condemning voice Judith called the "inner witch." The inner witch delivered judgments more scornful than Judith's mother, and this voice had twenty-four-hour access. Judith hoped to screen out the inner witch, as she'd screened her phone calls, but screening out an inner voice is no easy feat. She was stymied as to how to do it. When it came to the thoughts running through her own head, she felt entirely vulnerable.

Her first step was to closely observe the inner witch over the course of a week. This brought to focus a vicious cycle. Typically, the cycle started in the morning with the thought, "You won't accomplish anything today." Judith tried to combat such thoughts by setting meaningful goals. By late morning the goals would not have been met and the inner witch would come on strong: "You're incompetent, lazy, and useless." At this, Judith would often rebel. She'd seek to feel better through "sneaking" indulgences such as videos and chocolates which would bring a moment's pleasure, but the tactics inevitably backfired because they gave the inner witch more fuel for attack. The witchy voice would taunt, "See, that's proof. You're incompetent, lazy, and indulgent." Judith would then succumb to defeat and mope through the rest of her day, validating the inner witch's reproaches by accomplishing little. The inner witch so powerfully dominated her moods and actions, Judith felt helpless to divest her.

I suggested an old Jungian trick, answering back. "One can argue, or at least stick up for oneself, in an inner dialogue," I said.

Judith tried coming up with salient arguments to throw back at the inner witch: "Why can't you say something positive? I'm not as bad as you think." But she found her own arguments "lame" and the witch still came out ahead. For help mounting stronger arguments, she returned to Rapunzel, and studied the point in the story when Rapunzel first disobeyed the witch.

Visitors were strictly forbidden, as if all the world beyond the tower were tainted and foul. But the prince came to visit one day when the witch was gone, and Rapunzel learned he was companionable, gentle, and kind. This was a turning point in the story, for it marked the moment when Rapunzel began to think her own thoughts, separate from the witch. But she didn't immediately confront the witch with those thoughts. At first she held them close to her chest.

For Judith, Rapunzel's style seemed more workable than direct confrontation. We talked about how she might do it. The inner witch was almost always nagging, and during that particular session she was saying, "You're selfish. You're wasting John's hard-earned money in therapy and accomplishing nothing." Judith didn't answer back, but she shaped a comforting thought which she could secretly hold close to her chest: "Maybe things are going slowly, but my intentions are good. I want a good future for me and my family."

While we were focused on Rapunzel's princely visitor, another thought came to me. Receiving kindness helped to empower Rapunzel and might also help to empower Judith. Judith still walled off kindness when it came to her in the form of affection, compliments, or support from others. It seemed each time she tried to accept kindness from John or a friend, the inner witch interfered saying, "If they only knew what a bad person you are, they wouldn't be so nice," or "You don't deserve that kind of attention." To alter this pattern Judith and I developed a little exercise to help her receive kindness from others. When John or a friend offered kind words or gestures, Judith made a point to visualize the witch confined behind a stalwart wall. This made it easier to absorb a little drop of kindness.

At first she was like a dried up sponge, resistant to absorption, but as support kept coming, she moistened, and eventually soaked it up. There was great joy in this for her. She laughed more, but she also cried more. Soaking up good things caused her to realize how long she'd been dry. She sometimes burst into tears when people were kind to her. Other times she was overcome with sorrow for the lonely girl she had been as a child. She grieved on occasion for the woman she might have been had she not started out life with a narrow, dismal view of the world and of herself.

Over the next few months, Judith felt the full weight of her life's sadness. Early on, we'd discussed the duration of her therapy and the fact that she'd hoped to be "done" in two years. Now she felt she might need "four or five years" to root out ingrained witchiness and develop a more kindly inner rapport. Her attachment to me grew. I became increasingly important because, like the prince, I'd entered her lonely tower and hadn't condemned her. She was grateful to have a witness to her inner struggle, one who recognized even her small steps toward selfhood.

At times she became feistier with John, and occasionally warmer. But overall, the "frigidity" remained in place. She blamed herself for not changing, and sometimes took solace in remembering that Rapunzel remained desperately lonely for a very long time, even after the witch had exiled her from the tower.

Out of the blue one day Judith called for an emergency visit. Her nightmare had returned, but it was more than claustrophobic this time. It was terrifying and was accompanied by a feeling of dread. The dread felt so familiar she thought it must be some kind of memory and she wanted help with it before it faded. I had an opening that morning and Judith took it.

"In this version of the nightmare the room is cold and foreboding from the start," she said. "I feel really trapped and small. As the walls start to close in, I grow tinier by the second, until I'm nothing but a small speck on the floor. Then I see my mother's ankles and shoes, and hear her singing hymns in a loud, terrifying voice. It seems like she's going to step on me and I'll be obliterated. I can't get her attention and I can't speak to let her know I'm there. Then John shook me because I was moaning, and I woke up."

This version of the nightmare had the quality of an infant's memory—a vague, tactile, emotional imprint. I trusted it implicitly.

"It just seems so real," she said.

"Let's respect your sense that it's real," I said. "It conveys a true emotional reality—the reality of an infant's need for warmth and protection, and the terror an infant feels when a parent is oblivious and threatening."

"You think my infancy was like that?" she asked incredulously.

"You know your mom better than I do," I said. "Did your dad ever say anything about it?"

A fire sparked in Judith's eyes. "Yeah, he did, actually. Mom was carrying on one day, saying I spoiled Curt by holding him too much. Dad said every time he picked me up as a baby she'd said the same about me. She was terrible with Cindy and Curt as babies! She patted them too hard, and jiggled them unmercifully, and had no tolerance when they cried."

"As a mother, how did you feel about that?"

"I knew it was wrong." she said as certain as a mother bear. "And that makes me think of another thing. When Cindy was a newborn, Mom went to put her down for a nap one afternoon. She sang so loudly she made Cindy cry. I tell you, I have every reason to hate music. Other people think music is uplifting. Not me. Mom terrorized me with hymns!" I'd never heard Judith speak so vividly. She was on the scent of a whole trail of memories. She rooted after them like a hungry animal. "Do you know, when I was really little, I don't remember how old, a bee stung me on the knee while Mom was hanging out the wash. I started screaming and she didn't even help me. She just drowned out my screams with really loud hymns.

"Believe me, she was the loudest singer in the congregation, too. Even her singing voice was witchy. At home she yelled all the time. The neighbors thought she was nuts. They never allowed their kids to come to our house.

"Her religion was supposed to solve everything. To this day I hate those damn hymns! Talk about walls. She shut me out with her damn sermons and hymns! Imagine, preaching the fear of God to an infant." Judith's anger erupted from a hot molten core. Alive, lucid, and fierce, its heat forced clarity from vague moods and dim memories. I hoped it signaled the return of her vitality and would lead to a desire to reclaim the energetic, sensual, and creative parts of her which had long been in exile.

More stories flooded forth in distinct color. She used her mother's name for the first time, *Virginia*. I learned how religion had been Virginia's only hope to rise above a family history of incest, violence, and chaos. She prided herself on not using blows to control Judith, as her own mother had done with her. A constant bombardment of Bible warnings was aimed to protect Judith from the family's stained past, to shield her from the evil of the world, and root out the furtive wickedness in her soul.

Judith's father had been able to give her some hint of solace. He wasn't big on words, but he often looked at her with soft eyes. His parents had been farmers from Eastern Europe who'd immigrated when he was nineteen. Both died soon after. Virginia was the only girl he'd ever dated and he married her at twenty-one, Judith believed, out of grief, fear, and confusion. Ashamed of his accent, he nearly always let Virginia do the talking regardless of the situation. She even told the barber how to cut his hair. He never stood up to Virginia on Judith's behalf. "Putting up with Mom was his cross to bear," she said. "He was a silent martyr type. A couple of times he implied I'd be better off, the sooner I learned to 'put up and shut up,' like him."

Unlike her father, Judith didn't simply succumb to the stronger will of her mother. At a young age she'd learned how to even the score through procrastination, the art of resisting Virginia's dictates by dragging her heels at every turn. Whenever there were chores to be done she practiced the art of delay. It infuriated Virginia, and served to carve out a small arena in which Judith could exert personal power.

In the past I'd been the one to tell Judith her old defenses worked against her, but now she explained how procrastination contaminated all aspects of her life. She knew how to run her business, but as soon as she set her schedule of tasks, she felt oppressed by it. The schedule became the overbearing mother, and naturally, her resistance kicked in. Procrastination took over with a power greater than her most businesslike intentions. Many of these things had been examined before, but the heat of anger clarified the picture the way a kiln fire anneals crystal.

I believed heat from a similar depth would rekindle her sexual passion. Psychology has long studied the link between Eros and aggression. Mythology points to it as well. The Norse goddess, Freya, is the queen of love and war, as if the two were somehow tied at the core. Aphrodite, the Greek love goddess is irresistibly attracted to Mars, the god of war. I felt the key to Judith's repressed Eros was in her fire. It wasn't long before this theory proved true.

One day she began the session by reporting she'd seduced John and enjoyed intercourse. I listened carefully and learned this rare event had followed a fight. Releasing blocked anger had indeed cleared the way for Eros. I encouraged Judith to continue expressing anger directly, pointing out that the fight warmed things up, as opposed to procrastination and withdrawal which froze things over. Judith felt pressured by my encouragement, and it immediately brought up a wall of defense. She'd never seen marital anger expressed appropriately. Her mother's witchy rages and her father's quiet submission were all she could refer to. She despised herself for yelling at John and feared any angry words would sound exactly like Virginia.

I tried to convince her that steam can be blown off in moderate doses, without total devastation. I described movie scenes where heroines told heroes off with great aplomb, improving the situation, not destroying it. Judith nodded and humored me, but in actuality she dug in her heels and resisted, retaliating by canceling our next appointment.

When I called her on it, she admitted being mad at me for trying to change her. She said everything I'd said about anger rang true, but she didn't feel she could successfully get mad at John and she didn't like me pushing her toward failure. I asked if she could get mad at me for my meddlesome interference. "Nice, try, Erica," she teased, and then sadly explained, "Getting mad at you would be humiliating. It's nowhere near as powerful as getting even by canceling. I know that puts me back into the old power struggle with Mom. l can recognize it, but I don't seem to be able to change it."

I wondered, after all those months, if Judith was right back where she'd started, "Analyzing things to death without resolving anything." I didn't think so. This seemed to be the kind of regression that precedes a breakthrough. I had a hunch about it.

The Garden

The following week she told this dream: "A neighbor woman had been sort of flirty with John. His face lit up and it made me think she might be better for him than me. She grew these huge purple orchids in her garden. All her plants grew like magic. I was so taken with the orchids, I wanted to transplant some to my garden, which looked scroungy by comparison.

"I was too shy to ask if it was okay, so I sneaked into her garden at night to steal a few. Before I could dig them up, my mother arrived out of nowhere. Only it was *not* Virginia. In fact, she was the total opposite of Virginia. She was amazingly beautiful. She had incredible blonde braids and she rode on the back of a big prizewinning pig, you know, like at the county fair. It sounds weird, but in the dream it was natural and even sort of regal. She knew why I was there, and she grabbed a garden spade. All smiles, she said, 'Come on, Honey, I'll help you.' So, we started digging up these great purple orchids and putting them into a sack. Then she went over to the vegetable garden and started picking all kinds of greens, saying, 'These will be good for you, Dear.' The vegetables had special healing powers. It started to dawn on me that the mother-figure and the neighbor woman were one and the same. She was like a good witch who could change her form. I wasn't afraid. I realized there was no threat at all about her and John. She really wanted to help my marriage."

Despite all the positives in the dream, Judith examined it in a typically self-effacing manner. She felt ashamed for envying the neighbor woman and wanting to steal from her garden. I had no patience for the self-effacement. Finally Judith's dream psyche had

given her a nurturing dream figure, the type Jung called a "greater
personality maturing within," a mother-figure that blended the quali-
ties of two Norse goddesses of old—Freya, the flirty love goddess,
and Frigga, the guardian of marriage. Judith's ancestors were speaking to her through her bone and blood memory, showing how the
spark of flirtation and milk of kindness could break her self-im-
posed exile, and empower her as a woman. The moment held great
potential, and yet, I had to proceed with great delicacy in order not
to arouse her resistance. I asked the mother goddess in my own
Scandinavian blood to handle the dream as gently as a newborn
child. "Judith," I said, "this mother figure is very interesting. She
brings to mind the Norse goddesses Freya and Frigga."

In the past my mention of such things was met with Judith's
blank stare, but this time she smiled, "You're kidding, they ride pigs
or something?"

"Well, Freya rides a great golden boar, actually," I said, "and she
adores flowers."

"How about that?" she said, looking as if the idea rolled around
her psyche searching for a place to light. "So who is Freya, again?"

I reached to the bookshelf and took down a ragged copy of *Funk
and Wagnalls Standard Dictionary of Folklore, Mythology, and Leg-
end*. I flipped to the F's and handed the book to Judith. She scanned
the Freya section and learned Freya was the beautiful goddess of
love and fertility but also the goddess of war. "That's like what you
said before," Judith recalled. "Maybe if John and I can fight more
freely, we can love more freely?" Judith read on to discover Freya
was born of the sea and later married the sunshine with whom she
bore two fair children. "Listen to this," Judith said. "Early Chris-
tians declared Freya a witch and banished her to the mountains
where they say her demons still dance. A witch, imagine that, a
goddess reduced to a witch."

"Let's look under *witch*, and see what *Funk and Wagnalls* says, "
I suggested.

Judith turned to the back of the book. "Witch," she said, and
began scanning the page. "Wow, it says the wise woman of early
societies became, through the lens of Christianity, the 'malignant
witch' of later lore. How 'bout that? It's ironic, when you think of

it. Christ loved everyone, but Christianity is hard on women. Eve is blamed for the fall of man. Wise women are called evil witches. You know it's still going on today. Mom's pastor says feminists are brides of Satan. But it's so entrenched, how do we change it?"

"Your dream suggests the opposite trend."

"You mean the return of the good witch?"

I nodded.

"All my life, the power has been in the hands of bad witches, first Virginia, then the inner witch. But the dream is different. This Freya-type witch takes over."

"She welcomes you into the garden, gives you beautiful flowers, and nourishing food. Does that speak to your life right now?"

"Well, maybe you could say the ground of my being is changing hands? Maybe good witches are reclaiming the soil, you know, bringing the garden back to life."

"I'd say so," I said.

"It's got lots of implications if you think about it," Judith mused. "Like reclaiming Eden, or the garden in Rapunzel."

I got goose bumps from head to toe, and put in my two cents. "Or reclaiming the gardens of marriage, motherhood, and spirituality."

Judith nodded, smiling.

Weeks later, Judith reported an amusing series of events which could have been engineered by Frigga and Freya themselves. Judith's girlfriend, Val, had invited her on a shopping excursion. The two women met in their favorite department store, had coffee, and then, following Val's lead, headed for lingerie. Judith waited while Val tried on several items Judith had never tried garter belts, teddies, wonder bras. "I was amazed." Judith said. "I never realized there were so many things to make women feel sexy. Val tried to get me to try stuff on, but I couldn't relate. I just went over and bought a couple of pairs of pantyhose.

"Then Val said, 'What do you want to do?' So I took the lead. We looked at coats and then went to the pastry counter and shared a slice of chocolate torte. Val asked if I could keep a secret. I said sure, and she started telling me how she's going to fly to L.A. for the

weekend to meet this younger guy from work. He's real young—
twenty-three. Val's forty-four and has a twenty-year-old son. She's
embarrassed about having a fling with someone close to her son's
age. But this guy is so attractive, and has the hots for her too, so
they decided to meet at a hotel in L.A.

"Hearing the story made me feel more aroused than I can ever
recall. It made me envious. I told her how I felt, and she said she
envied me more, because John is a very sexy man, as well as a reliable husband, which she's never had. I admitted that all in all, I'm
the one with the better deal. Then, I can't even remember which
one of us suggested it, but the next thing I knew we were back to
lingerie and I was trying stuff on. I bought something in red because John likes red, and to make a long story short, I wore it to bed
and we had great sex. I really enjoyed it.

"But one thing makes me feel guilty," she said. "The whole time
I kept my eyes closed and pictured I was in L.A. with a younger
man."

"Did that spoil it for you?" I asked.

"No, it made it interesting," she said, "but it feels like cheating."

"I suppose cheating made it interesting," I said.

"Yeah," she said, "exactly. I hate that about myself. Why can't I
enjoy the things within reach? Why do I have to long for forbidden
fruit?"

"For-BID-den," I echoed, as if the word were a sip of fine wine
with several layers of taste.

"Yes. Like when I was little. The things I relished most were the
things Mom forbade. Rapunzel for one. She said fairy tales were
'devil's work,' so that made them all the more delightful. I read with
a flashlight under the covers and hung on every word.

"Then in high school she forbade me to date guys who weren't
'born again' so who did I fall for? Jews and Catholics, of course. She
hated that. And that made me pursue those boys all the more.

"Even nowadays, when I resolve not to eat sweets, that's when I
crave them the most—when they're forbidden. Is that sick or what?"

"It's like Rapunzel's mother," I said, "craving forbidden greens.
If everything you want is just a reaction against your mother, then,
yeah, that's a problem. But if in breaking a rule you discover your
heart's desire . . ."

"My *heart's desire,*" she mused. She closed her eyes and took a few deep breaths, going into herself to study desire. "Hmmm, I desire the feeling of a fresh start. No baggage. When I imagine making love with another man, it's good because there's no history of guilt. I excite him, he excites me. I don't have to feel ashamed for past disappointments.

"When I imagine it's a younger man, that's even better, because I feel in charge, like I'm teaching him. He's easy to please and wildly grateful."

Judith studied her fantasies in depth, and logically concluded that they hurt no one, in fact, John was overjoyed at the renewal of their love life. But this brought Judith to a pivotal point in her healing. She had to contend with the clamoring inner witch who condemned the adultery fantasy, shaming Judith almost to the point of resuming her former "frigidity." It was like the moment Rapunzel faced the witch and said, "I like the prince. He's good and I'm going forth with him."

To move forth, Judith needed support from good witches. It was my job to bless the renewed conjugal fire and offer an alternative to shame. "Judith," I said, "remember how the mother in the garden dream blended two goddesses, Freya and Frigga? Well, Frigga is the guardian of matrimony—the queen of fidelity, trust, and conjugal harmony. She's big on monogamy, and she'd approve that you've always been a faithful wife. Freya, of course, is the queen of flings and affairs. So, we're talking about two separate domains, but those domains overlap in one area: private fantasy. In the privacy of your own mind, either goddess can rule. In fantasy, even the best of wives can occasionally wander like Freya, no harm done."

The hint of a smile came to Judith's lips. The corners of her mouth curved upward like a Botticelli Madonna. A delicate blush spread from her chest, warming her neck and face, brightening the air around her. She took a deep breath that passed through her entire body like a sublime light—as if the sunshine himself had pledged love to her.

That afternoon she picked up the kids and they stopped off at the garden store on the way home. They bought bulbs for purple orchids and a terra cotta statue of a prize-winning pig. She took her spade out into the drizzly dusk and cleared an overgrown section of her garden. To remind her of good witches, she planted purple orchids, hearty winter kale, and placed the pig in the center like a guardian.

In the months to come she seduced John more often. Sometimes wearing red, sometimes not—sometimes thinking of another man, sometimes not. John seemed to take it for granted that all her sighs and moans were for him, and for the most part they were. John's new-found contentment filled the house. Cindy and Curt thrived in the nimbus of their parents' mended love. Whole days would pass by without much noise from the inner witch. Judith began to think of herself as a competent housewife and a good mother, and she liked it that way.

Home from Exile

"The only time I regress back to the tower is when Mom's around. When she and Dad stop over, her criticisms get me every time. She makes me feel four years old. John says I let her get under my skin, and it's hard on him and the kids. I know he's right. Mom and Dad are coming for dinner on Cindy's seventh birthday, and I'm uptight already."

Judith and I pragmatically reviewed all the trusty tools she'd developed during the four years we'd worked together. We broke it down to three basics: 1) Build protective walls in the right places; 2) Be receptive to love and support; 3) When all else fails, go out to the garden and ask Frigga and Freya for spiritual aid. I hoped these tools would help Judith through the birthday dinner.

The following week she sashayed into the office looking particularly bright. "Well," she said, "we had quite a dinner. Mom and Dad came over and Mom was uptight right away. She was annoyed at all the crumpled giftwrappings on the floor from when friends had stopped by earlier with gifts. She started bending over, picking up ribbons and paper saying, 'I'd think you'd have had a chance to tidy up by now.' I wanted to scream, but John piped up and said, 'Cheer up Virginia, there's more to birthdays than tidiness.' That sort of smoothed her feathers temporarily.

"Then the kids wanted to play with Grandpa like they always do. Of course Mom got uptight because they never gravitate to her. Dad kind of glossed that one over by saying, 'Let's play Monopoly so Grandma can play too.'

"Anyway, the kids don't even like Monopoly, but they played just to be good sports. They were being really great. John knew how bothered I was and he basted the turkey while I took a breather in the garden. Out there I just felt peaceful and decided no matter what, I'd hold my ground in my own home. When we sat down to eat, Mom hinted that it was unmanly of John to forget to say grace. She asked Dad to say it and of course, he did. The dinner was a little tense, but we were getting through it okay. Mom was on her best behavior. I served mashed potatoes, Cindy's favorite. I'd steamed some beets from the garden—the kids know they're supposed to eat at least one vegetable —but they were on good behavior too, so they ate both beans and beets. Cindy played around with the beet juice, and said, 'Look, Mom, I can write my initials.' She wrote CJ, CJ, CJ, over and over on the plate. It was harmless. But Mom couldn't stand it. She scolded, 'Shame on you Cindy! Show a little respect!' Tears immediately came to Cindy's eyes. John looked at me like he wanted to handle it, but these words came right out of my mouth, 'Mother, that's a little harsh. She's not hurting anything.' I took Cindy's hand and said, 'It's okay, Honey, Grandma's too strict sometimes. You didn't do anything wrong.'

"Mother stood up and hollered, 'Judy, how dare you show disrespect for me in front of this family and in the eyes of God!' Dad said, 'Leave it now, Virginia. Judy means no harm.' Then Mother turned to Dad, 'How could you let our daughter talk that way? You coward. This is the thanks I get for my good works—an immigrant husband and a heathen daughter!' John stood up. 'Virginia, that's enough. I won't have you talk that way in our home, do you understand?' Mom sat down glaring at Dad saying, 'Well at least John knows how to wear the pants in his family.'

"Cindy looked around with her eyes big as saucers wondering what to make of all this, then she looked at Virginia and said clear as a bell, 'My mom can wear pants if she wants to.' Then she looked wide-eyed at me and John to see how her remark would sit with us.

It was so sweet. She was completely assertive yet totally without guile. No adult could have been more firm and more tactful at the same time. I just burst into tears. Not because I was hurt, but because I saw my seven-year-old daughter was good through and through. I saw the kind of kids she and Curt are. They wish harm on no one, and they've got real courage. It was clear to me that with kids like that I must be a decent mother."

John said, 'That's right, Cindy, Mom dresses how she wants to.' He got up and came over to my chair, not knowing what to think. He bent down and whispered, 'Sweetheart, shall I tell them to go?' I said, 'No, honey, I'm crying because I'm happy. Look at Cindy and Curt. We've got the two sweetest kids on God's green earth and I'm just happy about it.'

"Curt turned to Mom and said, 'Are you happy with us, Grandma?' All eyes were on Mom. I don't think she'd ever told the kids she loved them or was happy with them. She was really on the spot. She looked like she wanted to say the right thing, but didn't know how. Dad whispered, 'Go ahead Virginia, tell the boy you're proud.' Mom cleared her throat—and then didn't say anything. l looked at John, realizing that later we might just have to explain to the kids that Grandma was a very unfortunate person who just couldn't show love. But finally Mom says, 'Why, Curt, you know Grandma's proud of you. I've always said so.' We all looked at each other, silently thinking, 'No, you never said so.' Finally Dad said, 'Kids like a word of encouragement now and then.' And Mom said, 'I'd give my right arm for these kids. Lord knows I would. This family is all I care about in the world.' And I knew that in its own twisted way, what she said was true. What followed after that was the most pleasant evening we've ever had with my folks. I wouldn't say Mom was sweet, but she wasn't nasty either. John said later, 'Maybe your mom's starting to mellow out in her old age.' It was a great night for me. I don't want to sound overconfident, but the way I feel now, I don't think seeing her will throw me off like it used to."

Judith and I both knew she no longer needed me. She was still a quiet homemaker trying to make a go of an iffy cottage industry, but she no longer hid behind a wall or lived in emotional exile. She'd become the heroine of her own life story. She gardened with a passion and devotedly tended to her family. She no longer gazed hungrily at other women's gardens. She tilled her own soil and cultivated her own prizewinning orchids. Her effect on the earth was like her effect on her husband and kids. As with the good Norse witches of old, there was a bit of magic in her touch—something inexplicable about the way things thrived in her care.

— 11 —

Battered Moon

Stories are to society what dreams are to individuals. Without them we go mad.

—Isabel Allende

The Family Tree's Most Luscious Fruit

When I first met Maria, North American city life suited her about as well as an oil spill suits a dolphin. "I'm miserable here," she said twisting a thick handful of lustrous hair, "but no way can I go back home." Home was a coffee farm in Central America where despite earthquakes, distant gunfire, and the smouldering volcano, her family enjoyed a prosperous life.

"In *sangre*, in blood, I'm part Maya Quiché," she said. "My grandmother is from a very old Quiché family."

Maria's talk of the Maya Quiché took me back twenty years, when as a college student, my search for living myths had led to her village. At that time few Quiché women traveled beyond the furthest avocado grove, and leaving the countryside was unheard of. Maria's tailored suit and Italian shoes contradicted my memory of the cheerful bands of barefoot Quiché women in colorful hand woven wraps,

212

deftly climbing steep hillsides with babes and water jugs in tow. Images of these women and their village flooded over me. The monster earthquake had struck during my stay, toppling buildings, filling the air with the stench of death, nixing basic resources like water, food, medicine, and gas. When the first rumblings hit one night, I woke to the sensation of being jostled as if my adobe hut were a freight car. Loose bricks pummeled down as I crawled to the door. Outside, neighbors ran about like panicked children, but key elders immediately began rituals in various parts of town. Fires were lit. Elders ceremoniously placed fragrant herbs into the flames. Aromatic cords of smoke wafted dizzying fumes. Prayers climbed skyward on the nimble incantations of old men. Old women sang laments and divined doom. I'd never forget these scenes, and the current of terror in the air.

After the big one, smaller tremors continued. I focused on the task of clearing the road and gathering supplies. The locals humored my efforts, but turned their attentions toward ritual. I wanted to participate, but the quakes had increased their wariness of outsiders. Some said the very presence of *Gringos* brought disruption and caused quakes. Villagers remained polite, but banned me from the rituals which had sustained their way of life over the centuries.

A few weeks later, when patched-up roads permitted my rough passage out, I said a bittersweet goodbye to Maria's homeland. My youthful heart swelled with unnamable longing and my head itched with unanswered questions. To this day, I believe the Mayan devotion to nature spirits and their unshakable faith in the cycle of life, death, and rebirth affords them a far more enviable wealth than their modern neighbors will ever know.

Now, with Maria in my office, worlds and decades away, my spiritual hunger was piqued and dozens of questions flooded to mind. Attuned to both modern and tribal ways, Maria could bridge my gaps in understanding. But her sad eyes shone like obsidian mirrors, calling me back to the tasks at hand: learning why she'd come, and how I could help. It took every ounce of psychic muscle I could muster to quell my hunger and keep on track.

My first step was to ask if she hoped to go home. She looked at me as if the question were too simple-minded to warrant response.

"When you hear my family story," she said, "then you'll begin to understand." I took the cue to hush up and listen.

"I told you my grandmother is Quiché, but my family is known as a *ladino* family, you know, aristocrats from Spain. When Mayan blood and Spanish blood mix, the Spanish blood takes over because they have money to take over the land." Maria's family farmland was first cleared early in the nineteenth century when her great, great grandfather, Don Diego, sold his dwindling estate in Spain and sailed to Central America, where his small Spanish fortune translated to big opportunity. He bought up virgin Quiché hills, clear-cut the forest, and sold the lumber as a means to regain lost family grandeur.

I was impressed with Maria's solid grasp of her family tree. Feeling certain that the roots of her problem lay entangled in the ancestral past, she bathed me in a recounting of her family's history in the Quiché hills. A proud Spaniard once told me that family roots are the seat of the soul. I prepared to hear soulful rustlings in the branches of Maria's family tree.

She went on to elaborate the family theme of the Spanish side "taking-over" the Quiché land and people. She expressed no scorn for the usurper or the usurped. Instead she gave a matter-of-fact history of the two diverse sources of her bloodline.

Don Diego's clear-cut hills were fringed by ancient Mayan farm terraces which had fed the Quiché people for centuries. Maria explained that the Quiché thought it inconceivable for even a great man to own the mountains and more incomprehensible was that he killed trees without consulting their Dueña. For according to their way of thinking, if anyone owned the mountains, it was the Dueña, a generous but stern mountain spirit whose guidance kept the balance. It was the Dueña who, through the local holy man, told them when to fast and when the stars were right to hunt bristle-backed boars for holy feasts. It was she who permitted them to tap her dark cisterns and loose her spring water down the mountain's serpentine channels to their crops. It was she who they thanked (along with the local gods) for the bounty of their region. They thought it obscene for their rich boss to bypass the Dueña and bless his new farm in the name of Jesus alone.

For the Maya, earthly harmony depended upon a sort of all-inclusive religious thoroughness, that is, honoring the many gods of worlds below and above this one. Had the locals been in charge of blessing the new farm, you can bet their prayers would have rung long into the night for many days, praising numerous gods and mystical beings such as the deer and jaguar.

But Don Diego had fixed his sights on a vision of his own. He aimed to see his own name on gold and red labels throughout the coffee shops of the world. But how could he accomplish this if his laborers were forever observing holy days, inhaling incense, and chanting to trees? Through a series of perfectly "legal" land swindles, he forced them to forsake their own crops to tend his acres of coffee. They were soon dependent upon the plantation system and in no position to argue when he forbade them to celebrate sacred days. The people wondered how fate allowed Don Diego to prosper, what with his bold disrespect for gods and customs. Some said his Quiché bride was his salvation.

Though the Maya frown on marrying outsiders, he managed to purchase or woo (family stories differ) a Mayan wife young enough to be his daughter. And though she quickly learned ladino ways, bread never took the place of tortillas at the family table; and though forbidden, the tenacious clicks and leisurely vowels of her mother tongue rang through the house when her man was away. Her whole life she secretly prayed like a proper Mayan and fed hungry villagers when times were bad. When her only son came of age and married a Quiché bride, Mayan traditions took root firmly, setting a tone for the homelife of the generations to come.

As young girls, Maria and her five sisters never had to work at learning the old tongue. They imbibed it while nestled against their grandmother's breast, drinking warm chocolate or helping her place tortillas on the grill. When their beloved father was home, they strove for the lisps and trills of proper Castillian Spanish. In their mid-teens they went off to the capital for the classical education of the privileged class where they added English and French to their repertoire.

At age twenty-two, Maria caught the eye of an older outsider, a clever entrepeneur from Chicago. He marketed agricultural chemi-

cals to third world farmers—a dubious, but wildly lucrative enter-
prise, not so different from that of Maria's founding father, Don
Diego, nearly two centuries before. All five sisters longed for the
northerner's touch and he was first on their father's too-short list of
eligible grooms. Maria was without doubt, the most luscious fruit
on the family tree, and when he shook the branch, she fell willingly.
"It is a family tradition," she told me with a shrug, "to find a prosperous man."

But now, three years later, Maria felt anything but prosperous.
She'd fled from the handsome Lake Michigan estate where her pub-
licly gallant husband had entrapped her in a private hell. Her family history conveyed the tale of two forces, one overt and autocratic,
the other subtle and enduring. These two forces had danced together for nearly two centuries, sometimes yielding joy, often veil-
ing anguish, always maintaining a strained balance. But when she
spoke of her own life, it was clear that the hurtful aspects of the
dance had come to a head in her marriage and could no longer be
endured. To end her part in it, Maria had done the unthinkable.
She'd left her husband, an act of degradation unheard of in the
family. She'd sought refuge with her Berkeley educated cousin,
Lucy, in the Pacific Northwest. Lucy had been Maria's role model
and dearest friend in childhood. Lucy's move north had opened
the door for Maria to risk leaving home, and now that her marriage had failed, there was no place for Maria to turn except to
Lucy. Maria felt like a fish out of water in Seattle, but there was no
place else for her to go.

It took several visits for the whole tale to unfold, for though she
spoke excellent English, when she was upset, she slipped into Spanish, the language we came to call her "father tongue." When she
was very upset, she slipped into Quiché, her "mother tongue." Quiché
offered the most comfort, being the language her grandmother
whispered while holding Maria close when she was small.
English, her "husband tongue," sometimes abondoned her entirely.
On occasion she'd intentionally throw me off with French, which
she'd mastered in college. I'd ask her to hold the French, and
she'd laugh—pleased to establish her edge on me. But her moods
were always easy to read, and with my rusty grasp of Spanish and
a dictionary in hand, I could usually keep up.

Her Prosperous Man

Though Maria was determined not to go back to her husband, he was still under her skin. She spoke of him at length, as if she could only stay away by repeatedly convincing herself the marriage was doomed. "I call him 'Big Boots,' because he wears really fine American cowboy boots. Everybody back home admires his boots and of course, the big Norte Americano–size foot. In public, Boots is a prince. All the women think I am so very lucky to have such a fine man. But when we are alone in our home, it is different. He beats me—the one he loves most in all the world. His 'Mayan treasure' he calls me. He uses booze and cocaine, but very discretely so no one knows. When he first hurt me I did not believe it was real. But one day he pushed me to the floor, then he bashed a dining room chair over my back and it broke to pieces. After that I stared at the busted up chair. I looked at the blood and bruises on me and I knew it was real. In the next year I lost count of the times he hit and punched me. I wore sunglasses everyday and always a big sweater to cover the bruises. He started hurting me so often, I could not tell anymore which lumps were new and which were still there from the time before. I got used to always having green skin, the color of old-bruises.

"One time he threw me against the bathtub and my shoulder snapped. It hurt like bloody murder and we both heard it crack loud. He thought he broke my shoulder and I said I need a doctor. He was afraid I was really hurt, and he carried me to the car. I was praying all the way to the clinic, 'Oh please, merciful mother of god, may the doctor be a good man who will see my problem and help me.' But Boots took me to his friend, a foot doctor who takes cocaine. Right away Boots said to him, 'Hey Buddy, help me out, eh? My wife fell down the stairs. Guess she had one too many toots.' The doctor just laughed and said, 'Do you know where I can get some? I bet Maria has good connections south of the border. Why don't you share a good thing?' Then he yanked my arm and snapped my shoulder back into place, the whole time making jokes to Boots about Mexican prostitutes.

"I was so sick of it and there was no one in Chicago who I could trust. The next day I phoned Lucy. I broke out in tears and told her everything. She said, 'I knew Boots was crazy! He's a sick man and you are sick to stay there a minute longer. Domestic violence is so fucked up, Maria!' I did not know they had a formal name for it—*domestic violence*. It sounds like all these nice things: domestic wine, domestic cheese, domestic wool, domestic arts. Sometimes English is very strange. Anyway, Lucy said, 'Maria, Get the hell out of there. Get a credit card out of his wallet. Get a ticket and get on a plane. and that is what I did. That is how I got here. And now I am talking to you. You see what my life has come to, Erica? Lucy says I made bad choices and that is why all this happened. But these were the decisions required of me, no?

"I have no money, no work, and no work papers. I have some-body who pays me cash to clean house, so now I am a scrub-woman. Before, people said I was beautiful, Erica, really. Now I am too fat and my heart is broken. Lucy says I am codependent, a battered wife. Where I come from when a wife gets beat up, we do not say she is codependent, we say 'pobrecita,' the poor dear. We try to help because it hurts to have a bad husband. The other women pray for her. I said to Lucy, 'What is this codependent?' She said, 'You de-pend on Boots for everything. You have nothing of your own. That is why he gets away with beating you. You need your own life.' But, Erica, you must understand, all my life I was told, 'A prosperous man will make you happy.' Now I am told I must have my own life. The rules changed overnight. Sure, I want to have my own life. But I am confused and so tired.

"Lucy says it takes two to tango. She says I must search my soul for my part in it. But every time I go over it, I see what a good wife I was. It was not me who put meanness into Boots. His mother says he was violent even as a boy."

Maria often traced the origins of Boots's brutality as if she needed to prove to herself that she hadn't caused it. I could have told her "It's not your fault," until I was blue in the face, and it wouldn't have mattered. She required time to sort through the question of responsibility and blame. Her preferred sorting tool was her slow, deliberate logic. I could have attacked her self-blame with agressive arguments, but that can backfire by driving it into the unconscious where it festers and generates more bad feelings. She was on the right track, so I made a point to be patient, to support her sorting and affirm her sound conclusions.

It was important not to dismiss the deeply confusing contradictions before her. She'd been reared to embody the gentle, enduring ways of her grandmother, but suddenly the traditional rug had been yanked out from under her, and her wifely virtue was now her downfall. Under the new rules, as interpreted by Cousin Lucy, salvation lay in Maria's ability to embody the overtly powerful ways of men like Don Diego, her father, and Boots. From now on, happiness was supposed to depend upon leaving her prosperous man and building her own life. No wonder she felt old at twenty-five. She'd leapt from the fifties to the nineties in one week.

Seeking clues to this new life, Maria punctiliously studied the personal evolution of Lucy, her lifelong role model. According to some, theirs would have been termed a codependent, enmeshed bond, but solidarity like theirs is the backbone of women's esteem and strength in their homeland. Their relationship—their love for and loyalty to each other—taught me much about the profound possibilities of female bonds. No matter how far apart their lives took them, they remained powerfully influential for each other. For this reason I endorsed Maria's request to bring Lucy to our next session.

The Cousins

Following Maria through the door, Lucy came to the office wearing practical, layered rain-gear and hiking boots. She wore her hair in a severe bob, stylish for the time. Aside from their drastically different styles, they could have been sisters with their identical handsome Mayan noses and strong Spanish brow lines resembling soaring eagles.

Maria introduced us and urged Lucy to tell her story. It unfolded deliberately as Maria's family story had unfolded weeks before. Maria interrupted whenever she felt Lucy was overmodest. She'd laud Lucy's genius, and the two would argue briefly until reaching an accurate medium. Then Lucy would go on. Their rapport was as fresh as raspberries on a July morning. It made me fall in love with my job.

Years earlier, Cousin Lucy had left home to embrace the call of higher education. She'd been a gifted student from the start. Like a falcon, she'd swooped and seized her subjects, devouring them whole. Soon after she arrived at Berkeley to feast at the Liberal Arts buffet, she made her mark as an outstanding, outspoken student. But regardless of the pressures on her during those years, she always found time to write to Maria, her beloved younger cousin back home.

One fateful day during Lucy's first year, a telegram from Maria arrived. The message rammed her gut. "Quiché farmers shot by green-suits. Everything is crazy. Grandmother weeps. Father is outraged." After that, Lucy could no longer accept the false calm of her upbringing. The distant gunshots she'd heard throughout childhood, now tore point-blank through her dreams at night.

Her Liberal Arts career careened suddenly away from English literature and dove headlong into Latin American studies. She became a fiend for its history, a glutton for its politics. But she was no longer content to simply store learning in the vault between her ears. She wanted knowledge to surge from her pen and blast through her lips to wake North America from its NutraSweet dream, long enough to gaze with clear eyes at the Yankee-sponsored nightmare in her homeland.

She sold her car to buy a computer for the Sanctuary program. She wrote leaflets and gave speeches. She found sanctuary for exiles. She rounded up blankets and clothing for widows and orphans back home. She discovered her genius for rallying grass-roots groups, inspiring volunteers, pooling resources, throwing concerts, art fairs, puppet shows—anything to raise funds. Once graduated with honors, she nailed a scholarship, no strings attached, and whipped through grad school in a year, nursing the cause all the while. Then, to be near trees again, and to go where the movement most needed her zeal, she moved further north, to Seattle.

Lucy had never liked Boots. She'd early on sized him up as the enemy, and when Maria married him, it didn't make her the enemy, but it made her a complacent, lost soul. She often pictured Maria zoned out in front of TV talk shows or wandering through department stores trying on shoes. She now saw things differently. Maria wasn't a rich housewife dulled by a life of excess, she was a defeated refugee with the hope pounded out of her. Lucy was both furious and exhilarated. Nothing would be more gratifying than rescuing her beloved cousin from the clutches of the enemy.

Before going to the airport to fetch Maria, she spent the morning at the library perusing women's studies subjects alphabetically, starting with abortion, addiction, Jane Austen, birth control, bulimia, breast cancer, childbirth, and Cleopatra, moving on to Mary Daly, daycare, divorce, domestic violence. Then as time ran short, she began skimming: motherhood, menopause, Georgia O'Keeffe, osteoporosis, poverty, Roe v. Wade, Sappho, tubal ligations, uterine cancer, wages, witch burnings, and the vote. She wondered how she'd heretofore avoided this topic. It hit her there in the 35334 isle, like a ton of hardbacks crashing down on her head. "Woman is the nigger of the world," as John Lennon had said. All those years she'd failed to address the one injustice that was most ingrained. Even in the movement, brilliant women made coffee and typed, while less brilliant men held rank. She counted the times her own ideas weren't respected until they were snatched up and restated by a man. Never, in all her learning, had a revelation been so suddenly and so sweepingly clear.

By the time Maria's plane arrived, Lucy had already formed the master plan. As these two had frolicked hand-in-hand over the hills of childhood, so they would conquer the rough terrains of womanhood together. They'd join the National Organization for Women and the Women's International League for Peace and Freedom. They'd head up fundraisers for rape relief and the shelter for battered women. Lucy thrilled with joy, almost skipping through the airport just to think of it: The cousins, together again, only now as two full-grown, first-class women warriors for peace and justice. They'd mobilize their mission immediately.

At the arrival gate, Lucy looked eagerly past the puffy, luteous, young woman dragging up the ramp. When she realized it was Maria, the breath caught in her throat and could go neither in nor out. She swallowed a gulp of air when Maria threw her bag down and ran to her in tears, looking like their fat cousin Rosa after they'd dropped her sweet-bread down the well, whimpering like Mother after her miscarriage.

Lucy's strategic plans disappeared like seedlings in a flash flood. Maria's sniffles and moans seemed neverending and Lucy grew jumpier with each baleful sound. Why couldn't her cousin get ahold of herself? They tried to talk, but their words jammed up their throats like red lights at rush hour. Where and what they would eat became a topic of enormous difficulty, fraught with monumental self-doubts, testy judgments, and hurtful withdrawals.

Lucy couldn't see one ounce of fierceness in Maria's weary flesh. She couldn't bear to think of Maria sitting around festering like a giant boil. She wouldn't get free of Boots without a fight, so they'd have to hire a lawyer with big guns. That night before bed, she tossed Maria a women's resource guide. Without so much as a drop of her usual eloquence, she grunted that Maria should look under "L" for "Legal" and get counsel. Lucy meant counsel as in attorney, *abogado* —a fierce courtroom lawyer. She'd been after Maria to press assault charges and sue for divorce on the grounds of physical and mental cruelty.

At this point in Lucy's story, Maria's eagle brows came together flanking an anger line splitting her forehead. Lucy backed off to let Maria take over. She explained that courtrooms were obscenely public, and completely out of the question. She'd watched reruns of *Divorce Court,* and knew how ruthless lawyers could be. Boots would convince the court that Maria had contrived charges, that she was merely conniving for citizenship and wealth. Even if things could be settled out of court, in her favor, as Lucy predicted, Maria hated the thought of official papers stating for all eternity that she was a battered wife.

She was intent on finding someone discrete to talk to—someone who'd listen to her whole story—someone on the order of Oprah Winfrey, say, but not so talkative and certainly not so public. Thumbing through the pages she came upon a heading under "C" for "Counselors and Therapists." The next day, after Lucy had gone to work, Maria took down the numbers of the female counselors with the most appealing names. Mine was fifth on her list. Lucy wrinkled her nose at Maria's version, but Maria threw her a fierce glance and she held her tongue.

I remembered the day Maria's call happened to catch me at lunch, halfway through a very juicy Reuben. I apologized for a couple of slurps. Now Maria explained to Lucy and me that the Reuben was one of two ingredients which had brought us together. "I chose Erica," she explained, "because I felt relaxed right away when you smacked your lips. And even though your Spanish is quite rusty, you had seen my homeland, and the Quiché people. I thought, 'Here is someone who will look at me and see more than a battered wife. She will think of lakes and mountains and handsome people when she sees me.' You and Lucy are perhaps the only ones who look at me and think good things." Now Lucy nodded in agreement, seeing the overall wisdom in her favorite cousin's roundabout ways.

What Grandmother Would Say

That first year, Maria lived on whatever cash she could earn cleaning. Paying me was a stretch. I decided to offer her my service free of charge, reasoning that it could take the place of a volunteer job I'd just finished. And besides, if you tallied up the amount of enjoyment I'd gained from the art and myths of her grandmother's people, I'd already come out ahead. What my reasoning overlooked, was Maria's already meager dignity. "Thank you, Erica," she said, "but as my grandmother would say, 'Charity fattens the belly and starves the pride.'" The soul-truth of Grandmother's proverb turned my offer upside down, and revealed it for what it was—a blatant error. Despite tough times, Maria saw paying for therapy as a step toward building her own life.

Shame was the worst part of poverty for Maria, and she fumed at the irony of Boots courting her from afar with expensive gifts. "The delivery boy who brings flowers is far better paid than me!" Maria exclaimed. "But he still stands there waiting for a tip. I wish he would deliver money instead. It is ridiculous to have fresh flowers when I can hardly pay rent." A month later she pawned a bracelet Boots sent for their anniversary and carefully apportioned the cash to get through the tough months to come.

Maria studied the tight confines of her dilemma: "I cannot go back to Boots, and I cannot go home, either. If I go home to my village like this, fat and beaten down, people will whisper about me for the rest of my life. If I could go home as a wife in mourning and say my husband died, I could meet someone new and start over. But everyone knows my husband. They buy from his company. I could never start over at home. I have to do it here, like Lucy, but I do not know how. Can you see, Erica?"

Sometimes I urged her to find traces of her own will in the picture. "Maria," I'd say, "maybe part of you wants a new life here, not just because old options are closed, but because life here intrigues you."

"You sound like Lucy. She says I am not helpless, I am a strong woman with a future of my own. I just do not see it. All I can see is my past in ruin." Like an earthquake victim, Maria scoured the scattered remains in disbelief, hoping to find meaning in her study of the rubble around her. Then one day, this powerful dream came to guide us:

"In this dream, I gaze at the moon in the night sky. It is so full and bright, it makes the clouds glow. It is so close, I reach up to touch it. Then what is beautiful goes wrong. The moon starts to melt. It drips like a broken egg. It runs down the hillside and then just evaporates into the dark. It gives me a sinking feeling like I have ruined everything. I woke up and couldn't go back to sleep after that. I fear that is what I've done to my life—ruined everything."

The full moon within reach must have been like the hopeful swell in her heart as she reached for a life with her prosperous man. But as she reached to possess its fullness, it melted into darkness. It seemed like something I'd seen before—a déjà vu, carrying a familiar dread. The dream could have been a lament sung in the soulful cante jondo of her Spanish ancestors. It also reminded me of the sad tale of IxChel, the Mayan moon goddess. Maria's grandmother came to mind, as one whose pithy wisdom might assist us.

"I wonder how your grandmother would interpret it," I said.

Maria didn't answer. She looked at me as if I'd offered something of substance for her to chew on. At last she said, "Grandmother might say the moon and I share something in common. Perhaps I am like the moon, growing dark and sad now, only to shine again when the time comes." This was the first bit of forward-looking optimism to come from Maria's lips that year. If I'd said it, it might have been dismissed as an effort to cheer her, but coming from Grandmother, it had an authoritative ring.

That day secured "Grandmother" as a central reference point in Maria's healing. Grandmother's words came to her via memories or equally vivid imaginings of what she might say were she questioned on a given matter. The timely probe, "What do you suppose Grandmother would say?"often opened the the right door at the right moment.

Maria's likeness to the moon turned out to be the single most significant door. Determined to make use of it, I scoured several texts and learned that the Mayan moon goddess, IxChel, did indeed have a great deal in common with Maria. She too, was a battered wife. Piecing together the tale, I felt I'd struck gold, or at least discovered good solid bedrock where Maria might hew the cornerstones of her new life. During our next visit, I asked if she knew the story. She recalled museum visits when she'd been drawn to a beautiful stone carving of IxChel's serene face. She was eager to hear the tale.

Her Former Brilliance

Long ago IxChel, the moon, shone as brightly as the sun. There was no such thing as darkness then, for her brilliance filled every corner of the night sky with light. Drawn to her beauty, fiery Sun came to woo her. But IxChel's possessive grandfather guarded her closely, and forbade male guests to visit Moon Palace.

To fool the old man, clever Sun changed himself to a hummingbird. He sampled the nectars in IxChel's garden and caught her eye by flashing ruby and green among tobacco blooms. But suspicious Grandfather shot the shape-shifter with clay pellets. Sun fell, exactly as he'd intended, into IxChel's tender hands. Shunning Grandfather's cruelty, she nursed the wounded bird and her

fondness for it grew. Her affection washed over him—a healing tonic, a love-balm.

As Sun healed, he couldn't conceal his surging heat. His passions exploded. IxChel lept willingly into the blaze and lost all sense of where she left off and he began. He swore they'd rule the heavens side by side, their love bombarding the universe, piercing the clouds, bathing the heavenly bodies in their luscious glow. IxChel followed willingly, leaving Moon Palace forever.

But Grandfather was no fool. He sent the storm god Chak in pursuit. IxChel and Sun fled up the cosmic stream in a dug-out canoe. When Chak threw lightning IxChel changed herself to a red crab and dove under. Sun changed himself to a mottled turtle and followed. Chak's lightning bolts penetrated the depths and struck IxChel. Lifeless, she sank to the bottomless dark.

Her admirers, the dragonflies, found her. They gathered by the thousands to mourn her, using her canoe as a coffin. They formed a cloud over IxChel and hummed dirges night and day. Their songs called her spirit back from the dead, and her glow slowly returned. Her former brilliance was at last restored. She and Sun set the sky ablaze—together again as the brightest couple in the universe. Grandfather conceded and sadly closed Moon Palace forever.

IxChel and Sun lit the heavens side by side for a short while. Then Sun grew tired of sharing the throne. He missed the days when his light alone awed the daytime sky. He grew to despise IxChel and brooded jealously when others gazed upon her. At first he threw fierce looks when guests lingered near. Later he began to shush her speech. He wanted no peer in heaven. To woo and win her, yes; to possess her as his jewel, of course; but to shine side by side; nevermore!

IxChel, knew nothing of dimness. She was born to shine brightly for all to see, and that she did. Sun's rage flared. He hit her again and again, dimming her brightness with each blow, until her hot light turned cool and pale.

But her radiant core couldn't be snuffed. Admirers still gazed at her with love. At last, he kicked full force, knocking her down from heaven, to the earth below. IxChel landed at the foot of a volcano, not far from your village.

"Yes, I know the volcano you mean," Maria nodded, "but what happened then? Surely she did not die."

No, indeed, she merely collapsed in exhaustion. It happened that the vulture king flew by overhead. He looked down and saw the fallen IxChel. Moved by her sorrow and beauty, he swept down, scooped her up and took her to the vulture palace high in the fog atop the mountain peak. There he cared tenderly for her. She accepted the vulture king's kindness and gradually came to love him.

When Sun learned of their contentment, he wanted to destroy it. He put his cunning to work on a new trick. He changed himself into a flea and hid in a deer carcass, knowing the vultures would deliver it to their king. As soon as they brought it to the palace, Sun burst forth in all his brilliance, speaking words of love to win IxChel. Though she loved the vulture king, he looked hollow and frail compared to her husband, the sun. Sun enticed her to join him once more.

But nothing really changed. It wasn't long before Sun's accusations again turned to blows. This time IxChel didn't wait to see how far it would go. She made up her mind to leave and never come near him again. She returned to her own realm, that of the night sky, where she still rules today. She vowed to lead a solitary life and travel on her own path ever after. She has never regained her former brightness, and this is how the darkness of night came to be.

IxChel remains a faint lantern in the night sky, shedding a pale glow, and people still call her the beauty of heaven. Sun still tries to pursue her, but she manages to keep her distance. She rules the sea, the tides, the rain, and the night. She rules women's fertile cycles, midwifery, and hand crafts such as weaving. Farmers, weavers, and expectant mothers still seek her blessings. IxChel is content with her own domain.

"It is good she found her domain," Maria said making fists, "but that bastard Sun infuriates me. He does not pay for his wrongs! Yet IxChel is punished for simply being herself. That is so true to life. Boots used to punish me for being myself. He said, 'Maria, you are pretty enough to marry, but too pretty to be any man's wife, that is your trouble. No man wants other guys gawking at his wife.' He blamed me if a man merely glanced my way. Perhaps men did admire me, but no harm came of it. In reality, Boots is the one who makes a show everywhere he goes. He speaks loudly and struts those fancy boots and hats. He is so full of contradictions. On the one hand I was to be his prize—something to show off. On the other hand I was to be invisible. How could I win, Erica?" The story uncorked Maria's long-stowed wrath. For a few moments she huffed and fumed.

"I'll tell you how bad it was. One time I handed our plumber his wrench, and Boots accused me of flirting with the poor man, a bald guy with a big fat ass and pants that hang down to here." She marked a spot halfway down her rump and cracked up laughing until the tears flowed. Then her eyes flared, "I tried so hard to be invisible when men were around, so he would not blame me if they looked my way. Imagine trying to be both attractive and invisible! No wonder I failed. Boots won, just like the sun. He won because he is still shining. Look at me. I am the one who faded."

I expected her tirade to continue, but she quickly shifted toward the ever-gnawing question of self-blame. I hoped the heat of her rage would melt it.

"Lucy says I made things worse by staying as long as I did. But you know, Erica, I felt obligated to stay. In my family the woman serves the man, even if the man is wrong. Besides, I felt sorry for him. I hoped to heal the heartbreak of his first marriage. Can you understand a love like that, Erica?"

"Yes," I said. "It must be like IxChel's attraction to the wounded bird."

"Dios Mio, yes! But why is a hurt man so attractive?" Maria covered her face like an embarrassed girl caught with her hand in the cookie jar. "I saw myself as the special one who could heal him with love. His first wife married him for money and he knew it. She ran off with someone else when she got the chance. I don't blame her. I often longed for a kinder man. Sometimes I wonder if Boots read my mind. I ask myself over and over, 'Did he beat me because I wished for another man? Did my secret thoughts poison our marriage?' I thought if I could love him enough he would become a better man."

She looked me in the eye as if I had the power to divine the truth. Had she unwittingly driven Boots to beat her? Had she failed to love him properly? Or was she, like IxChel, simply seduced into a marriage doomed from the start?

It was time for me to get tough. "Maria, how long are you going to blame yourself for failing to reform him? How long are you going to worry whether one person's thoughts cause another person's actions? Why are you so devoted to blaming yourself?"

Maria burst into tears. "I did not think it was necessary to talk about Joaquin. Now I see Lucy is right. I can never sort this out without talking about him. Love is so difficult. I am not ready to talk about this. Next week," she said with an enormous sob. "Next week I will talk about my *true* love. Dios mio, I am so confused. I no longer know what to think. Perhaps Joaquin is not my true love, either. Perhaps he too, is a wounded bird!" We were out of time, but neither of us would forget where she'd left off.

Hummingbird and Vulture King

She came to the next visit ready to delve into the hidden reaches of her story. "I never told you about Joaquin," she said sighing deeply, "because I hoped to have put him behind me. I hoped my love for him had nothing to do with my problems of today. But when you said I keep blaming myself, well, I realized that deep inside I blame my love for him. Joaquin was my first love. I never really let go of that love—not when I married Boots—not even to this day.

"I loved Joaquin since the age of seven. His mother had tuberculosis. I used to go to their house everyday with Grandmother to take them food and to help his mother bathe. My grandmother would make her bed and comb her hair. Joaquin and I played outside together. We made our own little house in the bamboo. We played we were married, and promised to be true to each other for life. When we played with other kids we played bandits or ball games. The rest was a secret just between us.

"When we got older, age thirteen, Joaquin got sick. He got TB and soon after that, his mother died. I wouldn't let my grandmother feed him. I wanted to do that myself. She bathed him and combed his hair, but I fed him. I thought of him night and day and was by his side as much as my parents would allow. The more he needed me, the more I loved him, like IxChel with the hummingbird. But it was different for Joaquin. My caring for him day by day did not cement his love for me. It hurt his pride and made him turn away from me. He recovered after a year, but it was never the same between us. He became stern and distant, denying our secrets. He seemed to care only about proving his strength to other boys.

"So you see, Boots was not the first to break my heart. In my teen years I believed Joaquin would get over his shame and we would be together again. But when we were nineteen, while I was away at school, he married someone else—a very quiet, pious woman. That squashed my hopes, of course. They had four kids last time I heard. Joaquin is running one of my father's farms now. But he is still cold and unfamiliar with me, and Grandmother says it is better that way." Maria stared out the window as if lost in the past.

"And this is tied to your self-blame about your marriage?" I asked, grasping the loose threads of the present.

"Yes. When Boots was cruel, I used to long for Joaquin. The more Boots hit me, the more I wished for Joaquin's gentle touch. It seemed like Boots read my mind, because those were the times he accused me of wanting another man."

Maria still longed for Joaquin—or rather, the ambrosial Joaquin rarefied by memory—whenever she felt depressed or lonely. When she was most downhearted, she plunged into lengthy "Joaquin fantasies" fueled by unspent desire. Fantasy scenarios began with Maria in the nursing role, approaching frail Joaquin's bedside. "Treatments" involved compresses and gentle massage, which lead to erotic caresses, followed by ecstatic lovemaking and blissful calm.

In reality, Boots was Maria's first and only sexual partner and his brutality had overshadowed their sex life. She longed for an adult version of the tender sexual feelings of her childhood. After much rumination on the Joaquin fantasies, Maria concluded that the role of the lustful nurse offered certain psychological advantages. The bedridden fantasy lover neither rejected nor bullied her as Joaquin and Boots had done. He allowed her to "be in charge" sexually, something she'd never experienced in life, but secretly longed for.

Maria felt embarrassed that she still found the "wounded bird" so compelling. She also feared wasting warm-blooded life passion on a dead-end fantasy. I asked Maria if the fantasy was a temporary haven, as the vulture palace was for IxChel, or if she planned to spend her life nursing a phantasm. Once she'd had a good laugh over the similarity of the words *phantasm* and *orgasm*, Maria nursed the notion that her fixation might be transitional. She added that food was another "vulture king." She fled to chocolate as a source of solace in the dark hours.

"What did your grandmother mean," I asked, "when she said it's best that you and Joaquin went separate ways?"

"Grandmother said I have more *face* than Joaquin." I must have looked puzzled for Maria explained without my having to ask, "She means I have more power, more spirit, I guess. She thinks my spirit is more matched to Lucy and that I adored Joaquin because he needed me, the way a woman loves a child."

"The way IxChel loved the hummingbird," I added.

"Yes, like that. She loves it because it is beautiful, and because hurt things attract a woman's love. I loved Joaquin like he was my wounded bird to nurse and protect. That love healed him but took away his pride. Then he had to find a woman he could protect, one who made him feel strong. Grandmother said his spirit is better matched to his wife."

"Is she right?" I asked.

"Yes, I think she is right."

"So in reality, you and Joaquin wouldn't make a good match?" I asked. Maria nodded. She had no qualms with the logical truth. I pushed to learn more about Grandmother's point of view. "What does your grandmother mean when she says you and Lucy have matched spirits?"

"She says we are sister-cousins, meant to learn from each other. She says everything we ever learned, we learned from watching the other. Walking, talking, reading, writing, driving, everything, one of us learned first, and the other followed.

"My parents feel it is very strange I stay in Seattle with Lucy, but Grandmother says it is natural. She feels my spirit will get strong again if I stay near Lucy. She says I will learn my own way of mastery around Lucy but not around Boots. She says a woman will share mastery with another woman, but a man like Boots will use his mastery to keep the woman down."

I wished I could hire Grandmother to lead a battered women's support group. "So, Grandmother feels you can learn your own way of mastery," I said. "What about you? Do you feel that?"

"When my spirit gets strong again, then I hope to learn my own way of mastery. Like IxChel, I hope to find my own domain. I think if I can do it, it will be better than trying to fit into Boots's domain, or Joaquin's. What I do not want any longer, is to try to make myself dim to put a man at ease. I do not want to pretend, like young girls do, to be weak or silly, to help a man feel strong. If I find another man, I hope he will be strong on his own—strong enough to appreciate my glow. Do you understand, Erica?"

I nodded. Maria had brought tears to my eyes. I understood everything she and Grandmother said about face, spirit, and mastery, not as a detached witness, but as a woman whose own faded parts sought repair. I felt my blood surge as if my grandmothers spoke from deep inside my veins, "Yes, yes, yes, Maria, we understand." That conversation marked a turning point. Maria's glow began to return, gradually but steadily dissipating the dank sorrow and self-blame, lighting the way toward her new life.

Her Own Domain

On the work scene, things started looking up. When the son of Maria's favorite cleaning client was flunking high school Spanish, Maria landed the job of helping him hoist his grades. When his girlfriend needed help with French, Maria got hired for the job. She had a knack for working with youngsters, and they helped her feel more a part of mainstream U.S.A. "The kids got me using English contractions," she said one day, implying that Lucy and I had left her out in the cold. Maria had all the skills to set up a legitimate tutoring service, but was barred from doing so because of interminable foul-ups with immigration papers and work permits. For months, she waited in limbo, keeping a low profile despite her growing popularity as a tutor. She felt uneasy accepting cash under the table, but providence was finally providing the cornerstone of her new life, and she felt it was no time to let red tape interfere.

Meanwhile Boots continued to make trouble. He pulled numerous tricks to perpetuate bungles at the Department of Immigrations, including losing the marriage license, telling authorities Maria had taken him for a ride, and insisting she was "only scamming citizenship." Luckily Lucy knew the ropes forward and back. She could unravel red tape as fast as Boots could ball it up.

Boots seemed to sense Maria was finding her own domain. "Either he has a sixth sense, or he has a spy after me," Maria said about his uncanny ability to "plant quicksand" in her path. The quicksand took many forms, including attempts to manipulate Maria's parents. At one point he had them believing Maria was in trouble, and it was in her best interest to go back to him. They wrote her an empty letter saying a woman's place is with her man. She read between the lines. "They know Boots is bad for me. That's why the words in this letter have no strength. They don't know how to help, so they write empty words."

The good of Boots's meddling was that it forced Maria to level with her parents: to tell them how wrong they'd been about Boots, and what a hellish mistake her marriage had been. They asked her to come home for "just a visit," but Maria said she needed to get better settled first.

Boots played every angle, including sending his mother to Seattle to pressure Maria to go back to him. The mother-in-law made
the mistake of warning Maria of the perils a "Chicana" faces without a white man to protect her. "I'm not a Chicana!" Maria fumed,
"Neither Boots nor his mother ever bothered to figure out who I
am. I'm not a Mexicana! My grandmother is an indigenous, Maya
Quiché woman! My parents are Ladinos with roots in Spain. Is that
so difficult?

"I told that hateful woman her son Boots has done everything
but protect me. I said I'd have been safer with Manuel Noriega. She
looked at me with a blank face and asked, 'Who is Man-Well Nor-
yay-gah, Dear?'! Erica, I ask you, what ever possessed me to marry
into such an ignorant family?"

But there was a brief spell when her firm resolve wavered. She
was broke due to her students' spring break and alone due to Lucy
jaunting off to the rain forest with her botanist sweetheart. Maria
stayed in bed all day that Friday and let the old Joaquin fantasies
roll. When the mail arrived around four, she received two parcels,
one from her parents and one from Boots. Her parents had sent an
Easter gift and a card with a news update. Joaquin's wife had just
birthed child number five and Grandmother was laid up with a
broken rib. A confusing panic came over Maria. Only later would
we sort it out as a mixture of envy and grief.

Her better judgment fell by the wayside and so did her policy of
returning Boots's gifts unopened. She tore open Boots's package
and found a basket laden with her favorite hand-made chocolate
eggs and a letter. She began devouring the eggs and read what she
later called "the most seductive letter Boots could have sent." In it
he took an unusually humble, contrite tone. He explained at length
that he'd given up booze and cocaine, and had undergone a complete metamorphosis. His new doctor had concluded that the toxic
nature of the drugs had altered his personality, causing him to have
"spells" in which he hurt Maria without realizing it. Now that he'd
sobered up, they could begin their happy life together. Enclosed
was a note from the doctor, verifying the same. For three days,
Maria kept the shades down, consumed two pounds of chocolate
eggs, and paced around in the dark, vacillating between grief, confusion, and fantastical hope.

On Monday Maria and I reviewed the episode together. Her dark weekend lingered like a strange, intense dream. Combing through it at length, we gained deeper insight into her greedy kinship to chocolate. Binges began as efforts to comfort herself, to recreate the warmth she felt while sitting on Grandmother's lap, sipping hot chocolate as a girl. The beverage of her childhood contained very little sweetener and only a shave of chocolate, thereby yielding warm milk's sedative effect. But the double-dark chocolate eggs from Boots were a different story. Heavy on sugar and caffeine, the dark chocolates fueled anxiety and upset her stomach. Their dark richness offered decadent consolations which Maria likened to the vulture palace—seductive, indulgent, but ultimately unsettling.

Discussing chocolate's hold on her seemed to break its spell. She went on to speak with pathos and humor about the other triggers which had set her off. "I was so broke, I couldn't even afford a movie. And Lucy pissed me off, flaunting her lover in my face. Then that letter from my parents . . . I burned with envy to read about Joaquin's fifth baby. It's not that I want a baby right away—it's just that my parents tout it as a symbol of completion—and I feel so incomplete! And on top of that . . . Grandmother's injury! It frightens me to know she's hurt and I'm not there to help her. With everything so uncertain, I find Boots's recovery very seductive. Perhaps there is hope for our marriage, after all."

Something told me her weekend crisis was not a setback, but perhaps the final, inevitable drama in the vulture palace. Before the old ghosts could let her go, they had to seize her tightly, and tempt her one last time. I made one suggestion. "Maria, since you're seduced by the thought of Boots's recovery, why don't you see if there's any truth to it?"

On her way home that day, Maria stopped at the library for a Chicago phone book. She looked up the new doctor and discovered the same address as Boots's old friend, the foot doctor. "You remember, *Dr. Cocaine*, don't you, Erica?" she asked later. "The one who fixed my shoulder. The one who smokes dope and sniffs cocaine with Boots. Boots must take me for a fool! I don't need to look any further into this 'recovery' to know it's completely bogus!" She emphasized the word *bogus* the way her students did, right out of a pop movie. Hearing a word once was all she needed to carve out a spot in her vocabulary and claim it as hers. I knew it wouldn't be long before she'd carved out her own domain and claimed her new life. She'd unveiled Boots's final enticement as a powerless ruse. His seductive spell over her was now completely broken.

Maria resumed the work of establishing her own domain. That meant lots of official paperwork: immigration papers, work permits, a business license, and a tax number. It also meant getting divorced. Boots's new girlfriend, eager to be his wife, pushed him to divorce Maria. Maria felt obligated to warn the woman of Boots's violent history, so she phoned her. "I could tell she was drunk by the way she slurred her words," Maria told me later. "She started attacking me, calling me a Mexican whore. I could see I might as well try to warn a viper, so I hung up. Perhaps they're suited for each other. If she doesn't already know about Boots, I guess she's going to learn the hard way."

In the end, the divorce went more smoothly than expected, and it looked as if the financial settlement would enable Maria, not only to get her business off the ground, but to invest in a duplex where she could live and run her business under one roof. She and Lucy were overjoyed discussing the possibilities. They intended to set up an office in the basement for their Sanctuary work aiding exiled Mayans.

When the divorce papers came through, Maria had another weekend panic. She again started to gorge on chocolate, but this time she stopped herself and phoned me, hoping to reroute her anxiety. She felt terrified of her new life and all the unknowns it created. She rattled off a litany of burdens she'd have to bear for evermore: the mortgage, the taxes, the billing statements, tutoring certification, advertising, insurance, getting a driver's license, and so on. She talked as if the bureaucratic details of her new life would be harsher than having the shine beat out of her. I reminded her that she'd attended to more difficult matters over the past months with Boots working against her and that all these bothersome duties would be easier with him out of her hair.

She burst into tears, "That's just it. When he was in my hair, at least I knew someone cared. Someone sought after me. Now I'll be forgotten. Think about it, Erica. When we say IxChel finds her own domain, we talk like that's a good thing, but it's very lonely. Can you see the moon outside your window?" I craned my neck to look out at the eastern sky. Sure enough, the wintry moon hung there in all her muted glory. "Look at that moon, Erica, and tell me it's not bleak."

Maria had a point. I hadn't anticipated the loss of Boots's bizarre attentions as cause for grief, but there it was. Like the previous weekend crisis, I figured this one indicated an old ghost's last stand: Maria the clinging bride, throwing a final fit at the loss of her prosperous man before embarking on her new life as a woman of stature in her own domain.

"Maria, divorce means you're free to pursue your new life. Is that so bleak?" Her silence made me wonder if the line had gone dead. It was time to call upon a higher authority. "If Grandmother were on the line, what would she say about it?"

"Well," Maria said finally, "Grandmother always said I'd be a teacher. When I was young, I made my sisters play school. In college I tutored North American students, not because I needed money, but because I love to teach."

"You're a single woman with a calling in life . . . like IxChel."

"Yes, a calling to teach, and to help Lucy with the Sanctuary program."

"It doesn't sound bleak to me."

"No," said Maria, "in truth, it's not bleak."

"What's your plan for the weekend?" I asked.

"Well, that's what's really making me nervous. We're having a fundraising dinner for Sanctuary."

"Who's we?"

"Oh, lots of people. But I'll be sitting with Lucy and her boyfriend and some faculty people from the university."

"Doesn't sound bleak, Maria."

"No, you're right, Erica, It's not bleak, but I have a new dress to wear, and I'm very nervous because several nice men will be there, and I don't know whether to be attractive or invisible. Can you understand?"

"Sure. What part of you wants to be invisible?"

"The terrified part."

"And what part wants to be attractive?"

"The part who wants new friends and a new life."

"Are you still looking at the moon?" I asked.

"Yes."

"When you look at the moon, which part do you see?"

"I see the part that wants to hide," Maria said, "but she's so exposed, she can't hide."

"I can see that too, but I also see something else. I see radiance that draws the eye, and reminds me why lovers gaze at the moon. Do you remember when you dreamt of the moon? You said you and she both had grown dim. The first hopeful thing I ever heard you say was that perhaps like the moon, you too, would shine again someday. Well, Maria, perhaps you're nervous because that day has arrived."

"Perhaps yes, Erica. All I know is, I'm going to wear a nice dress, and I'm terrified."

"And you probably won't be invisible."

"No, I never was any good at it, really."

Not long after that, Maria said that everything had shifted. She now stood squarely on her own two feet in her own domain. We both sensed it was the beginning of the end of our work. Much affection had grown between us, and we grew teary anticipating the end. But before leaving, she wanted to address one final issue: her weight. She'd managed to avoid chocolate for months and felt confident the binges were over, but her weight still stayed about twenty pounds above her "comfortable size."

I said weight could be a tricky completion goal. The part of her that wished to stay with me might thwart efforts to slim down as a way of sticking around. But Maria was two steps ahead. "What worries me Erica," she said grinning slyly, raising her eagle-wing brows, "is that the part of you who wants me to stick around will secretly support my overeating."

"Yes," I said, "that's possible too. What do you suppose your grandmother would say?" At this, she burst out laughing. The familiar koan which had once been our most profound tool, now seemed superfluous. The old question which had guided us through the dark, now made us laugh nostalgically at old times, and reminded us how far Maria had come. But in the final months, we did rely on the old, familiar grandmotherly guidance on two remaining issues: weight and Maria's relationship with Lucy.

The inner grandmother insisted the extra weight was due to the "bad food" up north. It was true that Maria nibbled junk food all day. In her youth, the family had sat down for large ladino meals, but Maria preferred to skip the dining room scene. She had snacked in the kitchen instead, chatting with Grandmother, freely nibbling vegetables, fruits, and tortillas. The weight gain had started up north, when Maria replaced fresh munchies with fatty processed snacks. Determined to slim down, she banished junk food and learned where to buy fresh tortillas, nice cuts of lean meat, beans, fresh vegies, and fruits. Getting back to traditional foods allowed her to nibble all day and still drop a pound every few weeks.

The new life also called for change in her relationship with Lucy. Maria started tutoring international business executives, a lucrative endeavor which allowed her to hire and train a small staff of Spanish-speaking tutors. Maria was proud of her expanding domain, and expected Lucy to be proud, too. After all, hadn't she managed to "build her own life?" And wasn't it wonderful to help minority employees do the same? Surely Lucy should appreciate this more than anyone. But as Maria's domain grew, so did Lucy's criticism. Maria's new status was suddenly subject to minute scrutiny, and Lucy found fault in her every move. "She taught me for many years," Maria observed. "Now she's mad at me because I have a few things to teach her." The inner grandmother urged Maria to "press Lucy" to respect her, not as a younger cousin, but as a peer. After a few snarly battles, and prolonged silences, the cousins amicably readjusted, easing into a womanly parity for the first time.

Maria and I said good-bye three and a half years after our first conversation. Occasionally I saw her ad in the local paper, and she phoned me once, for a referral for one of her troubled students. A year later, I got a letter from her, postmarked "Guatemala."

Querida Erica,

Lucy and I are visiting our grandmother back home on the finca. She is dying and she asked us to be with her. We closed up shop for a month to be by her side. Luckily none of my students have exams during that time!

We went over the whole story about Boots and me, and how I fled to Lucy. Grandmother wanted to know about you, and about how I started the business and all. We reminded her that we'd already written to the family about most of it, but she either forgot, or she just likes to hear it again. She says it's remarkable that today a woman can have her own life, and she thinks Lucy and I are wonderful. She was very impressed to learn you know Mayan stories. Sometimes she lapses and babbles and forgets. Then other times she remembers everything so clearly and says such wise things. Yesterday she said Lucy taught me how a woman could be strong and I taught her how a woman could make money! Lucy admitted it was true.

After she dies, Lucy and I plan to make a trip to Cozumel. Lucy's husband will come down to meet her and they plan to snorkel on the coral reef. I decided to go too. You probably know IxChel's shrine is there, and I think it would be fitting to say a prayer there for my grandmother before I come home. (Notice how the word "home" now means Seattle.)

Lucy's father, my parents, and my sisters are here too, of course. I was afraid my parents would treat me like a failure because of my divorce, but they have accepted it, and I think they're secretly proud of my self-reliance. My middle sister wants to come to Seattle and work with me, but is afraid to ask Mother and Father. Grandmother says, "Why not give it a try?" I am seriously considering it.

Lucy and I went to the capital to visit the Sanctuary office. All these years of sending money and blankets, we finally met the staff face to face. It's a really tiny basement office behind a bakery, but the woman who runs it, Paula, was in great spirits and it was a joy to finally shake her hand.

Joaquin's second son hangs out at my parent's house. He took to me right away. He looks so much like Joaquin, it was déjà vu. He asked if I could teach him English while I'm here. I said if his parents approved, yes. I was surprised when they said yes. Joaquin shows no sign of remembering our special friendship as children, and I myself feel very distant from my old feelings for him. He's a good man, but Grandmother was right. It's so obvious our spirits don't match. That's plain to see now.

Being here makes me realize how glad I am to have made my home up north. I'm getting serious about a very sweet man who teaches at the university. He writes wonderful poetry, and I think I mentioned him to you years ago. Don't be surprised if you get a wedding invitation from us one of these days!

Hope you are well and not depressed by the rain back home. I will say a prayer for you at IxChel's shrine.

Love and good wishes,

Maria

—— 12 ——

Irene and the Healing Powers of Story

A Pragmatic Teaching Tale for Those Hungry for Explanations as to How Healing Stories Work

A mythos is more than a theory, more than a plot. It is the tale of interaction between humans and the divine.

—James Hillman

"Every fall it hits," Irene groaned. "The daylight hours get briefer and briefer till I'm riding to work in the dark and coming home in the dark. The clouds close in and the rain starts. If I scrape together the fortitude to go out at lunch time, the wind sucks my umbrella inside out, flips my hat into the gutter, and whips the front of my coat up into my face. It's so depressing. If I win the lottery, I'll move to Mexico in a heartbeat, and I won't need you any more, Erica—no offense intended."

For years Irene had used special lamps, anti-depressants, herbs, and acupuncture to curb her seasonal depression. Gradually she'd come to suspect unresolved emotional issues played a part. At the age of twenty-seven, after a painful divorce she turned to therapy to help sort things out.

In college she'd studied mythology and had a love-hate relationship with Greek myths. Her father, an American of Greek origin, had abandoned her as a child. She found that Greek myths mirrored her own world view. As she put it, "Males have freedom and females pay the price." For several reasons she reacted strongly to the story of Kore* (KO-re) and Demeter (de-MEE-ter). Her great longing for security, warmth, and leisure was aroused when she imagined the abundant grain goddess, Demeter, strolling through sunny fields picking wild flowers with her daughter, Kore. The two goddesses passed each day of the never-ending summer in undisturbed joy and harmony. Irene felt jealous when she compared it to her own girlhood. "I was never carefree," she complained. "I never got enough of summertime or of my mother's attention." Irene felt her youth had been cut short. Her mother was forced to work long hours for minimum wage, just to keep a roof over their heads. Irene, an only child, had no choice but to cook, keep house, and spend long hours alone. The beginning of the story was the antithesis of her early years and brought up great longing. Other parts of the story repelled her: powerful males pulling rank, calling the shots, or using brute force against females. The intensity of her reaction was a sure sign that the story held therapeutic worth for her. *The first healing power of story is its ability to arouse strong emotions.* We heal best when we're powerfully engaged. When genuine emotions heat up and come to the surface, the psyche grows ripe for change, and new learning makes a deep impression.

The second healing power of story is that of identification. Irene had no trouble identifying with Kore. Demeter left Kore unprotected one day, leaving her quite vulnerable when Hades, god of the underworld, appeared without warning, raped and abducted her. Irene often felt unprotected and vulnerable to the dubious whims of others. Her mother remarried when she was twelve, and her teen years were plagued by her stepfather's sexual advances. Finding a mythic heroine who shared her pain decreased Irene's shame and isolation, and sparked hope for a positive future.

---

*See my retelling of the Greek myth of Kore in the appendix, p. 271.

*The third healing power of story is its way of helping us exter-
nalize a conflict.* Temporary distance makes room for reflection.
Irene gained perspective on her own dilemma by examining Kore's.
She studied the mother-daughter dynamics in the myth. For the
first time she looked at the possibility that like Demeter, her mother
may have failed to protect her. "Mom was so smitten with Al she
had blinders on. I know she heard him make sexual innuendoes
toward me, but she didn't want to admit there was a problem. I
didn't either, for that matter. Mom was looking for a bit of happiness and I didn't want to spoil it."

*The fourth healing power of story has to do with its ability to
activate long-term memory.* It does this by engaging imagination,
intellect, and feeling in a compelling narrative that is both causal
and mysterious. Not only did Irene remember the story in vivid
detail, it helped revivify her own memories and make sense of her
own story. Over a period of sixteen months she had dreams related
to mythic figures and wrote in her journal about it. As she did so,
she became less depressed and more expressive—more energized
with feelings of all kinds.

*Teaching people to trust emotions is the fifth healing power
of story.* Irene was brought up to hide her emotions. Her mother
told her never to raise her voice. When she cried, her mother scolded
that tears were self-indulgent. In the Catholic school she'd attended
she'd received physical punishment for expressing anger toward
one of the nuns. When she got angry at her stepfather, he mocked
and ridiculed her. As a result, all her strong emotions were accompanied by large doses of shame and humiliation. To avoid these,
she did her best to deny emotions, even to herself.

But looking at the story, she saw that powerful emotions such as
Demeter's rage at the loss of her daughter and Kore's loneliness
were not only justified, they were necessary motivators that led to
resolute action. Irene began to see how her denial of intense emotions had caused depression and added to the frustrations in her
marriage. She couldn't fault the goddesses for their strong reac-
tions to tough situations. This newly expanded tolerance for emotion transferred back to herself. She felt more permission to enter
realms of deep emotion. She wept, griped, fumed, and raged.

As her ire spewed forth, Irene likened her father and stepfather to Hades because their abandonment and abuse forced her into the underworld of depression. She likened her former husband to Zeus, the king of the gods, who surreptitiously allowed Hades to keep Kore in the underworld. "My husband told me not to be depressed, yet he constantly made cruel comments to kept me down." The abduction became a metaphor for depression, and the Zeus-Kore dynamic became a metaphor for her marriage. *This is the sixth healing power of story: providing metaphors for interpersonal dynamics.*

One night Irene dreamt she went to the doctor's office for antidepressant medication. A kind elderly nurse wearing a crescent-moon insignia asked, "What's the problem?" Irene answered, "Depression." But the old woman wrote the words *Self-abduction* under *diagnosis* on Irene's chart. When Irene woke, she wrote in her journal, "I abduct myself into depression." The kind old nurse, like grandmother Hecate in the myth, provided the missing information about abduction.

Irene shifted from blaming others to examining how the hurtful, rejecting voice also came from within. "Whenever I get hopeful or happy, like Kore picking flowers, this aggressive voice in my head starts in, 'Don't bother feeling cheerful, it won't last. You can't do anything right.' I just sink down and give up. Once I'm sunk, the depression is safe. It's like a cocoon. It's safer than trying, and it seems like it's all I deserve, anyway." Earlier, the myth had been a metaphor for her life circumstance. Now with the help of the old nurse, it went deeper. *This is the seventh healing power of story: providing metaphors for internal dynamics.*

In her journal, Irene dialogued with Zeus, the nurse, whom she called, "Crescent-Moon Hecate," and Hades, whom she described as "depression, my shadowy companion." She eventually came to an understanding with Zeus and formed alliances with Hecate and Hades. Hecate became a figure of wisdom and solace. Hades opened up an area of hidden emotion, loneliness, and desire. Irene no longer saw herself a victim of such energy. Instead she found within herself a strong desire to love and be loved. With the help of these two figures she came to feel she could conquer depression.

"I carry these two within me now, like a source of inner strength. Disappointments no longer mean I'm doomed to immobilization." *Internalizing wise, helpful, or comforting figures is the eighth way of drawing healing power from story.*

From Kore Irene learned patience and compromise, characteristics that served her career development and personal life. From Demeter she learned persistent assertiveness which she used in setting limits and protecting herself. *This is the ninth healing power of myth: modeling alternative attitudes and stances which help people cope with hardship and forge new paths.*

Irene equated Zeus with "the strict laws of life." She noted that without him, Kore might have remained a girl forever. As it was she became queen of dark and light domains. Irene saw justice and beauty in the compromise engineered at the end of the myth by Rhea, mother of the gods. She ruled that since Kore had eaten the fruits of the underworld, she was at least partially of the underworld. Part of the year she ruled there, and part of the year she returned to roam the meadows with her mother once again. It is Kore's return to the meadow that brings us springtime after each long winter. Irene saw this as an apt metaphor for life. She came to appreciate the interplay between joy and sorrow, discipline and leisure, aggression and surrender, companionship and solitude. She began to see life as cyclic, consisting of complimentary seasons—some warm and bright—others chilly and dark. *This is the tenth healing power of myth: helping people come to terms with duality, ambivalence, and strife, to move toward a philosophical perspective on life.*

Irene never did win the lottery or move to Mexico. But she did become a less reluctant Seattlite. She came to love the way huge yellow leaves carpet the streets in October, making the stored brightness of summer leap up at her from the autumnal ground. She harvested mushrooms from the woods in November and fresh nettles when their buds first poked through the forest floor come February. She said Kore returned to the Northwest every March, with the hearty crocuses that burst forth overnight and glowed brightly in morning's first light.

The myth of Demeter and Kore calls to many women, but not to all. Others are captivated by passion plays unraveling different themes. When Irene worked with this myth, it became her guide. It penetrated her psyche and activated sleeping potentials. It helped generate a deeper grasp of self, and led to a braver stance in the world.

While Irene worked with the myth, her heart and gut were its primary interpreters. The meaning she gleaned from it sprang forth from the place where her own experience and the myth overlapped. For others in other circumstances, the points of overlap vary, and therefore carry different meaning. This fluidity is precisely what keeps stories alive. The storytelling tradition remains vital because infinite meanings continue to hatch each time a story is told. *The eleventh healing power of story is its capacity to accommodate manifold interpretations, morals, and meanings.*

Irene found a wealth of personal meaning in the myth. But many women today find within it broadly apt universal messages. *The twelfth healing power of story is its applicability to the collective as well as the intricately personal.*

The thirteenth healing power of story is its containment of the sacred, and its conveyance of ancient wisdom. For many women Demeter and Kore have resurfaced as divine expressions of the mysterious cycle of life, death, and rebirth, thus returning the myth to its original function as a basis for ritual and a container for holy mysteries. Whether we're contemplating origin through a creation myth, studying ethics in Bible stories, gleaning psychology from fairy tales, or obtaining the spiritual secrets of sages from Brigid to Nasr-ed-Din, one thing is clear: We're tapping the wisdom of our ancestors. And if you believe as I do, in something called *spirit, muse,* or *inspiration,* then you believe that storytelling calls to life some third presence beyond storyteller and listener. A presence which connects our world to the place the Celts called the *other world,* the home of ancestors and gods. When the powers of both worlds join together, uncanny voices sing, old grudges mend, hard people soften, and silent ones speak. In the end we cannot fully explain why or how story speaks to the psyche and inspires change. Perhaps it has to do with the vast generativity of the imagination, or perhaps myth is simply our language of origin, the mother tongue of the human heart.

── 13 ──

By a
Thread

Stories differ from advice in that once you get them, they become a
fabric of your whole soul. That is why they heal you.

—Alice Walker

Personal stories, on occasion, can be as compelling as myths.
Thirty-some years later, elder storytellers, Fran and Vivian,
from "Peas and Beans," are now great-grandmothers. Fear
and frailty have soured Vivian on travel, so Fran spins this
yarn to lure her to Ireland.

Dearest Viv,

I beg of you, come join us in Erin. I know you had a lousy time
what with getting robbed when we were last here, but that's one
reason to stay home, and there are so many reasons to come. Life is
a risk, My Dear, so wouldn't you rather bump your head on a lamp
post in Dublin than on the bathroom door at home?

I won't pretend this adventure has been hazard-free. I was seized
by terror, in fact, the moment I set eyes on Maureen's rattletrap car.
It's more dilapidated than before. I'd assumed her grandson, Davey,

would drive to the airport to fetch me, but no, she'd driven alone all the way from Kildare. I wondered how in the world she held a license at her age. I tossed my luggage into the trunk and saw the latch is still broken. She rigged it shut with a string that wouldn't hold your shoe tied! Starting up the engine she saw my worry and sang in the most sanguine tone, "It's all held by a shoestring, Fran, a thread that could snap at any moment."

"What's held by a thread, Moe, Dear?" I asked, watching for my luggage to bounce out the back.

"Everything, Fran, everything: the car, the farm, Dermott's kidneys, my hair, the finances. Everything's falling apart. Your flight was so late I thought sure the jet was done for. It's everything, Love. Welcome to Ireland," she said, reaching her gnarled hand across to reassure me. From that moment, I accepted risk as part of the package.

Maureen needs us now more than ever, Viv. You'll be shocked to see how the past four years have worn her down. She looks like an ancient bird, a heron or a ragged stork—hunched, blotched, and dingy. Worst of all, she's bone tired, though she acts as cheerful as a wren. I wished her a happy birthday for you, and asked her age, knowing full well that she's eighty-two, twelve years younger than I. But when I asked, she tilted her head and chirped, "Seventy-four, isn't it, Fran? I can't keep track. Dermott is eighty, so I must be seventy-four. No, wait, his medicine costs eighty punt, that's it. I knew something about Dermott was eighty." Then she grinned at me and shrugged off the question altogether.

That first day I couldn't tell whether our dear friend was coy or confused. In the old days it would have been coy, but now it's hard to tell. We're getting old, Viv, all of us. Cora is extremely frail, and most of our other friends are confused or dead. It's depressing. At ninety-four, I'm the oldest remaining. As far as I can tell I'm not confused, and not the least bit dead. If anything, my wanderlust is at an all-time-high. I'd never imagined my old age would stretch toward the length of a century, but since it's doing just that, I intend to make the best of it, and urge you to join me. Death wouldn't need much of an excuse to take either of us, Viv. He could justifiably claim us at any moment, and with that in mind, we must pursue life like bird dogs.

Anyway, the ride through Dublin would prove well worth the risk. As we spiraled toward the parking exit, I prayed the car was road worthy, and marveled that the license bureau still allowed Moe to drive. If she couldn't recall her age, how could she find her way through Dublin? She peered out between the dash and the top of the wheel. I said she should sit on a cushion to give her some height, but she said she can't reach the pedals that way. She wrestled the wheel, maneuvering us to the exit. "Reach into my bag, Fran, Dear," she said. "See if you can find a punt for the car park." I squinted into her ragged old purse. The first thing I saw was her expired license, outdated by two years. No point in mentioning that now, I thought. A deeper rummage yielded up a handful of your favorite coins, imprinted with horses, harps, leaping salmon, and prancing bulls: perfect treasures for the great-grandkids. I splashed a punt's worth into Maureen's cupped hands, and she splashed them into the trough. The arm of the gate lifted, like a flag signaling the start of a race. My heart leapt as we sped into the turbulent flow of Dublin traffic.

As you know, there's no way around Dublin. One has to drive through it, and through it we went. Whitehall, Glasnevin, and Drumcondra still smell of coal fires, just like the north-end flat in the old days. We got behind a green double-decked bus and breathed its leaden fumes. Twin boys in Aran sweaters giggled and waved out the back window. Maureen's little car sputtered into the heart of Dublin, past Parnell Square, and over the River Liffey on O'Connell St. Bridge. She could have gone east right then, but she wanted me to see our favorite haunts before heading home to Kildare. We looped around the outer wall of Trinity College and on past St. Stephens Green. We motored down Leeson St. and crossed the Grand Canal. I swelled with pride to see Moe still knew the roads as well as a Dublin cabby.

Soon we chugged down the highway toward Naas, and then on to Newbridge and Kildare. Maureen revved past farm trucks when necessary, and neatly swerved to avoid oncoming "over takers" when they borrowed our lane to pass. Then out of the blue silence she said, "They would have revoked my license because of my age, so I decided not to apply for renewal."

"A wise choice, Dear," I approved. "They really never patrol the roads in Ireland, anyway, do they?"

"They never do," said Maureen. "I've got to keep my car running, and I've got to keep up my motoring skills. What with the phone on the blink half the time and the farm so far from the clinic, I can't rely on anyone but myself to rush Dermott to emergency when need be."

"A brave woman you are," I cheered. "Dermott's lucky having you for a wife." That night I got a taste of how lucky, and just what she meant about things hanging by a thread. Dermott's so ill, he can't tend the house or the farm, and it's all gone to the dogs, I'm sorry to say. The medicine he's on is considered experimental and their medical aid won't cover it. Moe pays for it with the grocery fund, which makes for frugal meals. We eat mostly a thin grey gruel Moe calls "stir-about." But the longer I stay, the more I realize these are precisely the reasons to be here, Viv, and I know it's in your heart to help.

You remember their grandson, Davey. Well, he's quite a man now, with a boy of his own. He watches Dermott on occasion so Moe can get away. No sooner had we come through the door, than Davey reported he'd had to diaper Granddad six times, and there were no clean ones left. Poor Dermott is not only incontinent, he's unconscious much of the time, often nodding off in the middle of a sentence. When he manages to stay awake, he keeps calling me, "Vivian," which irks me no end. (Men always remember you best!)

It's sad, though. You know I always had a crush on Dermott, always found him sexy, but not any more. When I look at this poor, balding, paunchy bundle of coughs and drools, I can scarcely connect him to the swarthy tenor who sang to us like a troubadour. Remember how he used to pitch hay? It made us see how the phrase, "making hay" earned a sexual connotation. I feel a twinge of guilt over the fact my vital organs still work. It doesn't seem fair I should be older and more fit, while Dermott is younger and falling apart. But these things are up to God and nature, Viv. All I can do is help out. Losing sleep over it won't do.

The first four days were miserable. I wondered if you hadn't been the wiser not to come. We had a nasty storm, and my old

bones don't shun the chill like they used to. Dermott can't drink, so
we were on the wagon which isn't my choice. Each day was consumed with cooking, washing up, keeping the rain out, and most
repetitive of all was the task of diapering Dermott. If I ever har-
bored a desire to see him naked, it has long since fizzled out of me.
I can't imagine anything I like less than helping Maureen roll him
this way and that, to wipe down his big buttocks and hairy testicles,
and rewrap him only so he can soil himself again. If it weren't for
my love of Moe and Dermott, and the brevity of my budget, I would
have sought lodgings elsewhere.

On the fifth day I was thinking of an early departure, and how
nice it would be to soak in my own bathtub back in Michigan, when
Maureen announced we'd all go to Dublin. "Dermott's medicine has
to be refilled," she said, "and Davey can't come watch him. We'll
pile Dermott into the car. It'll be grand, Fran. We'll put him in the
wheelchair and go to lunch at Bewley's Oriental Cafe, like old times."

That night before bed, I found Maureen at the kitchen sideboard
counting out coins from a tea tin. "We'll be going on a shoestring,
Fran," she sang. "The medication costs eighty punt, the petrol will
cost fifteen, and the lunch at Bewley's,"

"Lunch at Bewley's is on me," I insisted.

"Well, then," said Moe, "for now the shoestring won't break."
She wrapped the heavy coins in newspaper and placed them into
her purse. (By the way, she could surely use a sturdy coin purse, if
you could bring one.)

That night I had a funny dream. I dreamt you were with us, of
course. Dermott kept his own beautiful dairy cows, and Maureen
kept a vegetable patch, just like in better days. We all sang together
out in the barn, and passed a flask of Irish whiskey. A little man
resembling Davey popped out of the hay loft, only instead of being
young, he was ageless, like a leprechaun. He danced about and gave
us each a bundle of coins wrapped in newspaper. We all laughed
and danced, pushing each other into the hay and rousting each other
out again.

In the morning when I woke, Maureen was already dressed and
outside in the rain, bent under the hood of the car. She soon came
into the kitchen frowning. "What is it, Moe?" I asked.

"I just checked the oil," she said, wiping herself dry. "Davey says the car is burning oil."

"Is it low?"

"Yes, it's low," she scowled and whipped the back of a chair with the towel. It's so unlike her to get upset. We sat down and she started to cry, saying it was no good; the roof would collapse with the weight of the rain, and the car would explode. When I said it wasn't that bad she snapped, "If we have to buy oil, there'll be no lunch at Bewley's!" She was fed up with money constraints, and I don't blame her. We counted out what we had, and how much we'd need for the weeks ahead. It seemed we had enough for oil and tea, but not lunch. We resolved to watch the oil light all the way to Dublin and play it by ear. We padded Dermott with extra layers, and tucked him snugly into the back. He was pleased to get out of the house, but fell asleep within minutes of being on the road.

Just outside Newbridge, traffic came to a stop. We couldn't see why. "Too early for a ball game," said Maureen. After a good five minutes at a complete halt, she shut off the engine, and I got out to inquire. I spotted a gentleman at a bus stop. He looked dapper—the type to be well-informed—the sort you fall for. I walked up to him and noted he was no taller than I. Our eyes met just five feet above the ground. He tipped his hat and gave me a cordial nod. We struck up a chat, and I learned he was on his way to Dublin on business. A terrible accident had been blocking the road ahead for over an hour. No doubt his bus sat miles behind, and the delay would spoil his day's work.

I ventured, "Why don't you join us? We've got room in the back, and we'll drive you to Dublin as soon as the road clears." The gentleman didn't wish to impose, but I assured he'd be utterly welcome. "Do you know anything about cars?" I asked. Back at the car, I signaled Moe to release the hood latch. The gentleman removed his jacket and checked the oil. Within moments he was shaking his head saying it wouldn't do to drive another mile without more oil. He offered to scoot to the service station around the corner, and buy two liters for the journey. He insisted we let him pitch in for petrol as well, in exchange for the kindness of a ride to Dublin. He briskly disappeared around the corner. When he was out of sight

Maureen clapped her hands. "We're lucky today!" she crooned.

"That cinches the lunch at Bewley's," I said with a wink.

When the traffic started moving, and we were on the open road again, we felt exhilarated. The sun peeked through the clouds, the fields glistened, and the cows looked plump and surly. It had been ages since I'd been for a drive with a handsome man. Our passenger's name was Edgar Swan, an elegant name for an elegant man. You would have been flirting, Viv. He had a way of speaking formally, yet intimately, the way Alistair Cooke introduces *Masterpiece Theatre*. He asked all the details of Dermott's condition, as if he were a long lost cousin. Dermott awoke as we passed through Kill, and all the way to Dublin remained alert, even witty. He asked Moe and me for permission to tell a dirty limerick. "As long as it doesn't have our names in it," Moe insisted.

Dermott began, "Mr. Swan, to grasp the punch line of this limerick, you must know of Ireland's ancient stone figures which are called *Sheela-na-gigs*."

"I know the figures, well," Edgar Swan nodded politely.

But Dermott had to make sure Mr. Swan was not being merely agreeable, "Then you know a Sheela-na-gig is a woman-figure with an oversized vulva, poised for all to see."

Edgar calmly replied, "With great reverence for the Holy Mother, the ancients placed the figures on church doorways to remind us where we all came from."

"Ah, good then," sighed Dermott, greatly relieved. "You're prepared to enjoy my limerick.

> *There once was a woman from Skellig,*
> *Who fancied dancing a jig.*
> *She jumped so high,*
> *She exposed her thigh,*
> *And wound up a Sheela-na-gig."*

Maureen shook her head and said softly, "He hasn't told that one in years. I'd forgotten all about it."

I twisted 'round to look at Dermott's gleaming blue eyes, mad with pleasure. His frothy white brows spewed like a geyser. He began briskly smacking his knee, singing, *"All the way to Carlow."* His lips and cheeks twitched rebelliously, but his voice sparked strong and true, striking a firm tempo befitting the song.

When we reached Dublin we went as close to the center as we could, and parked the car. Edgar Swan insisted we not go out of our way to drop him off at his office. He had errands to run near the center of town, and was happy to get around on foot. Maureen offered, "We'll head back towards Kildare around half five, Mr. Swan. We'll be going right through Newbridge. If you'd like a lift, just meet us here at the car."

Edgar tipped his hat and smiled. He bid us good day, and disappeared into the crowd. I thought of him as we wheeled Dermott to the discount druggist. I'd noticed he'd worn no wedding ring. Earlier when I'd asked his line of business, he'd said, "Finance." He probably made smart investments, I thought. "How old do you think he is?" I asked Maureen.

"Sixty-five?" She guessed.

Dermott piped up, "He's seventy. He's seventy if he's a day!"

I hoped to see Edgar at five-thirty. It gave me something else to look forward to. I hoped to feel jubilant, riding home toward the setting sun. I imagined him driving the car, and me sitting beside him, conversing pleasantly while Moe and Dermott napped in the back. I'd probably never see him again, but why think of that? There was no pleasure in it. At my age, Viv, I've learned the value of nursing a pleasant thought.

You would have loved our day in Dublin. The sun shone brightly as we strolled over the wet cobbles of Grafton Street. Dermott was in great spirits and didn't mind jostling about over the bumps. At Bewley's we had the whole fry: sausage, bacon, ham, eggs, and fresh brown bread with lots of butter, just the way you like it. We walked through the Temple Bar, which has been greatly renewed by arty young folk. I bought postcards of graffiti art to send to the great-grandkids. We went to the museum to view the Ardagh Chalice. We'll drink from such a cup when we meet our maker, I'm sure.

At five-twenty or so we made our way back to the car. We had just fifteen punt to fill the gas tank, and not a penny more. Who should be at the car when we arrived but the garda, writing us a parking ticket. In all the excitement of arriving to Dublin, we'd failed to notice a small sign stating there was no parking after four. Dermott cursed out the copper, which didn't go over well at all. He wrote out a ticket for, imagine this: seventy-five punt! I feared driving with an expired license would land Moe a huge fine, more than the worth of the car. But before I could warn her, she told the garda she owned it, and began lamenting about the run-down farm in Kildare, "Everything hangs on a shoestring," she said, "a delicate thread." The garda steamed impatiently.

He looked us over. "Who's the driver, then? Surely not *you*," he said loudly looking with great incredulity at Maureen. Just when I feared our goose was cooked, Edgar Swan strode up, tidy as you please, and said, "I'm driving sir, and we've got to get Dermott home to his medication before he has a grand mal seizure." That changed the tune. The garda asked for his license, and Edgar whipped it out for examination. Satisfied, the garda gave it back, and said he'd still have to issue a parking ticket to the vehicle owner. He tore off one copy for Maureen and kept a copy for himself. He told us to hurry along. Edgar leaned toward him and asked if they could have a private word. It sounded as if he were whispering about the urgency of Dermott's condition. Then the garda offered to give us an escort to the edge of town. He got into his car and waited while we hurriedly loaded Dermott and the wheelchair into the car. Edgar took the driver's seat, I sat beside him, and Maureen snuggled Dermott in the back.

Off we went with the light flashing, following the garda escort toward the edge of Dublin. All that nasty traffic had to let us pass. It was thrilling, Viv, and yet how could we enjoy it with Maureen sobbing in the back? Then, at the next stop light, Edgar turned to her and said, "Don't worry, Mrs. Maureen. You'll never hear of it again."

But Moe went on blubbering, "Of course I will. If I don't pay it, they'll come after me."

"Don't trouble yourself, it will never happen," soothed Edgar.

"Mr. Swan, don't be a fool," Maureen howled. "The garda wrote my license number on that ticket. When he gets to his desk he'll learn everything's expired. They'll take the car. They'll arrest me."

Finally Edgar pulled something out of his vest pocket and waved it toward her in the back seat. "When the garda gets to his desk, he'll have nothing," he said. "I've got his copy of the ticket right here."

Maureen snatched it and read it in disbelief. "You're a saint, Mr. Swan, a magician, and a poet. You're Brendan, Fergus, and Yeats rolled into one," she said smiling through her tears.

"You filched it," said Dermott.

"Dermott, hush," Moe said.

"He's a pickpocket, he is," Dermott mumbled.

"And thank God for it!" Maureen scolded.

Mr. Swan glanced over at me. I put my hand on his and said, "You're a good man, Edgar. Your special skills have done us a world of good."

Just then the garda slowed down. I was afraid he'd stop us, but he just eased aside to let us pass. We'd reached the edge of Dublin. Dermott dozed off, and Moe kept thinking of songs to sing. Edgar and I sang along. Between songs Moe couldn't stop chattering about what a grand day it had been, and how Edgar Swan was an angel, and a gentleman. When we reached Newbridge, Moe said he should drive himself to his door, but he said he'd get out right where we'd met. When we came to the spot Dermott woke up. "You're a right rascal, you are, Edgar Swan," Dermott said. Moe carried on that he must promise to come to Kildare for tea some day soon. Edgar smiled, tipped his hat and thanked us, as dapper as could be. I knew that would be the last we'd see of him. He stood at the curb until we drove away.

I'm thinking of him a day later, Dear Viv, and two things come to mind, both concerning you. Firstly, he resembled Bertrand, your second/third? husband. Bertrand was my favorite of your husbands, so nicely understated—clever, but not presumptuous. Secondly, 1 thought Moe was right, he was a magician, a saint, or a leprechaun. Anyway, he seemed like the right remedy after what happened to you last time we were here. Getting knocked down and robbed as you did, you're the one he came for, but you stayed home, so he met us instead.

Now it's up to me, Dear Viv, to convey the story and implore you to join us. The sun has come out. Spring's here at last. Soon the lambs will be born. We're walking to the cathedral today. They've finally restored Brigid's fire shrine. Later we'll walk to the holy well to cure our aches and pains, but none of our jaunts will be right 'til you're here. Come soon, old girl! Don't make us wait.

Your loving friend,

Fran

Appendix

Tales and Myths

Rumpelstiltskin

Long ago there was a poor miller who had little to brag about except perhaps, the beauty and goodness of his daughter. By chance one day he happened to speak with the king, and striving to impress him the miller boasted, "My daughter can perform the wondrous feat of spinning straw into gold." The king replied, "That sort of skill greatly intrigues me. Bring your daughter to the palace tomorrow and I'll see for myself." The next day she arrived and the king led her to a room full of straw. He showed her the spinning wheel and ordered her to work. "I expect a room full of gold, when I return tomorrow morning," he said. "If you disappoint me, you'll die." Then he locked the door and left her alone in the room.

The miller's daughter had no idea what to do. She could no sooner spin straw into gold than she could sprout wings and fly or make the sun shine at night. The king had left her no leeway at all and the thought of losing her life over it terrified her. There was nothing to do but weep and so she wept. Suddenly the door popped open and a little man stepped in. "Good evening, Ms. Miller," he said. "Why do you weep as if the world were coming to an end?" "I'm supposed to spin straw into gold and I don't know how," she said. The little fellow asked, "If I spin it for you, what will you give me?" The girl put her hand to her throat, "My necklace," she replied. At that the little man took the necklace and sat down to spin. He turned the wheel three times, whir, whir, whir, and the spool was full of shimmering gold. Again he turned it three times, and a second spool was full of gold. All night he worked magic, until by morning each and every bit of straw was spun into gold.

Soon the king arrived. He was overjoyed to see spools of gold from wall to wall. The sight made him hungry for more, such was the greed in his heart. He whisked the miller's daughter to a larger room full of straw and said, "If you value your life, you'll spin all this into gold for my coffers." Again she found herself locked into a room facing an impossible task. Overcome with fatigue, she wept. Then the little man popped in as before. "Ms. Miller, if I spin the straw into gold, what will you give me?" She touched her hand and said, "The ring off my finger." The sprightly fellow took the ring and sat down to spin. All night he worked tirelessly, and by sunrise the room was full of shimmering gold. The king was delighted. Greedier than ever, he took the miller's daughter to a room with still larger heaps of straw and said, "If you manage to spin all this into gold, you shall live and I shall make you my bride." To himself he thought that though her origins were modest, in all the world there was no woman who could fill his coffers so swiftly.

When she found herself alone once again, the little man showed up for the third time and asked, "If I spin the gold, what will you give me?" The miller's daughter replied that she had nothing left to give. "Well then," said the little man, "promise me this: If you become queen, you'll give me your first-born child." Now the girl was in a bind. There was no telling what the future might bring, but unless she agreed, she'd have no future at all. "Very well," she said. Again the little man set nimbly and swiftly to work. By morning the king had his third room full of gold. He married the miller's beautiful daughter and she became queen.

In a year's time she gave birth to a lovely child. She'd nearly forgotten the little man, but one day he appeared in her room and said, "I've come for the child." The queen begged him to take jewels, gold, riches of all kinds, anything but her child. But he insisted, "I prefer a living thing to all the wealth in the world." Then the queen wept and protested so bitterly that the little man felt sorry for her. He proposed that if she could guess his name within three days' time, she could keep the child.

The queen stayed up all night, frantically racking her brains, going over all the names she'd ever heard. The next day she sent a messenger to inquire throughout the countryside about other names she might have missed. When the little man came, she rattled off the whole list from Algernon and Balthazar to Wagner and Zachary, but after each, the little man said no. The second day she sent servants to all the remote regions to collect the rarest of names. She tried Ribcage, Shortribs, Muttonchops, Lambchops, but none of these were correct, either. On the third day the messenger returned from his rounds and said, "At the end of the day I walked along the forest's edge, and rounding a bend I found myself at the foot of a hill. It was just the sort of spot where a fox and a hare might bid each other good evening. There was a rustic hut with a fire burning outside and a silly little man dancing around the fire. And here's what he sang. 'Today I brew, tomorrow I bake, the next day the queen's child I'll take. My name is Rumpelstiltskin, but guess it, no one can.'"

This news thrilled the queen. Soon the little man appeared to hear her final guesses. She said, "Perhaps your name is Tom." The little man shook his head no. "Well, maybe you're called Dick." No again. "Is your name, by chance, Harry?" asked the queen. "No, your Majesty," said the little man growing more cocky by the moment. "Hmmm," said the queen looking at her list, "Maybe you go by the name, Rumpelstiltskin."

"Fie!" said the little man flailing his arms. "How did you know? The devil told you!" he yelled and stamped his right foot with such fury he drove it into the ground up to his middle. Raging fiendishly, he yanked so hard on his left foot that he split himself in two. After that nothing came between the queen and her child.

Snow White and Rose Red

There was once a woman living in a cottage with her two daughters. The girls' father had long since died, and they made ends meet as best they could. In the garden out front grew two rosebushes, one with white roses and the other with red. Bearing resemblance to the rosebushes, the girls were called Snow White and Rose Red. In all the world there were never two children more kind and good, nor so willing and cheerful. Snow White liked to stay home helping their mother or reading aloud to her when the work was done. Rose Red liked to run in the fields chasing butterflies. The girls loved each other so dearly, they held hands wherever they went. They vowed never to be parted and their mother reminded them always to share between them whatever good things came their way.

The two sisters roamed the forest together, picking berries and making friends with the animals. The hare ate lettuce right out of their hands, while the doe browsed peacefully beside them. When the girls were near, the birds sang sweetly, and even the wary stag came out of his hiding place in the thicket to greet them. If by chance the girls should linger in the forest 'til overtaken by the night, they did not fear. They simply lay down side by side on the moss and slept 'til morning. Their mother knew they were safe and didn't fret.

One moonless night they slept in the woods, and awoke at dawn to see a beautiful child dressed in shining white robes. The child smiled upon them and quietly disappeared through the trees. Only then did they see they had slept near a cliff, and could easily have gone over the edge in the darkness. Later their mother said the child in white must have been a guardian angel who watched over them, keeping them from harm.

Snow White and Rose Red cleaned their mother's cottage 'til it was a joy to behold. Rose Red kept house in the summer. Every morning, she brought a rose from each bush to her mother's bedside. In winter Snow White tended the fire and polished the brass kettle 'til it shone like gold. In the evening, when snowflakes whirled around outside, their mother would say, "Bolt the door, Snow White." The girls would draw near the hearth and spin wool into yarn while their mother read aloud.

One winter evening there came a knock at the door. The mother said, "It must be a traveler seeking shelter. Rose Red, let him in." Rose Red drew back the bolt, and who should poke his head in, but a big black bear, covered with snow. Rose Red shrieked and leapt back. Snow White hid beneath the table. The bear said, "Don't be afraid. I won't harm you. All I ask is to sit by the fire." Pitying the half-frozen creature, the mother invited him to lie down at the hearth. She told her daughters the bear meant no harm, and gradually their fears faded. He asked the girls to brush the snow from his fur, so they swept his coat with a broom. Then he stretched out before the fire, sighing contentedly. Soon the girls got used to him and began to play. They put their feet on him and rolled him this way and that. They snatched at his fur, whipped him with a switch, and laughed when he growled playfully. The good-natured bear put up with much mischief, but when it got out of hand he cried, *"Children, children, let me live! Snow White and Rose Red, you'll thrash your suitor 'til he's dead!"* At bedtime, the mother invited the bear to rest beside the hearth until morning. At daybreak, the girls let him out and he lumbered across the snow and into the forest.

From then on, he came each evening to enjoy their company and the warmth of the fire. He always let the girls rough-house and tease him as much as they liked. They grew so fond of the bear, they looked forward to his visits each night and never latched the door until he arrived.

One morning they saw the snow had melted. The birds flitted about making new nests, and the forest and meadow were bursting with spring flowers and green buds. The bear said, "Snow White, I must leave and won't see you again until the winter returns and the ground freezes over." She asked, "Where will you go, Dear Bear?" The bear said he must go to the forest to guard his treasures from envious, thieving dwarfs. "In winter, they stay in their caves," said the bear, "but in summer, they ferret about, stealing whatever buried treasures they can find." Snow White bid him a sad farewell and opened the door for him to go. As he passed through, his fur caught on the latch and tore just slightly. Snow White thought she saw gold glimmer through the tiny hole, but it might have been the morning sunlight glinting in her eyes. Soon the big bear disappeared through the trees.

Some time later, the mother sent the girls to the forest to gather kindling. They found a fallen tree, from which to gather twigs. On the other side of the trunk, they heard rustling in the grass. As they drew near, they saw it was a dwarf with a shriveled face and a long snow white beard. The tip of his beard was caught in a cleft in the trunk, and the little man jumped furiously about trying to free himself. He glared with fiery eyes at the girls and shouted, "Don't just stand there like fools! Do something!" Rose Red asked, "How did your beard get snagged in the tree?" The dwarf snapped, "You nosy goose, if you must know, we dwarfs use only small bits of firewood to cook our modest meals—not like you greedy humans! I was trying to split the log, and when I drove the wedge in, my beard got caught. But you spoiled brats don't seem to care." Each girl took a turn, but it was no use, they couldn't free the dwarf's whiskers. "I'll go fetch help," said Rose Red. "Help indeed!" scoffed the dwarf, "There are two of you and that's too many." Snow White said, "Don't be so impatient, Mr. Dwarf. I have an idea." She took a pair of sewing scissors from her pocket and snipped the tip of the beard. The moment the dwarf was free, he reached under the tree and grasped a sack of gold that had been hidden beneath the roots. "The devil take you!" he growled, "How dare you snip my whiskers!" With that, the ungrateful fellow hoisted the sack to his shoulder and stomped away.

Some days later Snow White and Rose Red decided to catch some fish for supper. As they neared the stream, they saw something bounce toward the water like a large grasshopper. Coming closer they saw it was the dwarf. "Careful not to fall in, Sir," said Rose Red. "You idiot!" scolded the dwarf. "Can't you see the damned fish has me by the beard?" He'd been fishing, when along came a breeze that tangled his long white beard in the line. To make matters worse, a big fish had chomped on the bait and began a tug of war with the dwarf. He clutched at saplings on the bank, but the fish was stronger. Without help, the dwarf could easily drown. The girls grasped him tightly, and tried to unwind his beard, but it was badly tangled. What could they do but resort to the scissors? With all their strength and a bit of handiwork, they managed to cut through the matted mess and free the dwarf. "You wicked toads!"

he cried. "It wasn't enough for you to snip off the tip of my beautiful beard. You had to go and chop the best of it. You've disfigured me!" Then he picked up a bag of pearls that was hiding in the rushes. He slung it over his shoulder and stormed off without offering a word of thanks.

One day the mother sent the girls to buy needles, thread, lace, and ribbons at a nearby town. To get there, they walked across a rocky heath. A large bird of prey flew high overhead, slowly spiraling closer and closer to the earth. All of a sudden, it extended its talons and swooped down near a rock in front of them. They heard a bloodcurdling cry. They rushed forth to see the eagle had pounced on their old friend, Mr. Dwarf, and was about to fly off with him. The kindly girls held onto the dwarf with all their might, until at last the bird let go and flew away. The ungrateful dwarf shrieked, "You clumsy clods! Did you have to pull so hard? Look how you've wrinkled my jacket." Then he picked up a bag of jewels and disappeared into his cave beneath the rock. By then the girls were quite used to his cross tone and though it hadn't bothered them much before, it bothered them even less now.

They completed their errands in town, and headed back across the heath toward home. The dwarf hadn't expected anyone to pass by his cave so late in the day. When the girls walked past he had the jewels spread on the ground for counting. The dwarf looked up, quite startled to see them. The evening sun glistened brightly upon the many colored gems. The girls gazed in amazement. "Don't stand there gawking like ninnies!" he shouted, his face going crimson with rage. But before he could hurl more harsh words, they heard a growl, and a black bear came loping out of the forest. The dwarf leapt to his feet and tried to make for his cave, but instantly the bear was upon him. "Please spare me, Mr. Bear. These two girls are as plump as spring quail. They'd make a much tastier meal than my scrawny limbs. Eat them! Eat them!" The bear raised his great paw and smote the dwarf with one blow.

The sisters ran for cover. The bear called, "Snow White and Rose Red, wait, don't run away." They recognized the voice of their dear friend. When he caught up with them, his furry coat fell to the ground, and before them stood a handsome young man all dressed in gold. "I am a prince," he explained. "That envious dwarf stole all my treasures, and placed a curse on me, changing me to a bear. But now his death has restored my human form."

The prince reclaimed all his treasures from the cave. Snow White married the prince, and Rose Red married his brother. The sisters brought their mother to the palace. She left her old life behind, except for the two rosebushes, which she transplanted outside her new window. Every year the most beautiful roses bloomed, white from one bush, and red from the other. She lived there contentedly for many years to come.

Rapunzel

There was once a couple who longed for a child. Despite prolonged disappointment, the wife hoped beyond hope that her prayers would be answered. Behind their home was a garden wall, and beyond it, lay an enchanting garden belonging to a powerful witch. Everyone feared her, and no one dared trespass into her garden. The wife gazed down upon the garden from her back window, and spied a bed of rapunzel, a prized lettuce. It looked so crisp, fresh, and green that her mouth began to water. By the next day she could think of nothing else. Her craving grew until, feeling utterly deprived, she began to pine away. Her loving husband saw her suffering and grew concerned. "Dear wife, what's wrong?" he asked. "Oh," she replied, "I shall waste away unless I eat some of that rapunzel that grows in the witch's garden." The husband did not want to lose his wife, and so he ventured over the garden wall that very night. He picked a handful of rapunzel and returned. The wife quickly made a salad and gobbled it down. The rapunzel satisfied her so, that the next day her craving for it grew threefold. Her husband knew that nothing less than another visit to the garden would please her, so he went again that night. Just as he climbed down the other side of the garden wall, he saw the witch standing before him.

"How dare you creep into my garden!" she said scowling angrily. "You've been stealing my rapunzel and you'll be sorry!" The husband pleaded, "Old woman, be merciful. I had no choice. My wife was pining so, she would have died had she gone another day without the rapunzel." The old woman calmed down, "Very well," she said, "from now on you may help yourselves to as much rapunzel as you wish, but you must promise to give me your first child when it is born. I shall care for it like a mother and give it a good life." The man agreed to everything, such was his fear of the witch. Later, when his wife birthed a daughter, the witch named the infant Rapunzel and took her away.

Rapunzel grew more lovely each day until there was no lovelier child on the face of the earth. When she turned twelve years of age, the witch took her deep into the forest and shut her into a tower so as to keep her unspoiled by the world. This tower had no door and no stairs, only a single window at the top. When the witch wanted to visit she stood below and called, "Rapunzel, Rapunzel, let down your hair." Rapunzel had very long hair she wore in braids which she wrapped around her head like a crown. When the old witch called, Rapunzel unwound them, and hooked them over the window latch, allowing them to fall all the way to the ground below. The witch climbed the braids as if they were a ladder.

Some years later, a king's son happened to be passing through the forest on horseback. He heard sweet singing and followed the sound to the tower, where he stopped to enjoy Rapunzel's beautiful voice. She often sang to pass the time and break the spell of loneliness. He looked for a door that he might compliment the singer, but found none. Still, the voice had moved him so, he returned each day to listen. Once, as he stood behind a tree listening, the old witch came to the base of the tower and called, "Rapunzel, Rapunzel, let down your hair." Rapunzel lowered her braids, and the witch climbed up. Naturally, the prince was intrigued. This was a lesson he would not forget.

The following day he returned to the tower at dusk and called, "Rapunzel, Rapunzel, let down your hair." Her hair fell to the ground and the prince climbed just as the witch had done. Upon seeing him, Rapunzel was terrified. Never before had she seen a man! But the prince spoke softly and kindly, explaining how much he'd enjoyed her singing. Before long she forgot her fears and when he asked her to marry him, she thought to herself that he'd love her better than the old witch. She answered yes, and the two joined hands. "I'll go with you, Dear Prince, but how shall I get down?" Then an idea came to her. "I know," she said. "Each time you come, bring a skein of silk thread. With that I'll weave a ladder. When it's finished I'll climb down and off we'll go together, you and I." The prince agreed to visit her each night, as the witch came by day and was best avoided.

The witch knew nothing of the lovers until one day Rapunzel said, "Tell me Godmother, how come you take so long to climb my hair when the prince climbs up in seconds?" The witch shouted, "You wicked girl! You've deceived me. I tried to keep you shut away from the world!" In a rage she grabbed Rapunzel by the hair, snatched up a pair of scissors and lopped the long braids off just below her ears. Then the cruel witch exiled Rapunzel to a desert place where she would endure prolonged misery and loneliness.

That evening the witch tied the severed braids to the window latch. When the prince called "Rapunzel, Rapunzel, let down your hair," she lowered the braids to the ground where he stood. The prince climbed up the tower and into the window only to find Rapunzel gone and the vengeful witch in her place. "You've come for your wife, well, the bird is gone and there'll be no more singing in this nest! The cat has got rid of her, and will now scratch out your eyes! You'll never see Rapunzel again!" Overcome with grief and despair, the poor prince flung himself from the tower window before the witch could get at him. He fell to the brambles below. Though he survived, the sharp bramble thorns scratched his eyes and blinded him. After that he wandered through the woods for a very long time, subsisting on berries and roots, mourning over the loss of his wife. He wandered hopelessly until at last he came to the place where Rapunzel was living with the twins she had birthed, a girl and a boy. In the distance he heard singing, and the voice seemed familiar, so he moved toward it. As he neared, Rapunzel recognized her dear husband. She fell upon him, weeping profusely. Her tears spilled into his eyes, restoring his sight. They went to his kingdom and received a royal welcome. They all lived contentedly 'til the end of their days.

Kore, Queen of Darkness, Maiden of Light

Long ago, before the changing seasons ever showed their faces on this earth, there was but one season, that of summer. The dark hours of night passed quickly, while the daylight hours lingered, filling the sky with brightness. Trees remained forever laden with flowers and fruit. Hives stayed full of honey. Kore, the beautiful maiden, retained the freshness of a new blossom, and her mother, Demeter, the radiant goddess of ripe fields, remained forever in full bloom. They spent their days roaming the hills and groves of old Greece, bestowing their blessings upon fields of corn, enjoying perpetual mother-daughter harmony.

One day they briefly parted while Kore picked fragrant narcissus in a green meadow. All of a sudden, her ears were filled with the sound of thundering hooves. The ground trembled, and the earth split open at her feet. A blinding whirl of dust engulfed her. Powerful arms seized her, and no amount of struggle could keep her from being hauled down into the gaping darkness of the world below. There Hades, god of the underworld, asked her to dwell with him as his queen. Kore wept and refused, wishing only to return to her mother. Hades held her against her will and begged her to accept the wealth of his kingdom, but her tears and refusals did not cease.

As for Demeter, she searched for days without rest, without food or drink, calling, "Kore! Kore!" but found no trace of her beloved daughter. After nine days and nights she had but one clue. Old Hecate, guardian of crossroads, had heard Kore cry, "Rape!" but when she ran to the rescue, there was no one in sight.

At last, on the tenth day, Demeter heard substantial news when a herdsman described a frightful scene witnessed the day Kore had vanished. On that day, the earth shook, startling two herdsmen. A great chasm opened, and they could but watch in dismay as the gaping hole swallowed a herd of pigs. A thundering chariot drawn by black horses appeared and plunged into the chasm, the driver clasping to himself a shrieking girl. At this, Demeter grew furious, suspecting her brother, Hades, was the culprit.

Together, Demeter and Hecate approached the Sun who witnesses all events. The Sun confirmed their suspicions. Hades had raped and abducted Kore, probably with the covert blessing of his brother Zeus, chief of the gods. Seized by inconsolable grief, and unquenchable wrath toward her brothers, Demeter commenced to wander the earth, cursing the trees and fruits, forcing the human race to the brink of starvation. Zeus sent conciliatory messages and gifts, but Demeter swore the earth would stay barren until Kore returned.

Zeus had no choice but to order Hades to deliver Kore to her mother at Eleusis. At the same time he sent word to Demeter that Kore could return only if she had not tasted the food of the dead. Forced to accept these terms, Hades told Kore he was obliged to send her home. Upon hearing this, she stopped weeping. But Hades's gardener proclaimed he had seen Kore pick a pomegranate and eat a few juicy morsels of the fruit. He was sent to Eleusis to bear witness that she had indeed tasted the food of the dead.

At Eleusis, Demeter embraced Kore with momentary elation, but news of the pomegranate threatened their reunion. Furious Demeter refused to remove her curse from the land. Rhea, mother of the gods came forth to engineer a compromise. She said since Kore had eaten only a few bites of underworld fruit, it would not do to keep her in the underworld forever. Rhea proposed Kore spend part of the year ruling alongside Hades as underworld queen. During these months the land above would be barren, and her title would be "Persephone." The rest of the year she would return to Demeter's domain where mother and daughter would preside together over the growing season. All parties agreed.

Demeter restored prosperity to the land, and rewarded those who had helped her. Old Hecate offered to see that the agreement was kept. As keeper of crossroads, Hecate vowed to watch over Kore during seasonal shifts: in autumn when *Kore the Maiden* becomes *Persephone Queen of the Dead,* and in spring when she rises up from darkness to bless the fields with new life.

Index